The Good Representative

T0341376

To Houston, my love

The Good Representative

Suzanne Dovi
University of Arizona

WILEY-BLACKWELL

A John Wiley & Sons, Ltd., Publication

Registered Office
John Wiley & Sons, Ltd, The Atrium, Southern Gate, Chichester, West Sussex, PO19 8SQ,
United Kingdom

Editorial Offices
350 Main Street, Malden, MA 02148-5020, USA
9600 Garsington Road, Oxford, OX4 2DQ, UK
The Atrium, Southern Gate, Chichester, West Sussex, PO19 8SQ, UK

For details of our global editorial offices, for customer services, and for information about how
to apply for permission to reuse the copyright material in this book please see our website at
www.wiley.com/wiley-blackwell.

Library of Congress Cataloging-in-Publication Data
Dovi, Suzanne Lynn, 1966–
     The good representative / by Suzanne Dovi.
        p.   cm.
     Includes bibliographical references and index.
     ISBN: 978-1-4051-5578-6 (hardcover : alk. paper) ISBN: 978-1-118-36061-3
     (paperback : alk. paper)
  1. Representative government and representation.   I. Title.
     JF1051.D68 2007
     321.8—dc22
                                                2006022219
A catalogue record for this title is available from the British Library.

Contents

Preface

Is President George W. Bush a good or a bad representative? How about Russian President Vladimir Putin? Who is a better representative according to democratic standards: former Representative Tom DeLay or Senator Hillary Clinton? Contemporary political theorists do little, if anything, to help us answer such questions. Indeed, some treat citizens' preferences for representatives as sacrosanct, something that political theory should remain silent about.

However, as more and more nation states become democratic (at least in the sense that they hold elections), evaluating states simply by their institutional design is not enough to determine how democratic those states are. The actions of representatives need also to be evaluated. Political representatives matter. They matter a great deal. After all, political representatives can undermine democratic institutions by, for example, writing discrimination into constitutions. If democratic institutions are to survive, representatives need to resist the pull of extremism, and fight for the legitimacy of those institutions. And democratic citizens need to appreciate representatives who undertake such battles. Otherwise, representatives can and will give democracy a bad name.

In fact, what motivated me to write this book was my realization that democratic citizens can make very bad choices in selecting their representatives. When they choose their representatives simply by their looks, or by whom they would like to have a beer with, citizens put democratic institutions at risk. They should not ignore the impact that a representative is apt to have on those democratic institutions. And political theorists need to speak up about this risk.

We need to identify democratic standards for selecting representatives because the legitimacy of a polity's democratic institutions depends on the representatives and citizens who make up that polity. Everyone realizes that democratic institutions do not live up to their ideals. In fact, no democratic institution has ever lived up to democratic ideals. However, the ability of democratic institutions to approximate their ideals depends, in no small part, on *who* represents democratic citizens and *how* they represent them. Representatives and citizens alike need to know what it means to represent in a democratic fashion. And they need to be equipped with standards that help them differentiate the good representatives from the bad.

This book tries to do just that. It offers three distinctly democratic standards that democratic citizens should use in selecting their representatives. I do not expect everyone to agree with my standards. The goal of this book is not to settle all disagreements about who are good representatives. Rather, I will count the book a success if it starts a public dialogue about what democratic citizens should look for in a representative. My book argues that democratic citizens need to do more than apply existing standards of "moral character." They need to evaluate representatives by their ability to settle political conflicts fairly and justly. And this requires attending to three virtues of democratic representation: good representatives are fair-minded; good representatives develop critical trust; and good representatives are good gatekeepers.

When I say "good representatives," I mean good *democratic* representatives. I recognize that citizens choose representatives who they consider good for a wide variety of reasons: Some representatives are regarded as good because they make people rich. Other representatives are seen as good because they condemn sin when they see it. Some representatives are judged good because they are progressive. My understanding of the good representative differs. A good representative, in my sense, excels at representing in a democratic fashion. The three virtues of democratic representation specify what it means to be a good democratic representative. They serve as standards that citizens can use to identify those representatives who will allow democratic institutions to approximate their ideals.

The Good Representative will also be controversial because it argues that good democratic representation might not always be desirable. Of course, democratic representation offers a lot of *potential* benefits for democratic citizens. But democratic representation – even good democratic representation – suffers from certain problems. It takes time. It is inefficient. It can require sacrifices on the part of citizens. Sometimes, it is easier to let other people rule us than it is to monitor our representatives. What is more, democratic representation can be dangerous. Bad representatives can use democratic institutions as tools of domination. Democratic citizens need to choose their representatives with an eye on these problems. Under certain circumstances, it is not desirable to be represented in a democratic fashion. How much democratic representation is desirable will depend on the capacities of citizens and their representatives to sacrifice for the sake of their democratic institutions.

The three virtues that distinguish the good representatives from the bad make up the heart of this book. Chapters 4, 5, and 6 articulate these virtues, and explain how they serve as standards that citizens can use in evaluating their representatives. Those who want to cut to the chase, so to speak, may want to begin with Chapter 1 and then skip Chapters 2 and 3, to get to the detailed discussion of the three virtues. Chapter 2 deals with the relationship between descriptive representatives and democratic representatives. It suggests that the experiences of those who have been deeply betrayed by democratic institutions can teach us why it matters who represents us. The past experiences of certain groups show that all democratic citizens need to remain suspicious of their representatives. Chapter 3 is for the more philosophically minded. It provides a justification for my understanding of democratic representation and for my ethics of democratic representation. In particular, it shows that existing standards cannot explain why Tom DeLay is a bad democratic representative.

Chapter 7 considers whether the virtues of democratic representation are naïve – too idealistic for real-world politics. In particular, I argue that these democratic ideals are not a coherent bundle – sometimes, we need to choose among the virtues. Such choices are hard, but we need to attend to them – and not rest content with pointing fingers at the failings of our representatives. It is also important that democratic citizens have good enough choices. Not only do democratic citizens need to appreciate democratic representatives who are good enough; when a democratic system gives them uninspiring and anti-democratic choices, they need to demand alternatives. The rhetoric of politicians is not enough to make them democratic. I will argue that to represent in a democratic fashion, they need to advocate in a way that fosters the legitimacy of democratic institutions. And to be good democratic representatives, they need to do even more.

Suzanne Dovi

Acknowledgments

I could not have written this book without the help of many people. In fact, this book took such a long time to write that I have incurred a serious number of intellectual and personal debts in the process. I apologize in advance to those whom I have inadvertently forgotten. First and foremost, I need to thank my family for their love and support. As usual, my mom, Pat Dovi, went above and beyond maternal obligations. She provided help with the references, crucial babysitting services during the final stages of the book, and an endless supply of warmth and laughter. My dad, Sebastian Dovi, taught me how to argue about politics. My big sister, Patty Kent, and my little sister, Cynthia Bucalo, were dependable and loving, helping me keep the daunting project of writing a book in perspective. I have a long list of other relatives whose love has made all the difference: my grandparents, Mary and Vince Bresan; my brother, Sebastian Dovi; and also Kelli Young Dovi, Susan Kuzy, Sebastian Dovi, Shelbey Dovi, Skyler Dovi, Sydney Dovi, Jack Kent, Katie Kent, Sam Kent, Edna Smit, and Mary Smit. My son, Hayden, would have liked his mommy to work on the book less and play more. I cannot thank him enough for providing so many giggle breaks.

Second, I have also been blessed with truly great and inspiring teachers. This book grew out of my doctoral dissertation, completed in the Department of Politics at Princeton University under the supervision of Amy Gutmann, Jennifer Hochschild, George Kateb, and Gerry Mara. Each provided important insights that were incorporated into the book. Amy Gutmann taught me the importance of conceptual clarity and precise thinking. George Kateb taught me the importance of remaining skeptical toward ideals. His provocative questions helped keep me from simply taking for granted the importance of democratic community. Jennifer Hochschild taught me how political theory can be done in a way that balances empirical political science and normative theory. I have benefited tremendously from her constant supply of advice and her nose for interesting ideas. My conversations with Gerry Mara have been an enduring source of intellectual excitement. I would also like to acknowledge the support of Mark Warren, whose work and friendship have had an exceptional influence on my thinking. Finally, I would also like to thank my graduate and undergraduate teachers: Nancy Bermeo, Alisa Carse, John Diulio, Bruce Douglass, George Downs, Elizabeth Kiss, Roger Masters, Alan Ryan, Carol Swain, and Sue Thomas. Each of these teachers contributed to the thinking in this book in important ways. Of course, the mistakes and errors there are all mine.

Princeton University provided an exciting intellectual environment for developing one's ideas. I am particularly grateful to the Woodrow Wilson Foundation for a fellowship from 1996 to 1997, and to the Center of Human Values for a fellowship from 1995 to 1996. In addition, I would like to thank the Mellon Foundation and the Spencer Foundation for, respectively, a fellowship and a summer research grant. I would also like to thank my friends from graduate school: Jonathan Allen, Sharon Barrios, Dana Ansel, David Callahan, Hawley Fogg-Davis, Stephanie Jencks, Michael Jones-Correo, Victoria Kamsler, Jessie Klein, Jacob Levy, the late Moshe Levy, Tony Lucero, Brenda Lyshaug, Kimberly Morgan, Kris Palmer, Scarlett Soriano, Peter Rowinsky, Rueul Rogers, Dietlind Stolle, Carol Tracy, Alex Tuckness, David Wecker, Brian Williams, Andrew Zawecki, and particularly, the marvelous and irreplaceable Judy Failer.

I started turning the dissertation into a book as an Assistant Professor at the University of Arizona. My junior year sabbatical, funded by the College of Social and Behavioral Science, and a fellowship from the Udall Center gave me the time to make this transformation. For their helpful advice, support and conversations during this process, I would like to thank Denise Allyn, Julia Annas, Mark Chavez, Tom Christiano, Lis Clemens, Richard Dagger, Sally Deutsch, Bill Dixon, Tim Duvall, Martha Fenn, Caryl Flinn, John Garcia, David Gibbs, Gretchen Gibbs, Michael Gill, Gary Goertz, Sarah Griffiths, Bernard Harcourt, Kristen Hessler, Cindy Holder, Reeve Huston, Brad Jones, Kris Kanthak, Margaret Knight, Paulette Kurzer, Orsi Lazar, Colleen Loomis, Mike Mann, Bill Mishler, Ami Nagle, Cary Nederman, Cara Nine, Barbara Norrander, Antxon Olarrea, David Owen, Spike Peterson, Kathy Powers, Rob Reich, Mia Ruyter, Andy Sabl, David Schmidtz, John Schwarz, Sarah Soule, Bea Urrea, Tom Volgy, Chad

Westerland, Pat Willerton, and Christine Wolbrecht. I would like to thank the graduate and undergraduate students whose questions often fueled my own research. Deep appreciation for reading various parts of this book goes to Robin Brande, Sigal Ben-Porath, Ben Berger, Simone Chambers, Tom Christiano, Kristen Hessler, Jacob Levy, Cary Nederman, Andrew Rehfeld, Andrew Sabl, John Schwarz, Jeff Spinner-Halev, and Mark Tessler. Giorgios Sotiriou and Becky Wyatt were helpful research assistants. Melissa Williams made some crucial suggestions about using virtue theory at an early stage of the project.

I have presented bits and pieces of this project at a number of different academic forums. I would like to thank the audiences from the following departments of political science: the University of Notre Dame, Stanford University, the University of Colorado, Boulder, McGill University, Rochester University, Queens University in Belfast, Ireland, and the University of Arizona. I am also grateful to the participants in the 2003 meeting of the Cactus Political Theory League and to the participants in the workshop "The Transformation of Democratic Representation," organized by Mark Warren and Dario Castiglione and held at The Center for Democracy and the Third Sector at Georgetown University, Washington, DC, in 2004. I have also presented versions of this work to the American Political Science Association and to the Midwest Political Science Association. I am particularly grateful to Bill Bianco, Eileen Botting, Dario Castiglione, Yasmin Dawood, Richard Fenno, Russell Hardin, Jane Mansbridge, David Mapel, Patchen Markell, Horst Mewes, Susan Okin, Andrew Rehfeld, Jennifer Rubenstein, Dara Strolovitch, Alvin Tillery, Nadia Urbinati, Dorian Warren, Mark Warren, Laurel Weldon, and Iris Marion Young for their comments and criticisms on this project.

I also have many other dear friends to thank. My gratitude goes to Geeta Anand, Carrie Brennan, Jodi Washburn Christophe, David Earling, Gretchen Gibbs, Judith Greenberg, Ira Joseph, Matthew Lansburgh, Mike Mann, Jenny Raskin, and Nina Zitani. Without their encouragement and support, I would never have made it through this process. Robin Brande provided the carrots, or more specifically the chocolate, for finishing this project. Most of all, I would like to thank Sigal Ben-Porath, my dream friend and dream colleague, whose phone calls kept me going.

I literally could not have written this book if not for the childcare provided by Lisette DeMars, Loreen Jones, and Gabriela Novakova.

I am thankful to Patchen Markell and two anonymous reviewers for Blackwell Publishing for their incredibly helpful comments on the book.

Nick Bellorini was a wonderful editor, supportive and encouraging. My gratitude also goes to Geoffrey Palmer for this helpful copy editing.

Finally, I need to thank the person who literally made this book possible. Houston Smit read and commented on every word of this book. He talked through the various philosophical problems that I encountered. He had faith in the project when I lost mine. However, there's more. Houston took over the childcare duties when I needed time to work, let me sleep in when it wasn't my turn, and cooked delicious meals. For all that and more, I dedicate this book to Houston.

S. D.

Chapter 1

Who is a Good Representative?

Most everyone writing on democracy today agrees that democratic institutions must be representative in order for democracy to work. The size of nation states and the complexity of public policy issues rule out direct democracy. Democratic practices require representation. Or as David Plotke (1997) succinctly put it, "representation is democracy."

Despite this general agreement about the importance of representation for democratic practices, there is relatively little discussion of what it means to represent in a democratic fashion. There is an extensive literature evaluating democratic *institutions*.[1] And there is an extensive literature that discusses the proper behavior of representatives.[2] But theorists writing on representation have not focused on representing *in a democratic fashion*. As a result, theorists have overlooked the possibility that there are substantive and distinctively democratic standards for distinguishing good representatives from bad ones. The aim of this book is to offer just such standards, standards that democratic citizens ought to employ in evaluating their representatives.

Now, not everyone will agree that we need substantive democratic standards for evaluating representatives. After all, some theorists maintain that a good representative is simply one who advances the policy preferences of her constituents (provided that those policy preferences are lawful). Good representatives are good lackeys (the theoretical literature calls such representatives "delegates"). In fact, most contemporary empirical research on representation assumes that democratic representation occurs when a representative's actions reflect and respond to constituents' expressed policy preferences. According to this way of thinking, there is nothing more to representing in a democratic fashion than responsiveness to democratic citizens' policy preferences.

Others will reject the project of articulating a *single* set of distinctively democratic standards. For instance, Hanna Pitkin (1967) maintains that the concept of representation is paradoxical, and that as a consequence representatives are subject to multiple and conflicting standards of evaluation. Following Pitkin, many contemporary political theorists simply celebrate the diversity of standards that democratic citizens use in evaluating their representatives. That diversity is itself understood as a characteristic of democratic institutions (e.g., Mansbridge, 2002; Sabl, 2002, 2005). For this reason, political theorists often refrain from characterizing any particular choice of representatives as undemocratic. So long as other citizens have the opportunity to oppose that choice and/or citizens are presented with alternative candidates, democratic practices are sufficiently safeguarded. Those who, in this way, equate a commitment to democracy with a commitment to pluralism tend to hold that all criteria for identifying good representatives are contingent, varying with the particular opinions, interests, and perspectives of different democratic citizens. And they defend this position on the grounds that it is minimalist and inclusive. It is minimalist because it does not assume that any particular ethical outlook underlies a theory of good democratic representation. It is inclusive because it is consistent with all citizens' evaluations of their representatives.

However, on my view, democratic standards for evaluating representatives are more constraining. For such standards derive from an ethical outlook that privileges the legitimacy of democratic institutions. Consequently, these standards for evaluating representatives place substantive constraints on what good representatives can and should do. I call political representatives[3] within a democratic polity who meet these standards "good democratic representatives."[4] Such political representatives excel at representing in a democratic fashion. More specifically, good democratic representatives are those political representatives whose advocacy work maintains and advances the legitimacy of democratic institutions.[5] Such political representatives may be formal political actors, such as presidents,[6] senators, or other elected officials. But they may also be informal political actors, such as lobbyists or leaders of social movements. What matters is not a political actor's official title or her specific political office, but what she does.[7]

In particular, a representative acts as a good *democratic* representative only if her advocacy work fosters the norms and values distinctive of democratic institutions. These norms and values are crucial to the well-functioning of democratic institutions – that is, to their facilitating peaceful and just resolutions of political conflicts. Good democratic representatives, then, advance public policies on behalf of democratic citizens in ways that facilitate peaceful and just resolutions of political conflicts. The degree to which democratic institutions, through the agency of good democratic representatives, realize the norms and values distinctive of democratic institutions is the degree to which those institutions are fully democratic.[8] Three such norms and values are central to the purposes of this project: civic equality, self-governance, and inclusion.[9]

Other political values, such as liberty, toleration, the rule of law, or even piety, might coexist with democratic institutions, but they are not distinctive of democratic institutions. Consider, for example, that a benevolent dictator could support the norms and values of toleration and liberty, such as the freedom of religion, or the rule of law. A monarchy could promote a theocratic rule.

For a norm or value to be distinctive of democratic institutions, it must provide some guidelines for structuring formal political institutions as democratic institutions. It follows that these norms and values, including those of civic equality, self-governance, and inclusion, can only be fully realized in democratic institutions.

Of course, democratic governments do not always support or respect the norms and values of civic equality, self-governance, and inclusion. One only needs to survey the ways in which democratic governments have historically excluded or even enslaved certain groups to realize that democratic governments can violate these norms and values. However, we criticize such governments as *democratic* governments for failing to live up to these norms and values – a point that confirms that these norms and values are distinctive of democratic institutions.

So good democratic representatives are those who respect the norms and values distinctive of democratic political institutions. But this still leaves obscure the answer to the neglected question, "How should democratic citizens evaluate their representatives, as democratic representatives?"

Put simply, democratic citizens should evaluate their representatives by the way in which they advocate – that is, by how they advance public policies on behalf of democratic citizens. Democratic representatives represent democratically only when, in advancing public policies on behalf of their constituents, they aim to foster the legitimacy of democratic institutions, to promote citizens' participation, and to increase their identification with democratic institutions. Those who represent in a democratic fashion honor these constraints on their advocacy work.

Articulation of these constraints on democratic representation provides guidelines for determining when individual representatives are no longer representing in a democratic fashion. These constraints, then, draw a line that good democratic representatives do not cross. Moreover, corresponding to each of these constraints is a way of excelling at representing in a democratic fashion, a way in which representatives can, in advocating on behalf of their constituents, respect and foster these distinctively democratic norms and values. I will call these forms of political excellence the "virtues of democratic representation" or, simply, "the virtues." Each virtue provides a general criterion that democratic citizens ought to use in choosing their representatives. Together, these virtues provide a normative framework within which representatives should be evaluated.

That said, evaluations of democratic representatives cannot and should not be formulaic. Judgment plays an ineliminable role in the application of any criteria of good representation to particular democratic representatives. For example, it requires judgment to determine whether a particular president is, in meeting with the Black Congressional Caucus, reaching out to African-Americans and increasing their inclusion in the political process. After all, such a meeting could be just another "photo op." Moreover, judgment must, in any such application, be sensitive to an array of particular considerations that cannot possibly be codified, or captured in a formula. For this reason, any adequate ethics of democratic representation must permit a variety of opinions about who are good democratic representatives. At the same time, it should provide a general framework through which public debates about who are good democratic representatives can be properly conducted.

It is important to acknowledge the difficulties that the virtues of democratic representation may pose, ones that may complicate the task of distinguishing good democratic representatives from bad ones. Indeed, the difficulties posed by the virtues may be fundamental. As we shall see, the three virtues of democratic representation that I distinguish can be in tension with one another. Some democratic representatives, despite their best efforts and intentions, will face situations in which they can fulfill the demands of one virtue only at the cost of failing to fulfill those of another. Furthermore, there are circumstances under which pursuit of a virtue of democratic representation may pose a cost – which can potentially be prohibitive – to a polity. If democratic institutions are to resolve conflicts fairly and peacefully, a balanced approach to the virtues of democratic representation, one that attends to the problems they pose, as well as to the benefits they provide, is crucial.

Indeed, I hold that the purpose of democratic institutions simply is to resolve conflicts within a pluralist society fairly and peacefully. And the legitimacy of democratic institutions relies both on adjudicating these conflicts properly and on democratic citizens recognizing the fairness of these resolutions. So, to the extent that good democratic representation is crucial for the proper operation of democratic institutions, it is also crucial to the legitimacy of those institutions. The virtues serve as constraints on representatives that help to insure the fairness and legitimacy of democratic institutions.

Further, the stability and sometimes the survival of democratic institutions depend on citizens seeing that the institutions are adjudicating conflicts fairly. For if a disgruntled minority or majority holds that democratic institutions are unfair, then such groups are likely to employ undemocratic practices – for example, violence – to settle their political conflicts. Unfair and illegitimate democratic institutions are more likely to devolve into totalitarian and authoritarian forms of government.[10] And democratic citizens can, in turn, become accustomed to democratic institutions functioning as tools of domination.

A democratic society can only survive, let alone function properly, if it shows a kind of moderation toward the virtues of democratic representation. Here, too, it will be important to see that democratic representatives cannot always exhibit all of these virtues, but must sometimes choose among them. An examination of the various trade-offs among these virtues that good democratic representatives must make will help us to discern the requisite moderation. It will also suggest that good democratic representation might not always be possible.

The extent to which good democratic representatives can successfully negotiate the problems with democratic representation will depend, in part, on the capabilities of citizens and of their representatives. Sometimes a particular society might not be ready for democratic representation. Here, I follow John Stuart Mill (1991 [1861], 13), who recognizes that the appropriate form of government for any given society depends on the capacities of citizens. When citizens lack the proper capacities, democratic institutions cannot always function properly. Under such circumstances, democratic institutions can be used to dominate and oppress democratic citizens, and good democratic representation may even be undesirable. Good democratic representation is therefore a contingent political good. It is only desirable under certain conditions. Part of the job of good democratic representatives is to help make it possible for democratic institutions to function properly, by promoting conditions in which democratic citizens can come to appreciate the importance of having democratic representative institutions for settling disagreements among citizens fairly and peacefully.

The Good Representative proceeds on the working assumption that the norms and values that guide the design of institutional structures for democratic polities can also provide some guidance for the selection of the representatives who occupy positions within those institutions. Indeed, my argument draws on existing theoretical discussions of how formal institutions are to be designed in light of democratic norms and values to show how these norms and values should also inform citizens' choice of democratic representatives. And, in doing so, I further the insights of those who have recognized the importance of informal political actors in representative democracies.[11] In fact, one purpose of this book is to expand the scope of the theoretical literature on democratic representation beyond formal governmental institutions. Democratic representation is an activity of formal as well as informal representatives.

By identifying a function common to both formal and informal representatives – that is, the function of advocating public policies in ways consonant with democratic norms and values – I provide a common currency for evaluating all democratic representatives, one independent of their particular offices. Instead of focusing on the fairness of procedures for authorizing and holding representatives accountable, this book addresses an important, albeit often overlooked, question: What criteria should democratic citizens use in selecting democratic representatives? How democratic citizens answer that question will affect not only who is selected to serve as a representative, but also the performance of democratic institutions.

An Ethics of Democratic Representation

There are two basic questions that an ethics of democratic representation must address: What are the proper criteria for assessing democratic representatives and identifying the good ones? Are there any drawbacks to having good democratic representation? We will see that answering these two questions adequately turns on clarifying what it means to represent in a democratic fashion. And in clarifying that – in other words, the proper function, or characteristic activity, of democratic representatives – we also clarify what it means to be a good democratic representative – that is, one who excels at representing in a democratic fashion.

In focusing on the function, or characteristic activity, of democratic representatives, and deriving my account of a good representative from this function, I follow Aristotle. And I am assuming that there is a conceptual connection between the function, or characteristic activity, of a thing and its excellence as the thing that it is. Chapter 3 develops and defends this view. For now, it will suffice to see, quite generally, how virtues of a thing are read off of its function. For example, the function of a knife is to cut. A good knife is a knife that cuts well. The virtue, or excellence, of a knife, then, is sharpness. And, more generally, what it is for a thing to have the virtue or excellence proper to its kind is nothing other than its being disposed, in exercising its characteristic activity, to engage in that activity well. I am proposing that, in parallel fashion, the virtues of democratic representatives are to be read off of the function, or characteristic activity, of democratic representatives. (Compare, here, Aristotle's argument concerning the moral virtues at *Nicomachean Ethics* Book I Chapter 7, 1097b25–28: see Aristotle, 1970 [1831].)

The function of democratic representatives is to advocate on behalf of their constituents in ways that allow for the fair and peaceful resolution of political disagreements within a pluralist society. In other words, the characteristic activity of democratic representatives is *democratic advocacy*. The degree to which a democratic representative engages in this characteristic activity well is the degree to which that representative excels at representing in a democratic fashion. As we will see, to engage in democratic advocacy well, a democratic representative must realize three virtues: the virtue of *fair-mindedness*, through which a representative contributes to the realization of the value of *civic equality*; the virtue of *critical trust building*, through which a representative contributes to the realization of the value of *self-governance*; and, finally, the virtue of *good gatekeeping*, through which a representative contributes to the realization of the value of *inclusion*.

It is worth reemphasizing that my understanding of democratic representation applies to *all* political actors who advance public policies in democratic institutions. Informal as well as formal representatives perform the function of democratic representation.[12] My account of democratic representation, and the virtues of democratic representation, articulates a general ethical outlook that should underlie and inform the activity of all those who act as political advocates within a democratic polity.

In fact, a benefit of attending to democratic advocacy, as I conceive it, is that doing so provides standards for assessing informal, as well as formal,

representatives. Attending to the controversies surrounding advocacy, especially the advocacy of informal representatives, in light of my account of
democratic advocacy, reveals how democratic norms and values are to
be brought directly to bear in assessing democratic representatives. In the
case of many informal representatives, there is no temptation to try to settle
such controversies simply by appealing to formal procedures that authorize
the representative: after all, not all informal representatives are authorized
by formal procedures. Consequently, one cannot appeal to authorization
procedures to settle the matter of who is a legitimate, and therefore preferable, representative. Moreover, an examination of controversial instances
of political advocacy – specifically, instances of informal representation –
will put us in a better position to identify how and where representatives,
even when they are properly formally elected and abide by the law, can
nonetheless violate democratic norms and values.

To understand why democratic advocacy is the characteristic activity of
democratic representatives, it is useful to consider one of the most persuas-
ive arguments for the legitimacy of democratic authority. The argument,
made forcefully by Thomas Christiano (1996), is that democratic institutions are necessary under certain conditions of diversity. In particular,
democratic institutions are necessary to provide fair procedures for adjudicating disputes about public policy when citizens' interests, values, and
perspectives conflict. It is, I would argue, in virtue of realizing the norms
and values of civic equality, self-governance, and inclusion that democratic
institutions provide these procedures, and adjudicate conflicts and disagreements in ways that legitimate democratic authority. The function of
a democratic representative, then, is to advocate public policies for her constituents in a way that contributes to the fair adjudication of such disputes
within her society. A good democratic representative is one who performs
this function well. And, I will argue, a democratic representative performs
this function well only if her advocacy work is consonant with the norms
and values that underlie the legitimacy of democratic institutions.

Of course, not all democratic representatives do in fact engage in democratic advocacy. Anyone who is elected is thereby a democratic representative. And someone who is democratically elected could fail to engage in the
characteristic activity of democratic representatives. For instance, a democratically elected representative fails to advocate in a democratic fashion
when he refuses to deliberate with other citizens on the grounds that he is
obeying God's direct command to him and therefore would be corrupted
by attending to the opinions and perspectives of others. Moreover, some

representatives might be so corrupt or depraved that they do not care at all about conforming to fair procedures, or about the impact of the policies that they pursue on democratic institutions. They solicit citizens' opinions, not to pander, but to frame issues so that they can lower the potential electoral costs of their policy goals. They disguise the costs that their policies impose on democratic citizens and democratic institutions (cf., Jacobs and Shapiro, 2000). Such representatives might advocate, but they do not – and cannot – advocate in a democratic fashion. But, despite their failure, or even their inability, to advocate in a democratic fashion, and thus to engage in the activity characteristic of a democratic representative, these representatives nonetheless count as democratic representatives simply in virtue of being duly elected. Compare: a knife that is so dull that it cannot cut can still be a knife.

It should now be evident that any adequate ethics of democratic representation must address the ways in which representatives should advance public policies under conditions of pluralism. Given such conditions, democratic representatives will almost inevitably advance public policies that some citizens will endorse and others condemn.[13] A good democratic representative is not likely to be approved by, or even appreciated by, every one of her constituents, let alone by all citizens. Thus, my claim is not that a good democratic representative will be valued by every citizen (or even a majority of citizens); rather, my claim is that a good democratic representative will not be the unbridled advocate of her own constituents. In other words, a good democratic representative will constrain her advocacy in light of her appreciation of the conditions of pluralism, and of the demands that the norms and values of civic equality, self-governance, and inclusion place on all democratic representatives.

The Proper Scope of an Ethics of Democratic Representation

The Good Representative provides some guidance for the proper assessment of representatives: democratic representatives should, first and foremost, be assessed by the impact that their actions have on the legitimacy of democratic institutions. If a democratic institution loses legitimacy because the personal misconduct of representatives has contributed to the loss of trust in that institution, then those representatives are properly subject to severe criticism. And if the legitimacy of a democratic institution is compromised because it does not include representatives from marginalized groups, then its representatives are inadequate. In articulating the three virtues of democratic representation, my ethics of democratic representation offers citizens standards they can use in choosing among representatives, and a common set of norms that all good democratic representatives should follow. These virtues, moreover, can help settle contemporary controversies about representation by helping to resolve some of the conflicts about competing standards of good representation that underlie these controversies. These virtues help to resolve these conflicts by clarifying how the norms and values distinctive of democratic institutions are to be brought to bear in assessing the advocacy work of political representatives.

The Good Representative offers guidance for the assessment of democratic representatives by providing a normative framework for determining the extent to which an individual representative excels at representing in a democratic fashion. To be a good democratic representative is to have and exercise all three of the virtues of democratic representation – the virtue of fair-mindedness, the virtue of critical trust building, and the virtue of good gatekeeping – and to avoid the dangers associated with each of them. Consequently, representatives who advance public policies that undermine civic equality, limit the ability of citizens to govern themselves, or exclude certain groups from participation might be excellent delegates of democratic citizens who hold such preferences. However, such representatives are not good democratic representatives. For better or worse, democratic norms and values place certain constraints on the behavior that democratic representatives can engage in and still be considered good democratic representatives.

The virtues of democratic representation also require democratic representatives to advocate out of a correct understanding of their proper function. Now this function, as we saw, consists in contributing to the proper functioning of democratic institutions – providing a fair and peaceful resolution to political conflicts. Moreover, democratic institutions can provide such resolutions only by way of drawing on, and reinforcing, citizens' shared commitment to certain distinctively democratic norms and values, which justify preferring democratic institutions to nondemocratic ones. The good democratic representative is thus one whose advocacy work contributes, in and through the proper function of democratic institutions, to the realization of these norms and values in her polity.

Democratic citizens ought to prefer representatives who exhibit these three virtues over those who do not. And citizens ought to assess criticisms of, and controversies surrounding, representatives in light of the understanding of good democratic representation that a detailed articulation of these three virtues provides. Each of these virtues provides a different focal point for evaluating representatives. Those who are committed to democratic norms and values should look for representatives who not only exhibit these virtues, but who properly negotiate the problems associated with these virtues. In this way, the three virtues become normative tools of evaluation, assisting the critical assessments of democratic citizens.

My approach bears some important similarities to that of contemporary virtue theory.[14] After all, notions of function and excellence are central to virtue theory. Nonetheless, my theoretical aims and those of virtue theorists are fundamentally different. Virtue theorists aim to provide a moral theory within which morally right action is understood in terms of character: what makes an action a right action is that it is one that a morally virtuous agent would perform. My concern, however, is not with this general and fundamental debate among moral theorists concerning the relative priority of character and action.

My main concern is rather with *political* character – that is, the stable habits, dispositions, and attitudes of representatives that guide their actions as representatives. As recent empirical findings indicate, my focus on political character reflects an approach that US citizens actually commonly take in assessing their representatives: US citizens often select their representatives on the basis of what they perceive to be the representatives' moral character.[15] In concentrating on the virtues of democratic representatives, then, my ethics of democratic representation speaks to democratic citizens in terms they already use in selecting their representatives. Indeed, if we are to aid democratic citizens in their assessments of representatives, we cannot simply avoid talk of character.

One reason for framing an ethics of democratic representation in terms of the virtues is because I am inclined to think that representatives do have political character, and that it is in fact important for the proper operation of democratic institutions that a polity have representatives with democratically excellent political character. Another is that talking in this way is natural, given the way in which I derive standards of good democratic representation, in Aristotelian fashion, from an analysis of the proper, or characteristic, activities of democratic representatives. But the most important reason for talking in terms of political character is the fact it is no accident that democratic citizens assess their representatives in terms of their political character. Given the complexity of the actual policy debates that representatives in modern societies have to navigate, a complexity that makes it impractical for most citizens to follow these debates closely, a natural way of assessing representatives is by their political character. If a representative exhibits excellent political character in a given context in a fashion that a citizen can appreciate, it is not unreasonable for that citizen to support that representative, on the grounds that the representative will exhibit that excellent character in other contexts.

But the virtues of democratic representation are intended to articulate an ideal not only of character, but also of behavior, one that democratic representatives should strive to approximate. The virtues are also intended to provide citizens with critical tools necessary for assessing not only their representatives' political character, but also their actions, all according to democratic standards. The virtues also provide a general framework within which public deliberation that specifies what actions good democratic representation requires in a given situation can be fruitfully conducted.

Although I am inclined to believe that representatives who perform the actions that the virtues require of them will also possess these virtues of democratic representation – that is, a certain political character – one can imagine a representative who fakes possessing the virtues. Indeed, if we can watch and regulate someone enough, she might engage, much of the time, in the desired behavior, even if she lacks the character that would internally dispose her to that behavior. Call "truly excellent democratic representatives" those who themselves have the right character, one that would dispose them to act as the virtues require, independently of any extrinsic motivation. But a representative could, in principle, not in fact be truly excellent and still satisfy the criteria I have proposed for evaluating good democratic representatives. For my purposes, I want to set aside the question, "Which comes first, the behavior or the character?" I want instead to focus on describing democratic advocacy that exhibits the behavior that is usually indicative of a democratic representative's possessing the virtues of democratic representation.

Consequently, *The Good Representative* should be of interest even to those who do not want ultimately to do political theory using the language of political character.[16] For talking in terms of the virtues provides democratic citizens with the tools that facilitate their demanding representatives to do a good job of representing in a democratic fashion. If my ethics of democratic representation meets this goal, it will enable the selection of representatives who preserve and foster the legitimacy of democratic institutions. By assisting democratic citizens in their choice of representatives, an ethics of democratic representation puts representative democracies in a better position to realize good representation, and to avoid bad representation.

That said, I do not expect an ethics of democratic representation to eliminate all controversies about the proper behavior of good democratic representatives. Even if democratic citizens reach a consensus about an ethics of democratic representation, the messy work of applying the criteria articulated in that ethics to particular circumstances still needs to be done. Moreover, democratic citizens will need, through public deliberation and debate, to arrive at more determinate understandings of the norms and values that justify adopting democratic institutions.

The importance of articulating an ethics of democratic representation is underscored by the fact, evident in the course of the spread of democratic forms of government, that representative democratic institutions can be favored for unsavory reasons. Some may favor representative institutions because such institutions allow one group of citizens (e.g., a religious or ethnic majority) to dominate another group (e.g., a religious or ethnic minority). Others may favor democratic representative institutions as a way of insuring the charismatic rule of a particular individual; for example, Venezuela's Hugo Chavez. Given the variety of reasons that citizens can have for supporting representative institutions, political theorists should not assume that remaining silent about the criteria that democratic citizens should use to choose their representatives will necessarily promote pluralism or political freedom. It also means that political theorists should not endorse every norm or value that democratic citizens invoke to justify favoring democratic representative institutions. In order to choose their representatives more wisely, democratic citizens need to articulate and defend their conceptions of democratic norms and values, as well as how their understanding of good democratic representation is connected to the realization of those norms and values in their polity.

The articulation of general criteria for good democratic representatives – the virtues of democratic representation – will serve two purposes. It will help democratic citizens choose representatives who excel at representing in a democratic fashion. It will also help democratic representatives make better judgments about how to go about advancing public policies, judgments that are informed by democratic norms and values. Knowledge of the dangers associated with democratic representation will allow representatives to make better decisions.

Controversies about good representation are likely to intensify as a result
of my articulating an ethics of democratic representation. I fully expect *The
Good Representative* to be controversial. Some will disagree with my choice
of the virtues of democratic representation, while others will disagree with
how I understand and characterize a particular virtue. I welcome and invite
such disagreements, for it would be healthy for disagreements to replace
the existing silence about democratic standards for evaluating individual
representatives. An articulated ethics of democratic representation is, in
my opinion, vital to the health of any democratic polity, because democratic
citizens can and do choose bad representatives – that is, representatives who
actively undermine the legitimacy of democratic institutions. To remain
silent about the proper criteria for choosing representatives is to ignore
the fact that democratic citizens will not always bring proper standards
to bear in evaluating their representatives. Contemporary political theory
should not be afraid to challenge the judgments of democratic citizens by
offering guidelines for assessing individual representatives. By educating
democratic citizens about the importance of democratic institutions, the
distinctive values of democracy, and the proper way to represent in a democratic fashion, an ethics of democratic representation can change and,
hopefully, improve the criteria by which democratic citizens select their
representatives. If democratic citizens are to evaluate their representatives by whether they preserve or undermine the legitimacy of democratic
institutions, existing criteria such as "having a good moral character" or
"being willing to bring home the bacon" need to be refined. The purpose
of this book is not to eliminate disagreements about good democratic
representation; rather, it is to provide a framework within which these
debates are to be properly, and fruitfully, conducted.

Three Assumptions

There are three assumptions that underlie the argument of this book. The
first is that democratic norms and values should inform the institutional
design of a pluralist society. I take as a starting point that representative
democracies need to provide fair procedures for giving voice to concerns
of citizens and for authorizing binding decisions. This book, therefore,
is not an argument for the moral superiority of democracy (for such an
argument, see Barry, 1990 [1965]). Nor does it offer a justification for
democratic political institutions.

I will, to be sure, be questioning those who claim that theoretical discussions of democratic representation ought to focus *exclusively* on formal political institutions. But in doing so, I do not mean to deny a crucial operating assumption of that approach – namely, that fair elections are necessary features of democratic polities. I deny only that there is no more to a democratic polity's living up to democratic norms than its routinely providing fair elections. Indeed, we will see that the same democratic norms that should inform the institutional design of a pluralist society ought also to inform assessments of individual democratic representatives – and, indeed, the relations between citizens and their democratic representatives. That representatives advocate in conformity to these norms is, I argue, a crucial source of legitimacy both for democratic representatives and for democratic institutions. But for the record, this book rests on an assumption that democratic political institutions, although flawed, are the best source of political authority for pluralist societies. In fact, I derive my virtues of democratic representation from an already existing ethical outlook that endorses democratic values – specifically, civic equality, self-governance, and inclusion – that ground the preferability and legitimacy of democratic institutions. In deriving the virtues of democratic representation from this ethical outlook, I stand in agreement with Hanna Pitkin (1967) in an important respect. I take one's standards for evaluating representatives to depend on one's political world view. I should stress that, despite the fact that representatives who possess the virtues enhance both their legitimacy and the legitimacy of democratic institutions, the virtues are not meant to identify who is a democratic representative in respect of having authority to speak and act on behalf of citizens. Rather, isolating the distinctive kinds of political excellence that democratic representatives should realize as *democratic* representatives brings into clear relief both what makes for *good* representatives and what makes for *bad* representatives. Even representatives who enjoy authority may nonetheless be bad, if their activities threaten the health of our democracies and hinder our realizing the very values that make us care about having democratic institutions.

This leads to the second assumption of this book – namely, that, democratic norms and values should "condition" citizens' assessments of their representatives and the expectations they have of their representatives. Of course, not every aspect of life has to be governed by democratic norms and values. For instance, democratic citizens may consistently champion the democratic value of equality while accepting and even embracing certain inequalities in their personal relationships. Democratic theorists should resist the impulse to insist that democratic norms and values inform all aspects of citizens' lives. Here I concur with Ian Shapiro (1994) that democracy is a "subordinate foundational good." For Shapiro,

> although democracy is essential to ordering social relations justly, we should resist every suggestion that it is the only good for human beings, that it is the highest human good, or that is should dominate the activities we engage in. Democracy operates best when it conditions our lives without determining their course. (126)

Shapiro's discussion points to the fact that democratic citizens can, and perhaps should, hold some other values to be more important than democratic values. Consider the choice democratic citizens may face between a representative who realizes the three virtues and yet supports war and one who fails to realize the three virtues and yet is willing to do what it takes to avoid war. Citizens can justifiably prefer the latter representative, but my ethics of democratic representation spells out the potential costs for doing so. Democratic citizens who put other values first may directly or indirectly weaken the ability of democratic institutions to adjudicate political conflicts fairly and peacefully. They thereby put democratic institutions at risk of becoming tools for domination. Ultimately, democratic citizens need to decide how much good democratic representation they need.

Nevertheless, weighty reasons dictate that, given the conditions of pluralism, democratic norms and values guide the behavior of those who advance public policies on behalf of democratic citizens. Individuals may, under certain circumstances, reasonably regard a representative's ability to "bring home as much bacon as possible" to be more important than that representative's ability to excel at being a good democratic representative. However, being an effective advocate is not the same as being a good *democratic* representative. And if democratic institutions are to operate properly, democratic citizens cannot simply ignore instances in which their representatives – both formal and informal – violate democratic norms and values. They must pay some attention to whether their representatives are good democratic representatives. Substantive democratic norms should inform, and sometimes be the overriding factors in, their evaluations of the political actors who advocate in their name. In other words, citizens ought to reflect on and assess the degree to which the advocacy work of their representatives fosters democratic norms and values. The degree to which citizens simply prefer representatives who "take care of their own," whatever the cost to vital democratic norms and values, is the degree to which good democratic representation is at risk of being undermined. Thus, the democratic virtues are standards that democratic representatives should strive to achieve and standards to which democratic citizens ought to hold their representatives accountable.

The third and final assumption of this book is that democratic citizens will disagree not just about public policies, but also about the proper standards for identifying democratic representatives. Both sorts of disagreements are reflected, for instance, in public debates about the relative desirability of having George W. Bush or Bill Clinton as their president. Democratic citizens will possess multiple and sometimes opposing standards for identifying good representatives. Some want young and personable representatives, while others prefer mature and authoritative ones. Some citizens may prefer representatives who hold certain policy views; for example, those who denounce abortion or apply the affirmative action litmus test to judicial nominees. Such disagreement among citizens does not undermine my project. Rather, it helps to motivate it. Just as the fact of pluralism partially justifies the adoption of democratic institutions, so too the fact that citizens disagree about what makes for a good representative justifies appealing to democratic norms and values to help negotiate such disagreements.

This appeal to distinctively democratic norms and values yields standards of good democratic representation that should be used not just by democratic citizens in their selection and support of representatives, but also by those representatives themselves. Through these standards, democratic norms and values can and should inform representatives' thinking about their advocacy work. For instance, the democratic norms of transparency and accountability, rather than simply considerations of political advantage, should inform democratic representatives' conduct toward their critics. The democratic value of civic equality should inform representatives' attempts to balance the demands of their supporters with opposing demands made by their competitors. And the democratic value of autonomy should instruct democratic representatives to avoid monopolizing power, to keep democratic institutions from becoming tools of domination.

The Theoretical Contribution of *The Good Representative*

Democratic theorists like to argue about what are good democratic institutions, not about who are good democratic representatives. However, on my account, democratic representation is *not* a characteristic of formal representative institutions. In other words, we should not identify democratic representation simply by how political actors are authorized and held accountable through formal elections. Democratic representation needs to be understood, rather, as an activity on the part of representatives – political advocacy that has as its function enabling democratic institutions to settle political conflicts fairly and peacefully. Such an understanding of democratic representation contributes to two specific areas in democratic theory: treatments of deliberative democracy and debates about descriptive representation. Let me sketch these contributions by spelling out how this book situates itself in some of the more important recent work in both areas.

Deliberative democracy

In taking public deliberation to be vital to democracy, my project works with a conception of democracy that falls in the deliberative, or educative, as opposed to the aggregative, or economic, camp. The latter conception of democracy, most famously articulated by Joseph Schumpeter (1976) and Anthony Downs (1957), emphasizes the importance of competition. This conception remains neutral toward not only the substance of the public policies that representatives advance, but also to the manner in which they advance public policies. On this conception, representatives are democratic simply to the extent that they advance the policy preferences of their constituents. Competition among different representatives suffices to provide institutional incentives adequate to secure responsive and accountable representation. Aggregative theorists emphasize the importance of self-interest as motivating responsive and desirable political behavior. And they exhibit a minimalist approach to democratic theory that is well expressed by Ian Shapiro's notion of democracy as "limiting domination." For Shapiro, "Schumpeterian competition in public institutions is desirable not for its own sake but rather as the best available mechanism . . . to limiting domination" (2003, 75). While I agree that self-interest can be a democratically valuable motivation, and that democracy should work against domination, an aggregative or economic conception of democracy provides little guidance for debates over the preferability of different representatives. It ignores the role that citizens' evaluation and choice of representatives plays in maintaining public accountability (e.g., choosing representatives who provide accurate and available information to the public) and limiting domination (e.g., spurning representatives who eliminate democratic checks and balances for the sake of their political efficacy).

Consequently, relatively few contemporary democratic theorists concern themselves with the manner in which political representatives advance public policies on behalf of democratic citizens.[17] It is the *competition* among political representatives in setting the agenda and in implementing certain public policy preferences that is crucial to democratic representation. So long as the competitiveness of the political arena is preserved, informal democratic practices are sufficiently safeguarded. Most theorists hold that democratic citizens should be free to advance their public policies in ways commensurate with the intensity of their policy preferences, and so they have little to say about how political parties, interest groups, social movements, or political associations should advocate public policies. The more zealous the advocacy, the better. Instead of focusing on the advocacy of informal and formal political actors, most theorists follow James Madison (see Madison et al., 1987 [1788]) in assuming that institutional arrangements are sufficient constraints on representatives. Once institutional constraints are in place – foremost among them, institutional arrangements that secure fair elections or promote democratic deliberations – democratic citizens can use whatever criteria they prefer to select their representatives. The institutions will serve to balance out any unsavory motivations of political representatives.

Such a minimalist approach to democratic theory is clearly inadequate. The health of a democratic polity depends on its citizens discerning and demanding good democratic representation. And good democratic representation, in turn, requires individual representatives to attend, in their advocacy work, to the norms and values distinctive of democratic institutions. The economic theory of democracy needs to be supplemented with an ethics of democratic representation, an ethics that enables, and encourages, democratic citizens to choose representatives who advocate public policies in a democratic fashion – that is, representatives whose advocacy work is informed by fundamental democratic norms and values.

To argue that a framework is needed to identify good democratic representatives is not to deny that institutions play an important role in constraining the actions of individual representatives. I agree with Madison that institutions can provide incentives that constrain the unsavory motivations of politicians. Competition among representatives is certainly one way to provide democratic citizens with choices. However, it is important to recognize the role that democratic citizens have in selecting representatives and thereby in choosing representatives who are charged with protecting the legitimacy of democratic institutions. Truth be told, representatives have the power, collectively, if not individually, to undermine democratic institutions. Nancy Bermeo (2003) has recently shown that political elites can play a crucial role in preserving democratic institutions. Democratic citizens need to choose their representatives wisely – that is, in ways that support the reasons for preferring democratic to nondemocratic institutions.

In arguing that good democratic representation requires that the advocacy work of representatives be informed by fundamental democratic norms and values, I am thus arguing that the deliberative, or educative, conception of democracy is more adequate than the aggregative, or economic, conception. But I am also developing further the more substantive conception of good democratic representation championed by deliberative democrats. Most deliberative democrats recognize that modern democracies cannot do without elected representatives. For example, Amy Gutmann and Dennis Thompson report that most deliberative democrats "favor some form of representative democracy. On these versions of the theory, citizens rely on their representatives to do their deliberating for them" (2004, 30). According to Gutmann and Thompson, the advantage of having representatives is "that deliberation by leaders who have been tested by experience (if only by political campaigns) is likely to be more informed, effective, and relevant (if not more sophisticated)" (ibid.). Implicit in this view is that the quality of democratic deliberations depends on the quality of the representatives. But deliberative democrats have not, I believe, said enough about what makes for a good democratic representative. In particular, deliberative democrats need an account of good democratic representation that gives more weight to the norms and values distinctive of democratic institutions, for example, civic equality, self-governance, and inclusion: good democratic representatives advance public policies in ways that attend to such values. Deliberative democrats also need to provide a detailed account of how democratic citizens should take such values into account in their choice of representatives. An understanding of democratic representation as democratic advocacy provides just such an account.

It also expands the scope of discussion of good representation to encompass more than the deliberative activity of representatives. In putting the question, "How should good democratic representatives advocate?" front and center, I encourage political theorists to attend to the entire range of activities proper to democratic representatives. This shift is important for two reasons. First, it acknowledges the relatively minor role that deliberation actually plays in the public policy-making processes in most modern democracies, including the United States. As Amy Gutmann and Dennis Thompson (2004) and Bruce Ackerman and John Fishkin (2002) point out, there is very little deliberation in contemporary politics, dominated as it is by superficial television commercials and public relations campaigns. Consequently, any adequate account of democratic representation must attend not just to deliberation, but to other ways in which political representatives advance public policies – for example, through lobbying, fundraising, and mobilizing citizens (for a discussion of non-deliberative political activities, see Walzer, 1999). Second, the quality and efficacy of the public deliberation engaged in by democratic representatives needs to be assessed in the context of all of their advocacy work. The public deliberation of good democratic representation encourages the active, informed, and critical participation of the electorate both in that public deliberation and, more generally, in the entire political process. Indeed, good democratic representation should, by increasing such participation on the part of the electorate, expand and enhance the role that public deliberation plays in the life of a democratic polity. By shifting the discussion to advocacy, citizens gain additional grounds for assessing the performance of their representatives.

Descriptive representation for historically disadvantaged groups

Historically disadvantaged groups know the importance of good representation, for such groups have often been betrayed by their representatives. Moreover, democraticization has not always meant progress for some groups, for example, women (di Stefano, 1997, 206). An understanding of democratic representation from groups that have been denied the right to vote as well as groups that have won and then lost the right to run for office changes how one sees democratic representation. In fact, a growing literature has revised the meaning of democratic representation in light of the experiences of historically disadvantaged groups. Theorists such as Iris Marion Young (2000) and Melissa Williams (1998) have proposed alternative understandings of representation that can account for why historically disadvantaged groups need representatives from those groups. Young's understanding of representation as "a differentiated relationship" and William's understanding of "representation as mediation" allow us to see problems with the existing ways in which citizens are being represented in democratic polities. Such understandings of democratic representation support institutional reforms aimed at increasing the presence of historic-ally disadvantaged groups, for example, reserved seats, party list quotas, and group vetoes.

But in concentrating on the institutional reforms adopted to increase the number of descriptive representatives, this literature has failed to articulate standards for assessing the performance of individual repres-entatives. Such an omission is startling because both Williams and Young recognize that members of historically disadvantaged groups do not always represent other members of those groups. For example, Young explicitly recognizes how improving the representation of Latinos can work against improving the representation of gay and lesbian Latinos. Young is acutely aware that descriptive representatives can marginalize further certain members of historically disadvantaged groups' interests. Similarly, Melissa Williams (1998, 6) states that "it would be absurd to claim that a representative, simply because she is a woman, therefore represents the interests or perspectives of women generally, or that an African-American representative is automatically representative of all African-Americans. The mere presence of members of marginalized groups in legislatures is not *sufficient* for the fair representation of citizens from those groups, even though it is often *necessary*." Without specifying who counts as a preferable descriptive representative, institutional reforms aimed at increas-ing the number of descriptive representatives can cause further damage – increasing the vulnerability of some who have already been marginalized by democratic institutions.

Consequently, we need a better account of the relationship between democratic representation and descriptive representation. Understand-ing the distinctive role of descriptive representatives for historically dis-advantaged groups within a democratic polity, by situating the account of such representatives within a more general account of democratic rep-resentatives, is the first step. Standards for assessing the performance of individual descriptive representatives for historically disadvantaged groups are best understood within an account of the standards that should inform the assessment of all democratic representatives. Moreover, none of the recent works on democratic representation have adequately acknowledged the importance of democratic advocacy to good democratic representa-tion. As a result, these works are not in a position to assess adequately the extent to which an individual representative – whether a descriptive representative of a historically disadvantaged group or a descriptive rep-resentative of a privileged group – excels at representing in a democratic fashion. The provision of criteria for assessing descriptive representatives of historically disadvantaged groups specifically, as well as criteria for assessing democratic representatives more generally, is an important way of increasing accountability to historically disadvantaged groups.

The Structure of *The Good Representative*

The book begins by discussing one way in which good democratic representatives are typically identified – that is, by their membership in historically disadvantaged groups. Most theorists do recognize that members of certain groups must be present in democratic institutions in order for good democratic representation to take place. In other words, descriptive representation is considered necessary, albeit not sufficient, for good democratic representation. By descriptive representation, I mean the representation of historically disadvantaged groups by members from those groups. In Chapter 2, I examine the arguments theorists have offered for descriptive representation and show how, properly understood, these arguments show why *all* democratic citizens should worry about who acts and advocates in their name. The arguments for descriptive representation all turn on the contention that a commitment to distinctively democratic norms and values requires that historically disadvantaged groups be represented by members of those groups. Properly understood, these arguments generate constraints, not only on what democratic representatives should look like, but also on how descriptive representatives ought to advocate public policies on behalf of their constituents. Moreover, these arguments generate constraints on advocacy that apply not only to descriptive representatives, but to democratic representatives more generally: the good representative is one whose advocacy fosters fundamental democratic norms and values within the polity.

Chapter 3 articulates and defends my understanding of democratic advocacy. I begin by arguing that the scope of democratic representation should be expanded to include all political actors – be they formal or informal representatives – who engage in democratic advocacy. Democratic standards need to apply to those representatives who play important functions in democratic polities, functions vital to the proper operation of democratic institutions. I defend this proposal by identifying several sources of authority for democratic representatives, as well as mechanisms of accountability other than that of formal elections, and argue that these sources and mechanisms apply to informal representatives. I then situate my understanding of democratic representation within the existing literature on good representation, revealing that the existing theoretical literature cannot provide an adequate account of what it means to excel at representing in a democratic fashion. In other words, the existing literature does not identify the standards that govern democratic representatives as *democratic* representatives. I derive these standards from an analysis of the characteristic activity of democratic representatives. In particular, I distinguish three aspects to this activity – aims, methods, and relationships – and argue that the three virtues correspond to each of these aspects. I conclude by articulating my understanding of the relationship between democratic representation and the preferences of democratic citizens.

In Chapter 4, I introduce the first virtue of democratic representation, what I call the virtue of fair-mindedness. In doing so, I draw on my claim that democratic advocacy aims toward the well-functioning of democratic institutions. Democratic advocacy thus exhibits concern for the impact of public policies not only on one's constituents, but also on the democratic citizenry as a whole. More specifically, in engaging in democratic advocacy, a representative assesses her activity in light of its impact on the legitimacy of democratic institutions. Now, the preservation of civic equality is crucial for preserving the legitimacy of democratic institutions. For this reason, good democratic representatives are ones who have and act effectively on a proper understanding of civic equality – specifically in respect of how the realization of civic equality in a democratic polity can legitimate democratic authority.

To be properly sensitive to civic equality, in turn, is to further civic equality in light of the ways in which civic equality legitimates democratic authority. I distinguish three different approaches to civic equality: the *formal approach*, the *gap approach*, and the *threshold approach*. The formal approach conceives of civic equality as occurring when citizens have the same rights and entitlements. The gap approach identifies civic equality as being achieved when differences among citizens' control of political resources are minimized. The threshold approach understands civic equality as requiring all citizens to possess the minimal political resources necessary for exercising their rights and privileges as citizens. Distinguishing these approaches will show that good democratic representatives seek not only to protect the formal political rights and privileges of all citizens, but also to counterbalance the accumulation of power that, in producing systemic inequalities, undermines the legitimacy of democratic institutions. Good democratic representatives must balance all three approaches to civic equality.

Chapter 5 explores the meaning of the second virtue of democratic representation, the virtue of critical trust building. Good democratic representatives do not merely employ the methods characteristic of democratic advocacy; that is, the methods that increase the participation of democratic citizens. Rather, good democratic representatives employ these methods properly. More specifically, the methods of good democratic representatives develop citizens' capacities to have critical trust in their government. Thus, good democratic representatives employ methods with the aim of developing and utilizing the critical capacities of all citizens, so that citizens can be self-governing.

In Chapter 6, I argue that good democratic representatives exhibit the virtue of good gatekeeping when they excel at cultivating and sustaining political relationships with marginalized citizens, which makes the polity more inclusive. The relevant political relationship with citizens is one in which there is a kind of reciprocated recognition among citizens and their representatives. A significant part of this chapter is devoted to defining this political relationship, one that I term "a mutual relationship." With this definition in place, I argue that good democratic representatives advocate in a democratic fashion when they seek mutual relations that maximize inclusion. In particular, they need to seek mutual relations with their political opponents, the dispossessed, and the marginalized. Moreover, good democratic representatives can also promote mutual recognition that consciously excludes some citizens in the service of including others.

In Chapter 7, I conclude by examining how the virtues of democratic representation apply to democratic representatives faced with nonideal circumstances. I contend that the virtues should be used for identifying *preferable* democratic representatives. After defining what I mean by preferable, I examine how judgments of preferable democratic representatives are system-dependent. I then highlight one difficulty facing good democratic representatives – namely, that the three virtues of democratic representation can come into tension with one another. In the real world, it is not easy to be a good democratic representative. The tensions that can, in nonideal circumstances, arise between these different virtues require good democratic representatives to understand the distinctive dangers posed by democratic representation, as well as the benefits that it promises. When the virtues come into conflict with each other, good democratic representatives balance the different virtues in ways that negotiate the dangers of each. Chapter 7 also examines the distinctive problems that these conflicts can pose for descriptive representatives.

In light of these problems, one might be tempted to conclude that the democratic virtues are too idealistic for existing political realities. But that would be a mistake. Even in nonideal circumstances, the virtues can still guide citizens in their choice among available representatives. They can also help citizens avoid bad democratic representatives. Moreover, an understanding of ways in which, under nonideal circumstances, the virtues can pull a representative in opposing directions will help democratic citizens assess their representatives appropriately, in light of those circumstances.

Chapter 2

Moving beyond Descriptive Representation

My position, put simply, is that it matters who represents democratic citizens. The ability of democratic institutions to flourish, or even to survive, depends on who deliberates on behalf of, advocates and stands for, democratic citizens. Consequently, democratic citizens need to choose their representatives wisely. Moreover, political theorists can and should assist democratic citizens in their choices of representatives. Unfortunately, the tendency among contemporary theorists has been to remain silent about how democratic citizens, or whatever party is responsible for the selection of informal representatives, should go about deciding who are better and worse representatives. Political theorists emphasize the freedom to choose, at the expense of articulating standards for choosing representatives well.

Granted, there is one place in political theory where theorists acknowledge the importance of who represents democratic citizens. I have in mind the literature on descriptive representation. In its broadest sense, "descriptive representation" refers to the representation of groups by members of those groups. Descriptive representatives are representatives who look like, or at least have experiences and interests similar to, the people they represent. In contemporary political theory, the term "descriptive representation" is often understood in a more restrictive sense; specifically, to refer to the representation of historically disadvantaged groups by members of those groups.[1] However, for the purposes of this book, I shall adopt this broad understanding of the term, unless explicitly stated otherwise. In the literature on descriptive representation of historically disadvantaged groups, there has been extensive discussion about the meaning and importance of good democratic representation; specifically, theorists have made a case that good democratic representation sometimes requires having members of historically disadvantaged groups as representatives.[2]

In this chapter, I explore the literature on descriptive representation of historically disadvantaged groups in order to identify arguments for why it matters who represents. I then propose that these arguments can be generalized to show why *all* democratic citizens should worry about who acts and advocates in their name. Historically disadvantaged groups might be particularly vulnerable to having bad representatives inflicted on them. But the arguments that show why marginalized groups need representatives from their groups also explain why democratic citizens need good democratic representatives.

The arguments for descriptive representation of historically disadvantaged groups all turn on the contention that a commitment to distinctively democratic norms and values requires that historically disadvantaged groups be represented by members of those groups. Properly understood, these arguments generate constraints, not only on what democratic representatives should look like, but on how descriptive representatives of historically disadvantaged groups ought to advocate on behalf of their constituents. Moreover, these arguments generate constraints on advocacy that apply not only to descriptive representatives of historically disadvantaged groups, but to democratic representation more generally: the good representative is one who in her advocacy is willing and able to further the realizing of fundamental democratic norms and values within the polity. What is more, the recognition that the arguments for descriptive representation of historically disadvantaged groups can be generalized in this way deepens our understanding of good democratic representation. We can only fully appreciate what makes for a good *descriptive* representative by understanding what makes for a good *democratic* representative. Good descriptive representatives of historically disadvantaged groups, like all good democratic representatives, must advocate out of a commitment to the norms and values distinctive of democratic institutions. And the selection of such descriptive representatives, like that of all democratic representatives, needs also to be informed by the commitment to these norms and values.

Democratic Representation and Descriptive Representation

Democratic theory has long recognized the need for descriptive representation, at least under certain conditions. By descriptive representation, I mean the idea that representatives should look like or possess shared experiences with those who they represent. In the United States, the idea of descriptive representation dates back to the American Revolution. In particular, John Adams argued that a representative legislature "should be an exact portrait, in miniature, of the people at large, as it should think, feel, reason and act like them" (1852–65, 195). For Adams, the best way for representative democracies to avoid the corruption and tyrannical practices of monarchies was to include a broad range of citizens in those institutions. Descriptive representatives who had certain occupations (e.g., lawyers or farmers) or who were from certain locations (e.g., urban versus rural or small states versus big states) were necessary for the people in their diversity to be represented. Bringing "the people" into governmental institutions would insure good democratic representation. Implicit in Adams's view is a claim about the relationship between having certain people acting as representatives and having good democratic representation; namely, having an "exact portrait" of the people at large in the legislature will increase the responsiveness of democratic representative institutions and thereby improve political accountability.

Not everyone would agree.[3] In particular, Hanna Pitkin (1967, 89) maintained that descriptive representation is, in fact, incompatible with accountability. As she put the point, descriptive representation allows "no room for representation as accountability." For Pitkin, placing too much importance on what a representative looks like can prevent those being represented from paying adequate attention to what a representative does. This line of reasoning – namely, one that sees a tension between accountability and descriptive representation – has defined the theoretical problem facing proponents of descriptive representation.

In response to Pitkin's characterization of descriptive representation, an extremely rich and insightful theoretical literature has developed about the representation of historically disadvantaged groups by members of those groups (e.g., Diamond and Hartsock, 1981; Sapiro, 1981; Young, 1990, 2000; Phillips, 1991, 1995, 1998; Gould, 1996; Williams, 1998; Mansbridge,

1999).[4] For example, early proponents of descriptive representation of historically disadvantaged groups focused on the conflicting interests of privileged and relatively less privileged groups. Most notably, Virginia Sapiro (1981) showed that trusting some groups to protect another group's interests – for example, letting husbands take care of their wives' interests – was and continues to be foolhardy. The reoccurring betrayals of historically disadvantaged groups by relatively privileged groups partially explain why citizens should pay attention to the looks and experiences of their representatives: privileged representatives have proven to betray the trust of historically disadvantaged groups. Traditional mechanisms of accountability are insufficient for historically disadvantaged groups. Descriptive representation of historically disadvantaged groups would strengthen, as opposed to weakening, democratic accountability to members of historically disadvantaged groups.

Anne Phillips (1991) provides a helpful overview of the literature when she identifies four arguments that show why descriptive representation of historically disadvantaged groups is necessary. The first of these, which Phillips calls "the role model argument," claims that members of historically disadvantaged groups benefit from seeing members of their group in positions of power. For instance, having women in public office – for example, Nancy Pelosi or Elizabeth Dole – increases women's self-esteem and thereby their capacity to assume leadership roles. Having descriptive representatives of historically disadvantaged groups expands a historically disadvantaged group's sense of the possible, opening up different career paths and contradicting existing stereotypes of their acceptable roles. According to Natasha Walter, having female representatives such as Margaret Thatcher allowed British women "to celebrate their ability not just to be nurturing or caring or life-affirming but also to be deeply unpleasant, to be cruel, to be death-dealing, to be egotistic" (cited by Pilger, 1998, 91). This first argument stresses the importance of having representatives as role models.

The second argument Phillips gives for the necessity of descriptive representation, one she dubs "the justice argument," maintains that descriptive representation of historically disadvantaged groups compensates for past and continued injustices toward certain groups. For Phillips, it is "patently and grotesquely unfair" for the rich, the whites, or the men to "monopolize" representation. The justice argument examines patterns of inequality to reveal the need for descriptive representation. These arguments appeal to evidence ranging from formal political exclusions (e.g., the disenfranchisement of certain groups) to economic disparities (e.g., mean incomes falling below the mean incomes of other groups). Such evidence challenges the assumption that all groups in representative democracies always enjoy the political equality that democratic commitments demand.

Phillips's third argument for descriptive representation of historically disadvantaged groups focuses on "overlooked interests." According to this argument, such descriptive representation allows historically excluded groups to get onto the political agenda their interests, opinions, and perspectives that have been previously ignored. More generally, deliberations about public policy will be improved by having a more diverse set of representatives. Implicit in this argument is the claim that privileged citizens are not always aware of how public policies impact disadvantaged groups.

Finally, Phillips advances the "revitalized democracy" argument, which asserts that a commitment to diverse representation is necessary for more ambitious and transformative purposes – making democratic institutions more participatory and accountable. The presence of descriptive representatives is necessary according to this fourth argument because it has the potential to "disperse power through a wider range of decision-making assemblies, and changing the balance between participation and representation." Thus, having descriptive representatives of historically disadvantaged groups is expected to increase the participation of marginalized groups and thereby increase the legitimacy of democratic institutions.

These four arguments explain why good democratic representation requires, at least under some conditions, descriptive representation of historically disadvantaged groups.[5] Democratic societies that have systemically marginalized and oppressed certain groups need to have representatives who are members of those groups. The provision of descriptive representatives for these groups can play an important role in compensating past and present inequalities.

In light of these points, it is not surprising that one of the most common methods of assessing representative institutions is by the gender, ethnicity, and race of elected representatives (e.g., Guinier, 1994; Paolino, 1995).[6] Implicit in these evaluations is the assumption that democratic political institutions that lack any representatives from historically disadvantaged groups are unjust. Moreover, these evaluations often assume that an increase in the number of representatives from historically disadvantaged groups can contribute to the substantive representation of those groups (e.g., Thomas, 1991). This method of evaluating good democratic representation often assumes that the more women, blacks, and Latinos there are, the better it is for democratic institutions.

These assumptions justify the political practice of setting aside certain political and institutional positions for members of historically disadvantaged groups. Given this commitment, representative democracies must, at least in many circumstances, take active steps to increase the number of descriptive representatives from historically disadvantaged groups. For example, representative democracies could enact institutional reforms such as party list quotas, caucuses, racial districting, and schemes for proportional representation.

Having members of marginalized and historically disadvantaged groups represent themselves in democratic institutions is vital for good democratic representation. Descriptive representation of historically disadvantaged groups is necessary, albeit certainly not sufficient, for good democratic representation in any society with a history of oppressing those groups. Nevertheless, current accounts of how descriptive representation (and, more generally, democratic representation) is to be assessed are radically incomplete. They are incomplete because they fail to provide any framework for evaluating the performance of individual representatives. They provide little discussion of any general guidelines for assessing the actions of descriptive representatives for historically disadvantaged groups in a democratic polity – that is, for assessing how they advance public policies on behalf of those groups.[7] Moreover, current accounts of descriptive representation fail to consider whether the actions of such descriptive representatives are consonant with good democratic representation. As a result of these omissions, theoretical discussions of democratic representation are devoted almost exclusively to the proper design of formal governmental institutions, for example, the proper design for elections.

But not all descriptive representatives for historically disadvantaged groups are the same: some descriptive representatives of historically disadvantaged groups are preferable to others, in virtue of being better democratic representatives. I maintain that democratic citizens should select their representatives – both descriptive and nondescriptive ones – based, at least in part, on the degree to which representatives excel at representing in a democratic fashion. More specifically, democratic citizens should select representatives whose advocacy is consonant with the norms and values distinctive of democratic institutions. Moreover, the reasons why democratic citizens prefer some representatives to others really do matter, because these reasons can have a substantive impact on the performance of democratic institutions.[8] But citizens' choice of representatives also matters to the degree that having bad democratic representatives can undermine the legitimacy of representative democracies. Democratic citizens – especially vulnerable citizens – need to value and choose representatives who seek to preserve and strengthen the legitimacy of their democratic institutions. The legitimacy of democratic institutions – that is, the perception that democratic institutions are the ones citizens ought to choose – depends on citizens and representatives consciously making decisions in ways that are sensitive to the impact of their decisions on the legitimacy of democratic institutions. Because not all preferences held by democratic citizens and not all actions taken by representatives are compatible with democratic norms and values, the legitimacy of representative democracies depends on democratic citizens being able to make good decisions about who is going to represent them – or at least being able to correct their bad decisions. Notice that this line of reasoning suggests that the lack of adequate and commonly recognized criteria for evaluating representatives is a problem for all democratic representation, and not simply a problem for descriptive representation.

Despite these important insights into why descriptive representation of historically disadvantaged groups is crucial to good democratic representation, there is a lacuna in the existing literature. This lacuna will become evident when I address a tension within the current literature; namely, that between the reasons offered for descriptive representation of historically disadvantaged groups and the recognition that not every descriptive representative of historically disadvantaged groups is a good representative for those groups. Although proponents of descriptive representation of historically disadvantaged groups recognize that it matters who occupies the institutional positions that were created to increase descriptive representation of those groups, they are extremely reluctant to specify any criteria – however general – for identifying good descriptive representatives. After outlining briefly the reasons for this reluctance, I argue that not only proponents of descriptive representation of historically disadvantaged groups, but also democratic theorists more generally, need to provide certain highly general criteria of good democratic representatives. Such criteria constitute a framework within which democratic citizens can fruitfully go about specifying more determinant criteria that serve to identify good democratic representatives.

Two Problems with Descriptive Representation

Not every member of a historically disadvantaged group is committed to advancing the interests, opinions, and perspectives of the group to which he or she belongs. Some members of disadvantaged groups resent, denounce, and reject wholeheartedly any particular obligation to disadvantaged groups. Almost all political theorists who endorse some form of descriptive representation of historically disadvantaged groups recognize that not every member of a disadvantaged group is a good descriptive representative for those groups. For instance, Melissa Williams (1998, 6) states that "it would be absurd to claim that a representative, simply because she is a woman, therefore represents the interests or perspectives of women generally, or that an African-American representative is automatically representative of all African-Americans. The mere presence of members of marginalized groups in legislatures is not *sufficient* for the fair representation of citizens from those groups, even though it is often *necessary*." The diversity within historically disadvantaged groups means that one descriptive representative cannot adequately represent all the members of a historically disadvantaged group. Iris Marion Young (1997, 351) notes that "women are everywhere and differ so vastly along so many dimensions that it seems absurd to suggest that women who might attain positions as representatives can legitimately speak for other women." Implicit in the above comments is the insight that historically disadvantaged groups can have deep disagreements about the proper interests, opinions, and perspectives of the group. Members of historically disadvantaged groups are therefore likely to disagree about who are desirable representatives for their group (and what their descriptive representatives should be doing).

As mentioned above, a tension thus emerges in the literature on descriptive representation of historically disadvantaged groups. On the one hand, theorists of descriptive representation have argued that certain patterns of inequalities justify having an institutionalized voice of historically disadvantaged groups (the justice argument). Such arguments emphasize the *shared* obstacles facing members of those groups, obstacles that prevent members of these groups being present in the political arena in equitable numbers. On the other hand, these theorists increasingly acknowledge the diversity within historically marginalized groups. This diversity can seemingly undermine the presumption that historically disadvantaged groups will be served by increasing the number of descriptive representatives from those groups, for it suggests that some such representatives lack the desire or the experiences necessary for satisfying the reasons why descriptive representation of those groups is necessary for good democratic representation.

This tension highlights two important problems with the institutional reforms proposed by theorists of descriptive representation of historically disadvantaged groups. The first problem is *the problem of intra-group conflict*. According to this problem, attempts to bring in certain members of historically disadvantaged groups can have the effect of marginalizing other members of those groups. Most notably, Iris Marion Young cautions that attempts to include more voices in the political arena can inadvertently suppress other voices. She illustrates this point using the example of a Latino representative who might inadvertently represent straight Latinos at the expense of gay and lesbian Latinos (1997, 350). Similarly, Cathy Cohen (1999) demonstrates how descriptive representatives of historically disadvantaged groups can advance public policies in ways that ignore the vulnerable subgroups of historically disadvantaged groups. In particular, Cohen found that although black representatives generally supported AIDS education, they did not support the needle-exchange programs that would benefit only certain subgroups of the African-American community – that is, black IV-drug users. Cohen's study warns against secondary marginalization – that is, against the regulation and policing of the less privileged members of historically disadvantaged groups by the more privileged members of that group. Cohen's discussion of secondary marginalization shows that having descriptive representatives of historically disadvantaged groups does not guarantee that the overlooked interests of certain subgroups will be advanced.

This leads to the second problem with institutional reforms designed to increase descriptive representatives of historically disadvantaged groups. Bringing in descriptive representatives from one historically disadvantaged group – for example, Latinos – can exclude the presence of descriptive representatives from other groups – for example, African-Americans. I call this second problem *the problem of inter-group conflict*. Some institutional reforms aimed at increasing descriptive representatives of historically disadvantaged groups can favor one marginalized group over another. For instance, district-at-large voting schemes tend to favor mainly white women, while single-member districts can support the presence of African-Americans in elected bodies (Matland and Studlar, 1998). Within the literature on descriptive representation of historically disadvantaged groups, there is insufficient discussion of how democratic citizens should choose which historically disadvantaged groups deserve more or less voice within representational institutions. Typically, the literature assumes that the choice facing democratic citizens is between a descriptive representative from a historically disadvantaged group and a representative from a privileged group, for example, between a black representative and a white representative. The literature identifies groups that need additional representation as ones that have been historical excluded, for instance, groups that have been legally prohibited from holding public office or voting.[9] Since democratic citizens can also face choices between representatives who both belong to historically disadvantaged groups – for example, between a black representative and a Latino representative – some additional criteria are obviously needed. A reliance solely on historical exclusions to determine which groups require a presence in democratic institutions is insufficient, because often *all* of the historically disadvantaged groups have faced some form of historical exclusion.

The problems of intra-group and inter-group conflict partially account for why patterns of inequality, overlooked interests, and low participation rates in democratic institutions often persist even when descriptive representatives of marginalized groups are present in the political arena. These problems indicate that simply having such representatives is not enough to satisfy the considerations that drive political theorists to insist that descriptive representation of marginalized groups is necessary. Some descriptive representatives might come from the wrong groups. They might advance the interests, opinions, and perspectives of relatively privileged constituents. Some descriptive representatives might come from the right group, but not be committed to advancing the concerns and interests of their group. More worrisomely, some descriptive representatives can further marginalize the more vulnerable members of historically disadvantaged groups. Consequently, both problems point to the need for the presence of the right descriptive representatives of historically disadvantaged groups in institutional positions designed to increase the diversity of democratic institutions. Unfortunately, most proponents of descriptive representation of historically disadvantaged groups have remained silent about the criteria for evaluating descriptive representatives.

Justifying the Silence about Criteria

The silence about the criteria for identifying preferable descriptive representatives of historically disadvantaged groups is by no means accidental. In fact, the related literature has offered two kinds of arguments to justify this silence. I call these two arguments *the autonomy argument* and *the contingency argument*.

According to *the autonomy argument*, members of historically disadvantaged groups should decide for themselves who is a preferable descriptive representative. This argument assumes that autonomy is best equated with being left alone – at least in the case of a historically disadvantaged group's choice of its representatives. In particular, on this line of thinking, respecting the autonomy of historically disadvantaged groups requires theorists to refrain from advancing criteria for evaluating descriptive representatives of historically disadvantaged groups. This argument has two main versions. The first suggests that articulating criteria for judging such representatives attributes to historically disadvantaged groups a fixed identity, thereby violating the autonomy of all members of that group. The second emphasizes the autonomy of the representative.

The first version of the autonomy argument asserts that any proposed criterion for evaluating descriptive representatives of historically disadvantaged groups presupposes that a historically disadvantaged group has an essential nature. In other words, it presupposes that such a group has a "fixed essence given once and for all, and with traits that are homogeneously distributed among all the group members" (Gould, 1996, 182). Such an assumption places undesirable constraints on the behavior of members of historically disadvantaged groups. According to Williams, "No defensible claim for group representation can rest on assertions of the essential identity of women or minorities; such assertions do violence to the empirical facts of diversity as well as to the agency of individuals to define the meaning of their social and biological traits" (1998, 6). To explain why some members are less suitable descriptive representatives of historically disadvantaged groups is to question the authenticity of those members' identity. Such explanations make an implicit charge that "she isn't really a woman" or "he isn't really black." In this way, discussions about the criteria for selecting descriptive representatives of historically disadvantaged groups are often interpreted as attacks on the "authenticity" of descriptive representatives. The problem with such discussions is not merely that they may be overly divisive (Jones, 1993; Stasiulis, 1993): more fundamentally, such discussions of standards prevent the group from determining its own boundaries. What concerns the first version of the autonomy argument, then, is the claim that members of historically disadvantaged groups should define for themselves the meaning of their group identity, as well as choosing the criteria for evaluating their descriptive representatives.

In contrast, the second version of the autonomy argument emphasizes the autonomy of *descriptive representatives* of historically disadvantaged groups. Phillips, in particular, argues that specifying the criteria for evaluating descriptive representatives of historically disadvantaged groups would, in undermining the autonomy of descriptive representatives, undermine the arguments for descriptive representation. It is misguided to provide a laundry list of "good policies" that a female representative should support and to insist that preferable female representatives can vote only in ways consistent with that list. After all, male representatives could also vote according to a laundry list. For Phillips, descriptive representation of historically disadvantaged groups is justified only to the extent to which representatives have some discretion about their political decisions. It is because representatives have this discretion that descriptive representatives need to be present where political decisions are being made. To uphold standards of "strict accountability" – that is, to require descriptive representatives of historically disadvantaged groups to follow a particular policy agenda, such as requiring female representatives to endorse pro-choice policies – is, for Phillips, to neglect what is the primary reason for requiring that certain historically disadvantaged groups have representatives from those groups; namely, that democratic representatives are not mere puppets of their constituents, but must exercise their own judgment. To suppose that there is a fixed set of criteria by which descriptive representatives of historically disadvantaged groups should be judged is to fail to appreciate how the *autonomy* afforded to representatives is what justifies descriptive representation. Indeed, the more we can say about how a descriptive representative of historically disadvantaged groups should act, the less it is necessary to have a descriptive representative for those groups. Such reasoning led Jane Mansbridge (1999, 630) to conclude that descriptive representatives of historically disadvantaged groups become less necessary when interests have crystallized. The more we know what historically disadvantaged groups want, the less descriptive representation is necessary.

The second kind of argument for remaining silent about the criteria for judging descriptive representatives of historically disadvantaged groups is *the contingency argument*. According to this argument, it is impossible to articulate any general criteria that should be used to evaluate such descriptive representatives because context matters. Any attempt to articulate such criteria cannot do justice to the relevance of certain particularities – for example, the differences between groups or the particular issue at hand

– in determining how descriptive representatives should act. The proper behavior of descriptive representatives of historically disadvantaged groups depends on contingencies. Some theorists of descriptive representation, such as Melissa Williams (1998, 17), stress that particular historical developments play "an important role in defining the groups whose moral claims are strongest." For Williams, which groups have justifiable claims on representatives will depend on historical contingencies. Others stress that the experiences of historically disadvantaged groups defy generalizations, so that variations across groups prevent adopting any one set of criteria. *A priori* proposals for criteria will either be irrelevant because they ignore the experiences of some group or do more harm than good by advancing the interests of some groups at the expense of others.

In summary, proponents of descriptive representation refuse to specify any criteria for evaluating descriptive representatives of historically disadvantaged groups for two good reasons. First, they see offering such criteria as violations of the autonomy of historically disadvantaged groups and/or their descriptive representatives, and second, they view such criteria as insensitive to contextual variation. For these reasons, these theorists avoid a tough question: Who is a preferable descriptive representative for a historically disadvantaged group? It is not easy to answer this question, because it requires privileging the interests, opinions, and perspectives of certain members of historically disadvantaged groups over those of other members. Answers to this question can therefore have the effect of downplaying, if not excluding, certain interests, opinions, and perspectives. For this reason, answers to the above question are more likely to be disputed than answers to the question, "Why have descriptive representatives from historically disadvantaged groups?"

The Need for Criteria

Underlying both the autonomy and contingency arguments is a legitimate concern about who gets to decide which criteria are best. The impulse to speak for others can be and often is paternalistic and imperialistic (Alcoff, 1995). Standards for assessing political performance have often been used to disqualify historically disadvantaged groups from political participation. To articulate criteria for evaluating descriptive representatives of historically disadvantaged groups is to run the risk that those criteria can be used in unanticipated and possibly harmful ways. Some fear that articulating such criteria might also unduly influence members of historically disadvantaged groups.

Such concerns are understandable, but ultimately unpersuasive. After all, to articulate such criteria is not necessarily to assume that all members of a historically disadvantaged group have some essential identity. In fact, the very real and politically relevant differences among members of historically marginalized groups point to the desperate need for a theoretical discussion of criteria. To assume that "any black, Latino, or woman will do" ignores the very real danger of secondary marginalization.

Besides, there is a difference between articulating particular policies that a descriptive representative of a historically disadvantaged group must endorse in order to count as a *legitimate* descriptive representative of that group and articulating a general framework for identifying *preferable* representatives. For instance, proponents of descriptive representation for historically disadvantaged groups have agreed that institutional reforms are necessary because historically disadvantaged groups possess overlooked interests. To maintain that a descriptive representative for a historically disadvantaged group should pay special attention to overlooked interests does not require that she possess a particular view about those interests. Such a descriptive representative has autonomy to the extent that she can reasonably interpret those interests in a variety of ways. However, to say that descriptive representatives of historically disadvantaged groups can legitimately interpret their group's interests in multiple ways is not to say that anything goes. Descriptive representatives who were to denounce their group affiliations or who were to deny that they had any particular obligation to their group would fail to achieve the ends for which descriptive representation was introduced (cf., Phillips's four arguments). Descriptive representatives who claim to represent only the common good might be desirable representatives for other reasons; however, they do not satisfy Phillips's "overlooked interests" argument. Such descriptive representatives might be legitimate representatives – for example, fairly elected to their public office – however, such representatives would not be preferable descriptive representatives according to my account, to the extent that they do not satisfy the considerations that drive political theorists to insist that descriptive representation is necessary.[10] More specifically, such representatives do not carry out the proper functions of descriptive representatives.

One can articulate criteria for evaluating descriptive representatives of historically disadvantaged groups without violating the autonomy of either those groups or their descriptive representatives. After all, to propose criteria for judging descriptive representatives is not the same as imposing those criteria on members of historically disadvantaged groups. Obviously, to impose criteria on such groups, or on democratic citizens more generally, is wrong-headed. It is crucial, according to my view, that members of historically disadvantaged groups retain the ability to choose to adopt any proposed criterion.

Proponents of the autonomy argument may respond that articulating criteria for evaluating descriptive representatives of historically disadvantaged groups – though offered without any obvious coercion to adopt such criteria – might nonetheless exercise an undue influence on those groups. However, such a response by proponents ignores the fact that members of historically disadvantaged groups are not always the ones who select descriptive representatives for those groups.[11] Privileged citizens are frequently in charge of selecting political appointees and nominating candidates for public office. More worrisome, privileged citizens can nominate and appoint candidates from historically disadvantaged groups as a way of undermining and constraining democratic representation. For appointing or nominating a member of an historically disadvantaged group to a political office can be one strategy for curtailing democratic deliberations or, at least, diverting discussions away from substantive policy issues. The identities of political representatives can be invoked as a way to insulate those in power from criticism. For example, when members of the Klu Klux Klan hire an African-American lawyer to defend them against hate crimes, their choice of legal representation is meant to demonstrate to the jury that their organization is not racist – or at least, not morally repugnant to all African-Americans. Similarly, formal representatives are often judged by the race and gender of the people who they choose to be in their administration. The identities of staff, advisers, and legislative aides are important, because these underlings are often the agents who deliberate. Moreover, the identity of those persons taking certain public policy positions can be treated as reasons for supporting or opposing certain positions. For example, Pro-Life advocates often broadcast the fact that the child from the *Roe v. Wade* case does not support abortion. The identity of a speaker can, and often does, affect the meaning of a statement (Alcoff, 1995).

After all, having a representative from a historically disadvantaged group advance policies that adversely affect most members of that group can be one way to deflect criticism of those policies. This is especially true if democratic citizens are reluctant to criticize speakers who are members of historically disadvantaged groups. This leads to one of the most troubling problems with remaining silent about the criteria for evaluating descriptive representatives of historically disadvantaged groups: those in power can appoint, nominate, and support those descriptive representatives in order to make it seem as though they respect democratic norms, while actually weakening and undermining democratic commitments. Given that those in power can appoint and nominate descriptive representatives of historically disadvantaged groups in order to constrain the autonomy of those groups, proponents of the autonomy argument need to reconsider their silence about the proper criteria for selecting descriptive representatives.

To assume that not articulating the criteria for selecting descriptive representatives for committees or party lists is the best way to protect the autonomy of historically disadvantaged groups ignores the power that privileged groups currently hold. As Audre Lorde (1984, 41) aptly warned, "your silence will not protect you." Silence about controversial subjects does not necessarily protect the autonomy of historically disadvantaged groups, or automatically bring about desired outcomes.

Besides, citizens inevitably bring their general standards of representation to bear on their choice of representatives. A critical evaluation of the standards for descriptive representatives can facilitate deliberations by democratic citizens, thereby assisting, and not infringing on, the autonomy of historically disadvantaged groups. It is important to stress that articulating criteria for assessing descriptive representatives does not make the exercise of judgment unnecessary; rather, deliberations about these criteria can help refine those judgments. Theorists can offer criteria for choosing among descriptive representatives of historically disadvantaged groups and still leave it up to the members of historically disadvantaged groups to determine for themselves how those criteria are to be applied in any particular case, or even whether a specific criterion is appropriate at any particular moment. This leads to the second argument for remaining silent: the role of contingencies in evaluations of descriptive representation.

Context undeniably does matter. Evaluations of descriptive representatives of historically disadvantaged groups, like arguments for a politics of presence, depend on "historically specific analysis of the existing arrangements for representation" (Phillips, 1995, 46). For instance, who is a preferable descriptive representative for a historically disadvantaged group might depend on whose interests, opinions, and perspectives are currently being stigmatized and marginalized by existing political norms and institutional processes. "Because group identity is orchestrated and produced in part through political institutional processes" (Bickford, 1999, 86), citizens should consider the unjust effects of those processes as relevant to assessments of preferable descriptive representatives.

Espousing criteria is not the same as requiring that certain criteria be applied in all circumstances. Like most theorists of descriptive representation, I share the suspicion of a cookie-cutter approach to evaluating descriptive representatives. It would be foolhardy to propose a set of criteria that did not require sensitivity to context, or that did not require individuals to use their own judgment to determine whether the criteria apply to the particular case at hand. Good descriptive representatives should not be identified by matching their policy positions against some predetermined list – for example, a liberal or conservative policy agenda. To hold such a view would be to deny that representatives need to be evaluated according to the particular political context. But recognizing the importance of particularities does not preclude articulating criteria for evaluation. It requires having criteria that are sensitive to those particularities.

The criteria for evaluating descriptive representatives of historically disadvantaged groups that, I believe, most need to be articulated – criteria that exhibit the requisite sensitivity to particular context – are those that derive from the demands of democratic commitments. One begins to appreciate this need when one recognizes that not all members of historically disadvantaged groups agree about who should represent them.

Consider the controversies within the African-American community over Louis Farrakhan's leadership. Consider too how, as Angela Dillard (2001, 4) notes, conservatives among women (e.g., Phyllis Schlaffly) and minorities (e.g., Thomas Sowell and Richard Rodriguez) "have been dismissed as traitors, as sell-outs, as self-loathing reactionaries who are little more than dupes of powerful white, male, heterosexual conservatives." Recently, Lee Freed, a female president of the Manitoba chapter of the First Nations Accountability Coalition in Canada, accused the male tribal leadership of corruption and nepotism.

Such contemporary controversies within historically disadvantaged groups over the leadership of these groups confirm that members of a historically disadvantaged group can possess different understandings about who should be their representatives. But more importantly, these examples raise the concern that simply having descriptive representatives of historically disadvantaged groups is not sufficient to meet the requirements of a democratic commitment to the concerns of those groups. For not all members of historically disadvantaged groups are committed to democratic norms and values. Since members of disadvantaged groups can espouse inegalitarian and xenophobic views – descriptive representatives for these groups can also adopt positions that significantly undermine and weaken democratic commitments. Some descriptive representatives of historically disadvantaged groups might, for example, advance views that contradict a democratic commitment to human rights, such as protection from the use of torture, or equal protection before the law. The appointment of descriptive representatives of historically disadvantaged groups cannot be assumed to be good for democratic ends. Such appointments can be used by foes of democracy as a diversionary tactic to distract attention from their substantive anti-democratic agendas. Moreover, the appointment of such descriptive representatives can provide cover for such agendas, by creating the appearance of some minimal commitment to democratic representation. Criteria for identifying those descriptive representatives of historically disadvantaged groups who genuinely advance democratic commitments can help democratic citizens guard against such cynical ploys and tactics.

The Need for Democratic Standards

Implicit in the literature on descriptive representation of historically disadvantaged groups is a prior commitment to good democratic representation. After all, two of the best arguments for such descriptive representation will only resonate with those who care about democratic norms and values. The overlooked interests argument will appeal only to those who are committed to reconciling differences through democratic deliberation. The revitalized democracy argument will have purchase only for those who care about the well-functioning of democratic institutions. Proponents of descriptive representation of historically disadvantaged groups, however, have not explicitly recognized the extent to which their arguments for descriptive representation rely on a preexisting particular ethical outlook – an ethics of democratic representation. It seems likely that this reliance has been obscured from the proponents of descriptive representation as a result of their commitment to observing a studied silence about criteria for the selection of descriptive representatives. In any case, proponents of descriptive representation have failed to recognize that such criteria can be derived from this ethics, criteria that can, and should, inform both the activity of descriptive representatives of historically disadvantaged groups and the choice of descriptive representatives on the part of members of those groups.

In the chapters that follow, I want to generalize the argument found within the literature on descriptive representation of historically disadvantaged groups – namely, that it matters who represents democratic citizens – to articulate criteria that should inform the selection not only of descriptive representatives, but of democratic representatives more generally. Indeed, we shall see that articulating criteria for good democratic representatives helps to clarify criteria for good descriptive representatives of historically disadvantaged groups. These criteria will help all democratic representatives – descriptive representatives of historically disadvantaged groups as well as descriptive representatives of privileged groups – make better judgments about how to go about advancing public policies, policies that are informed by democratic norms and values.

As will be seen, there is a considerable amount of overlap between the criteria that govern good democratic representatives and those that govern good descriptive representatives of historically disadvantaged groups. Indeed, preferable descriptive representatives of those groups are good democratic representatives. Of course, descriptive representatives of historically disadvantaged groups might have particular duties or obligations to their groups that other representatives might not have. Nevertheless, all representatives who advocate – that is, advance public policies on the behalf of some citizen at the expense of others – need to be assessed, in large part, by the extent to which they foster the democratic norms and values that justify the legitimacy of democratic institutions.

My position is admittedly controversial. After all, some political theorists simply deny that the lack of any clear standards for identifying good representatives is a problem for democratic theory. In fact, the reluctance of democratic citizens to endorse their representatives is considered by these theorists to be an advantage of democratic institutions, what George Kateb (1992, 37) refers to the "radical chastening of political authority." Kateb interprets democratic citizens' reluctance to endorse their representatives as a healthy form of skepticism toward government, one that is vital for promoting a more active citizenship. Such skepticism can encourage democratic citizens to become more vigilant about their own political beliefs and interests. According to this line of reasoning, democratic institutions flourish when citizens exercise their own judgment about who is a good representative and create their own standards for evaluating the performance of representatives. Confusion about what representatives should be doing fosters democratic instincts in citizens. In particular, confusion over the proper standards by which citizens should judge their public officials motivates citizens to develop their capacities to represent themselves. To propose any one set of criteria for evaluating representatives would unduly constrain those capacities (and risk damaging citizens' democratic instincts). Democratic theory should not constrain the choices of citizens; rather, democratic theory should accommodate those differences by remaining silent about the criteria for evaluating representatives.

Moreover, for many democratic theorists, the existence of and competition among different and conflicting conceptions of the good – what John Rawls (1971) called "the fact of pluralism" – is itself an indication that a society is living according to democratic norms. Theorists such as Andrew Sabl (2002) and Jane Mansbridge (1999) equate valuing pluralism with being democratic. For them, democratic standards are ones that, in leaving room for diverse conceptions of the good, allow diverse standards for identifying good democratic representatives to flourish. It follows from such a position that standards for selecting democratic representatives are to some degree a matter of individual taste. Democracy should cultivate the pluralization of tastes in the name of freedom (Connolly, 1995), and not try to domesticate those tastes by subjecting them to democratic norms. According to this view, standards that discourage – let alone stigmatize – certain citizens' way of identifying good representatives would be in some sense undemocratic.

Certainly, political representatives in a democratic polity can face conflicting standards about how to excel as democratic representatives. Furthermore, democratic citizens are likely to disagree about who are good representatives. Like descriptive representatives of historically disadvantaged groups, democratic representatives must negotiate the problem of intra-group and inter-group conflict. For instance, members of Congress must negotiate the disagreements among their supporters from their electoral districts (intra-group conflicts) as well as conflicts between local and national interests (inter-group conflicts). As Iris Marion Young has insightfully pointed out, all representatives must confront the problem arising from one person representing the many. For Iris Marion Young (2000, 127), "no one person can stand for and speak as a plurality of other persons." She contends that we should not insist on representatives speaking *as* the constituents. For Young, "It is no criticism of the representative that he or she is separate and distinct from the constituents." Evidence that some democratic citizens disapprove of a representative's actions is not sufficient to determine whether that representative has violated democratic norms and values. After all, individual representatives will inevitably face conflicts with the people they claim to represent, as well as with citizens whom they don't claim to represent.

Moreover, democratic citizens should not reject their representatives simply because they differ from those whom they represent in respect to their interests, opinions, and perspectives. However, it is important to acknowledge that the substantive content of the criticisms filed against representatives matters. In other words, it makes a difference whether a representative is being criticized simply for adopting a particular policy with which her constituents disagree – for example, agricultural subsidies – or whether a representative is being criticized because her advocacy work undermines the equal political standing of democratic citizens. Some kinds of separation and differences between representatives and their constituents provide genuine reasons for criticizing and rejecting a particular representative as failing to abide by constraints that democratic norms and values place on good democratic representatives.

The recognition of the problem of one person representing the many is certainly an important insight. However, the failure to recognize how some kinds of separations or differences between representatives and their constituents are a problem for democratic modes of representation leaves representatives with too much wiggle room. To ignore this problem is to ignore the fact that representatives can adversely impact the capacities of citizens to hold their representatives accountable, and thereby undermine the legitimacy of democratic institutions. Moreover, differences between representatives and their constituents might not be the basis for legitimate criticism of democratic representatives. Democratic citizens might, out of excessive fear, agree with their representatives' taking measures that undermine the legitimacy of democratic institutions. I will argue that, in taking such measures, representatives would still be violating standards of good democratic representation to which they are subject. The main purpose of this book is to articulate a general framework for identifying the types of considerations, grounded in democratic norms and values, that democratic citizens should use in assessing individual representatives.

To say that democratic institutions should promote the pluralization of tastes is also not enough.[12] William Connolly (1995) is wrong to claim that that democratic institutions should try to *cultivate* the pluralization of tastes – whatever those tastes may be – in the name of freedom. For the pluralization of tastes is not in and of itself always consonant with democratic norms and values. For example, increasing the variety of racist and sexist values held by democratic citizens does not strengthen democratic institutions. The substantive content of citizens' norms and values is relevant to the assessment of the strength of democratic institutions.[13] It matters, for instance, whether democratic citizens increasingly prefer representatives who hold racist views. Similarly, it matters whether citizens seek representatives who advance their own narrow self-interests at the expense of preserving the fairness and legitimacy of democratic institutions. Simply equating the pluralization of values with the upholding of democratic commitments ignores how some values justify and promote unfair and unjust democratic practices.

However, the main problem with a radically pluralist conception of democracy – that is, an understanding of democratic commitments as requiring the toleration of diverse views regardless of the content of those views – is that it provides no framework for understanding how individual representatives should be assessed in light of democratic values. For such pluralism eschews specifying what makes any particular standard for evaluating representatives democratic. And radical pluralists are thus not in a position to articulate any distinctively democratic standards that govern the behavior of all democratic representatives.

Much more can be said about the standards for identifying good democratic representatives than simply that democratic citizens possess different and sometimes conflicting standards for evaluating their representatives. In particular, we can, and should, specify an ethical framework within which the performance of individual representatives can be evaluated in light of distinctively democratic norms and values. This framework would specify criteria for identifying representatives who excel at representing in a democratic fashion. Such a framework is necessary for at least three reasons.

First, such an ethical framework would improve the ability of democratic citizens to hold their representatives accountable. To assume that any standard for identifying good representatives (provided that it is lawful) is acceptable from the perspective of democratic norms and values is to ignore the dangers of bad democratic representatives. It is not good enough to treat the decision to vote for a particular candidate as simply a matter of individual taste, because that decision can have a significantly detrimental impact on how democratic institutions function. Democratic citizens need to consider whether their representatives have violated, or are likely to violate, democratic norms and values. And, in order to help democratic citizens make such assessments of their representatives, it is important to identify and defend the standards they should bring to bear in making these assessments. In holding their representatives accountable to these standards, democratic citizens can help preserve the legitimacy of democratic institutions.

This leads to the second reason why democratic standards for assessing representatives need to be specified: the absence of such standards can weaken democratic citizens' commitment to representative institutions. Consider the fact that Americans tend to love their Congressional representative more than their Congress (Parker and Davidson, 1979). One possible explanation for this discrepancy is that they mistakenly blame the institution of Congress for the misdeeds of individuals. Put frankly, democratic citizens may not distinguish adequately whether particular representatives or the institution as a whole is to blame for bad public policy. Do bad public policies result from the failure of individual representatives to live up to their duties (e.g., representatives selling out their constituents' interests to the highest bidder) or do the institutional norms of Congress prevent representatives from making good public policies? There are reasons for ascribing much bad policy-making to the latter. For instance, the Congressional practice of declaring bills "emergencies" does not allow for representatives to have time to read the bills that they are voting on, let alone consult their constituents about how legislation would adversely affect them.[14] Similarly, the extent to which Congress spends its time on activities such as naming post offices or congratulating sports teams can detract from its addressing substantive policy issues. By identifying the characteristic activity of democratic representatives, democratic citizens will be in a better position to differentiate between the faults of representative institutions (e.g., improper norms or procedures for determining policies) and the bad performance of individual representatives. Democratic citizens need to know when representatives are acting as bad democratic representatives – that is, when the advocacy of individual representatives undermines the legitimacy of democratic institutions. Otherwise, democratic citizens will continue to overvalue their own representatives and undervalue Congress.

A third and final reason for providing a general framework for evaluating individual democratic representatives returns to my earlier claim that any fully adequate treatment of descriptive representation of marginalized groups needs to recognize how an ethics of democratic representation underlies arguments for that descriptive representation. In particular, the failure to articulate democratic standards for the assessment of representatives can lead to the political abandonment, and further marginalization, of historically disadvantaged groups. An overly vague and, I would argue, inadequate, understanding of the need for descriptive representation of historically disadvantaged groups can lead to the insistence that such groups be represented *only* by group members – and this can drive out of the political arena important allies of those groups.

For example, consider the controversy over the white participation in an interracial civil rights organization, the Student Nonviolent Coordinating Committee (SNCC). SNCC, whose aim was to support student protests against segregation and to promote registration of black voters in the rural South, had always been black-led. However, increasingly, the presence of whites in SNCC had become problematic. Blacks were known to move from one project to another, fleeing the presence of "too many" whites.[15] SNCC's activities, especially its local branch programs, were seriously siderailed by internal debates about the legitimacy of white participants. For example, some black staff members at the Atlanta project would continuously interrupt organizational meetings, demanding that "whites had to go" (Carson, 1982, 240). On December 1, 1966, SNCC passed a resolution excluding whites by a vote of 19 for and 18 against, with 24 abstaining (all of the white members abstained). The December 1 decision to kick out white staff members was the culmination of a debate concerning the ability of some people (whites) to act on behalf of, and thereby to represent, others (African-Americans).

Consider some likely consequences of the dynamics that this example illustrates. First, standards for good representatives can encourage privileged citizens to withdraw from participation in democratic politics. These controversies promote what Linda Alcoff (1995) has called the "Crisis of Retreat." Political actors flee the political arena rather than be accused of abusing their privileged status by speaking on the behalf of the less privileged. The tendency to retreat from the political arena is particularly acute for those actors who are sensitive to the past and present injustices experienced by certain groups. Democratic citizens who are concerned about existing inequalities and injustices in their society can be made to be uncertain about (and sometimes afraid of) trying to advance the policy preferences of others.

Another problem with discouraging privileged citizens from representing less privileged groups is that identities of citizens are sufficiently complex that practically every individual can be disqualified as a legitimate representative according to some privileged dimension of his or her identity. Members of disadvantaged groups who have more education, fairer skin, or belong to mainstream religious groups would be disqualified from advancing public policies on behalf of other members of that group who are less educated, have darker skin, or are from a marginalized religious group. While the retreat of these privileged representatives might provide opportunities for less privileged members of historically disadvantaged groups to represent themselves, such retreats could also contribute to these privileged citizens irresponsibly abdicating their civic responsibilities. This is an especially worrisome phenomena in cases in which the only advocates available from within some historically disadvantaged groups – for example, illegal immigrants – are themselves privileged.

Thus, democratic theory needs a general framework through which the performance of individual representatives can be assessed in light of fundamental democratic norms and values. This framework needs to take into consideration the extent to which democratic representatives will have to negotiate intra-group and inter-group conflict. The absence of disapproval is not what separates good democratic representatives from bad ones. What does, rather, is the way in which representatives negotiate intra- and inter-group conflicts: good democratic representatives negotiate these conflicts in ways consonant with democratic norms and values. Of course, how an individual representative should balance these norms and values in a particular case will depend on the particular context and issues facing that representative. Sometimes, good democratic representatives will need to attend to the policies that are significant to the most marginalized in order to act in accordance with democratic virtues. At other times, a good democratic representative will act in ways consistent with the preferences of the majority. Genuine obligations can conflict, and such conflicts give democratic representatives some leeway for determining whose preferences they should prioritize.

However, there are standards that good democratic representatives will never violate. To acknowledge that democratic representatives can face conflicting obligations is not to say that "anything goes." The fact that representatives gain their authority from democratic institutions produces a particular set of ethical constraints that a representative must respect, if she is to be a good democratic representative. But before I turn to identifying these proper constraints on good democratic representatives, I need first to consider the function of democratic representatives. And that is the task of Chapter 3.

Chapter 3

Democratic Advocacy and Good Democratic Representation

Many political scientists simply equate being a democratic representative with being duly voted into a public office of a democratic polity. On this view, only duly elected officials can engage in democratic representation. Such a view is mistaken: informal, as well as formal, representatives can be democratic representatives, and can engage in the advocacy that constitutes democratic representation.

On my view, democratic representation includes more than simply the activities of elected officials. For democratic representation is properly understood as political advocacy, on the part of a representative with the requisite authority and accountability, that fulfills a certain function in democratic polities. More specifically, democratic representation is best understood as such advocacy that has a distinctive function within the democratic polity, one that requires that the representative employ certain aims, methods, and relationships. Moreover, democratic representation is an activity that not only has a distinctive proper function, but also characteristic effects, within a democratic polity. Democratic representation is *democratic advocacy*.

The main purpose of this chapter is to explicate my understanding of democratic advocacy and to sketch the theoretical landscape that informs my understanding of good democratic representation. I begin by arguing that the scope of democratic representation should be expanded to include all political actors – be they formal or informal representatives – who engage in democratic advocacy. My argument then turns to identifying the sources of authority and mechanisms of accountability available to democratic representatives. This discussion defends my proposal to extend the scope of democratic representatives to include informal representatives from the objection that only formal representatives can have the authority and accountability essential to democratic representation. Next, I locate my positions on democratic representation within the existing literature on good representation. As will be seen, although an extensive theoretical literature deals with the proper behavior of representatives, this literature does not adequately discuss what it means to excel at representing in a democratic fashion. In other words, the existing literature does not identify the standards that govern democratic representatives as democratic representatives.

After making the case that we need specifically democratic standards for evaluating representatives, I posit that such standards need to be grounded in the distinctive function of democratic representatives, namely democratic advocacy. In particular, I provide an account of democratic advocacy that distinguishes three moments, or aspects, of democratic advocacy – its distinctive aims, methods, and relationships. As will be seen, each of these moments corresponds to a different virtue of democratic representation, virtues that provide distinctively democratic standards for evaluating democratic representation. This chapter concludes by examining the relationship between democratic standards and the preferences of democratic citizens.

The Scope of Democratic Representation

Contemporary democratic theorists writing about representation have treated democratic representation as a characteristic of formal governmental institutions. Put bluntly, most democratic theorists assume that democratic representation requires direct mechanisms of authorization and accountability, specifically those of electoral institutions. According to this way of thinking, democratic representation occurs when fair procedures of authorization and accountability are in place. Implicitly, such democratic theorists subscribe to a minimalist view of democracy, one that identifies democratic representation with the representation that takes place when fair elections, basic liberties, and the rule of law obtain. Such an understanding of democratic representation naturally focuses on what it means for an official to be legitimately elected.[1] Moreover, on such an understanding, a democratic representative is considered to be only as good, or as bad, as the procedures that authorize her to act on behalf of democratic citizens and the mechanisms that hold her accountable to those citizens.

Of course, formal political institutions, such as elections, are central to any adequate understanding of contemporary democratic representation. After all, formal elections play a constitutive role in modern definitions of democracy. And formal elections do so not only because they authorize officials, but also because they allow democratic citizens to sanction representatives who have failed them. To the extent that our understanding of democracy is tied to formal elections, we can recognize as democratic only representation that occurs in a political context in which formal elections take place.

However, it does not follow that the proper exercise of formal electoral procedures is what constitutes democratic representation, or that only those who are elected through the proper exercise of formal electoral procedures can be democratic representatives. Democratic representation can, and should be, understood more broadly. One can acknowledge the centrality of elections to democratic representation and still understand democratic representation as an activity of political advocates, as opposed to a characteristic of formal governmental institutions. Moreover, one can acknowledge the centrality of elections to democratic representation and still understand democratic representation as the activity that performs a function that contributes to the proper operation of democratic institutions.

One reason why political scientists are led to equate being a democratic representative with being duly elected is that they equate democratic representation with a duly elected representative's advocating public policy preferences on behalf of her constituents. Now, being duly elected into a public office of a democratic polity is sufficient for someone to be a democratic representative. However, not just any effort to advocate a public policy agenda by such a duly elected representative constitutes democratic representation. In other words, the fact that the person engaging in political advocacy has been voted into public office in a democratic polity is not sufficient, let alone necessary and sufficient, for her advocacy to be democratic.

After all, on my view, informal representatives can also be democratic representatives. If one were to list the political actors who represent democratic citizens' policy preferences, that list would include informal representatives. Members of political parties, civic associations, labor unions, interest groups, nongovernmental organizations (NGOs), and social movements all plausibly claim to "represent" democratic citizens in pressing formal representatives to adopt certain public policies.[2] Moreover, such actors are now often responsible for writing, implementing, and even monitoring legislation. Since democratic governments "contract" out state functions, informal representatives often perform the tasks that were traditionally reserved for formal representatives.[3] In the United States, the work of formal representatives is often done by informal representatives. The latter can, and within contemporary democratic governments do to a considerable and growing extent, advocate public policies on behalf of democratic citizens and thereby serve as their political representatives.[4]

Indeed, there is some evidence that democratic citizens trust and identify more with informal representatives than with their formally elected ones. So when *The Washington Post* asked citizens to rate different political actors on environmental issues, environmental groups beat out both local government and the Environmental Protection Agency (EPA). Put bluntly, we trust the Sierra Club to be our advocates more than we trust local representatives or even the EPA (Greider, 1992, 170). The question is: Can at least some of this advocacy work by informal representatives count as democratic representation?

In answering this question, it is instructive to see that political advocacy on the part of these informal representatives can play a crucial role in promoting the proper functioning of democratic institutions. One such role is the correction of social injustices committed in and by representative democracies. Consider, for instance, the work of Stephen Bright, Executive Director of the Southern Center of Human Rights. Bright works to insure that those facing the death penalty receive adequate legal representation. He also leads a campaign to improve the living conditions of prisoners in the South, including providing healthcare to HIV-positive prisoners. In these ways, Bright advocates on behalf of, and thereby represents, many citizens who are marginalized by democratic processes. Other informal representatives directly foster democratic institutions; for example, individuals who work for NGOs whose primary purpose is to promote democracy through the development of civil society (MacDonald, 1997). Such informal actors may or may not be formally authorized by democratic citizens. However, if we attend to what they *do*, we can see that they act as representatives of democratic citizens, promoting the well-functioning of the democratic institutions in distinctive ways. Indeed, as we shall see, the advocacy of informal representatives, just as much as that of formal representatives, can violate democratic norms. These points indicate that at least some political advocacy on the part of informal representatives constitutes democratic representation, and that these representatives count as democratic representatives.

Now consider the role that debate in the public sphere – outside of formal, governmental institutions – plays in the process of democratic public policy-making. Take, for example, debates of public policy issues on news shows such as PBS's *News Hour with Jim Lehrer* or Fox News's *The O'Reilly Factor*. Such debates affect policy-making directly, by influencing legislators, and – perhaps more importantly – indirectly, by way of influencing public opinion. Participants in these debates, more often than not, act as advocates of particular public policies. Moreover, in doing so they often speak as representatives of particular groups of democratic citizens – as, for example, a spokesperson of the American Civil Liberties Union (ACLU) does in arguing that certain provisions of the Patriot Act undermine important civil liberties. Such advocacy on the part of an informal representative, insofar as it contributes to an informed and critical public debate about the relative importance of civil liberties and security, plays an important function in the proper operation of democratic institutions. It thus counts as democratic advocacy, in my sense, and it constitutes democratic representation, on my account.

Granted, for all I have said so far, one can recognize that some informal representation contributes to the proper functioning of democratic institutions without conceding that such representation should itself be classified as democratic. The issue remains murky, in large part because there has been little theoretical discussion of what it means to represent in a democratic fashion. The neglect of this question has been costly, for without an adequate discussion one cannot understand what it means to excel at representing in a democratic fashion. So this is our situation. We know that democratic citizens are being represented by a wide range of political actors, including informal representatives. Indeed, we know that informal representatives are playing an increasingly crucial role in representing democratic citizens. But we do not know whether, and if so how, democratic standards apply to the activities of these actors. And as a result, political theory has offered democratic citizens little guidance about how they should go about determining whether individual formal representatives are good or bad democratic representatives.[5] And it has offered democratic citizens virtually no guidance for the assessment of informal representatives.[6] So when Senator Robert W. Packwood (R-OR) was exposed by *The Washington Post* for making unwanted sexual advances on ten women, we know his actions might have forced his resignation, but there is no consensus about whether his actions violated democratic standards. Similarly, we have no way of assessing whether the advocacy work of the National Rifle Association or of those protesting against the activities of the World Trade Organization is consistent with democratic standards.[7]

My attempt to make up for these omissions, and to provide a general account of the democratic standards to which informal as well as formal representatives are to be held, turns on what I describe as the central function or characteristic activity of democratic representatives, the distinctive work that democratic representatives contribute to the proper operation of democratic institutions and thus to the health of a democratic polity. I call this function *democratic advocacy*. With this account of democratic advocacy before us, we will be a position not only to see that informal representatives can engage in democratic advocacy, but also to recognize what, in general, constitutes excellent democratic advocacy.

On this alternative understanding that I favor, democratic representation occurs whenever and wherever political representatives – be they duly elected officials or leaders of social movements, lobbyists for interest groups, or presidents of civic associations – engage in democratic advocacy. So when Stephen Bright challenges the cruel and unusual conditions in which 11 Southern states incarcerate their prisoners, his advocacy work holds formal representatives accountable for those conditions and educates the public about the interests and needs of a marginalized community. Bright's actions insure the proper operation of democratic institutions, protecting the rights of citizens who are prisoners and raising the awareness of citizens who are not imprisoned of the actions taken in their name. Of course, Bright is not the only informal representative to engage in democratic advocacy. Organizations such as the American Association of Retired People (AARP), which provides services and benefits to elderly citizens, the Christian Action Network (CAN), which holds that the US can be led to peace, prosperity, freedom, and unalienable rights through the principles established in the Bible, or Mothers Against Drunk Driving (MADD), which is devoted to preventing drunk driving, can provide vital educative and political functions, shaping the identities of their members and encouraging forms of political activities. But so can organizations such as the Coalition for Equal Access to Medicines, a union of poor people, minority members, and public health advocates that was established with the help of the Pharmaceutical Manufacturers Association. Even lobbyists for the AAA, who protested raising the federal gas tax in 1991 because some of the tax money would have gone to public transit, and lobbyists for the National Cattleman's Beef Association, which opposes superfund regulation for manure, can serve a critical role in the proper functioning of democratic institutions. (Again, not every act of advocacy on behalf of democratic citizens constitutes democratic representation. Only advocacy that advances public policies on behalf of democratic citizens in a particular fashion constitutes democratic representation.) Such an understanding of democratic representation includes political advocacy by some agents that are not duly elected representatives. It thus expands the scope of democratic representation to encompass the advocacy work of some informal representatives, as well as that of formal representatives.

My proposal to expand our understanding of the scope of democratic representation reflects a growing realization that the public sphere is a differentiated and multidimensional space.[8] The public sphere is not demarcated solely by the activities of formal governmental institutions. For example, it can include the actions of the media. After all, the media not only keeps the workings of government transparent and provides the public information relevant to public policy debates, but it also provides a space within the public sphere for public policy debates. Moreover, civic associations that may not be formal, let alone governmental, constitute part of the public sphere. Democratic representation can pervade all these areas of the public sphere, insofar as the political advocacy performed by informal representatives draws on political capital from these different areas, and that advocacy influences the processes of making and instituting public policy that contribute to the proper operation of democratic institutions. And insofar as civic associations and organizations (such as the Southern Center for Human Rights) demarcate areas of the public sphere from which political actors (such as Stephen Bright) can exercise such influence, they combine to provide valuable political arenas to the democratic polity, arenas within which democratic citizens can debate and contest public policy issues.

A rich literature on the role that civic associations play in democracy gives us an initial sense of the different important functions that informal representatives can play to promote the proper operation of democratic institutions. Consider, in particular, how in the course of his discussion of civic associations, Mark Warren (2001a) identifies three general ways in which such associations contribute to the proper functioning of democratic institutions: in producing developmental effects, public-sphere effects, and institutional effects. Associations produce developmental effects when they "contribute to forming, enhancing and supporting the capacities of democratic citizens" (61). Associations produce public sphere effects when they contribute to the formation of public opinion and political judgments by "providing infrastructure of public spheres that develop agendas, test ideas, embody deliberations and provide voice" (ibid.). Finally, associations produce institutional effects when they provide political representation by "enabling pressure and resistance, organizing political processes, facilitating cooperation and serving as alternative venues of governance" (ibid.). Political actors who qualify as informal representatives by virtue of their location within civic associations can act as agents of all three sorts of effects. Warren's discussion thus delineates three distinct ways in which informal representatives can act on behalf of democratic citizens. And in each of these ways they can function to contribute to the proper operation of democratic institutions, insofar as they advocate in ways that support citizens' power to make collective decisions and help preserve the autonomy of individual citizens. In short, because civic associations support democratic institutions, we need to understand how informal representatives contribute to those institutions.

We may add that, understood as an activity of representatives, as opposed to a formal characteristic of institutions, democratic representation generally – thus including that of informal representatives – has the function of fostering citizens' loyalty to the democratic institutions that they share as members of a single democratic polity. Done right, democratic representation binds democratic citizens to their democratic institutions. Furthermore, democratic representation has the function not only of connecting citizens to their political institutions but also of linking different political arenas. Democratic representation thus serves as the connective tissue of a democratic polity, binding citizens to the institutions and political practices that give meaning to democratic commitments.

One benefit of this expansive understanding of the scope of democratic representation is that it covers the wide range of ways in which democratic citizens are currently being represented, ways that are crucial to the proper operation of democratic institutions. Here it is important to see not only that the ways of representing democratic citizens are changing, but also that the number of representatives are proliferating as the number of points of access to governmental institutions has increased. An increased number of subcommittees, a weakening of national political parties, and a loss of power by committee chairs – all have contributed to increasing the number of formal representatives who have the potential of playing key roles in public policy-making, and whose activities democratic citizens thus need to monitor and seek to influence.[9] Moreover, a corresponding explosion of interest groups that work to target these points of access introduces more political representatives, informal ones, who claim to act on behalf of democratic citizens. Democratic citizens are thus now represented by so many formal and informal representatives that they often don't even know the names or numbers of the political actors who advocate on their behalf.[10]

The proliferation of political representatives has changed the forms of control that democratic citizens can exercise over their representatives. In the case of formal representatives, traditional methods of authorization and accountability no longer work effectively, and they do not even apply to informal representatives. Indeed, even if we restrict our attention to the activity of formal representatives, representation is arguably no longer promissory – in the sense that representatives are selected for their campaign pledges and held responsible for their pledges by voters (Mansbridge, 2002). Thus, democratic citizens would be wrong to assume that they have given formal authorization to those who advance public policies in their name.[11] They would also be mistaken to assume that the formal characteristics of their legislatures can secure the proper operation of their democratic institutions. Only if democratic citizens attend to the activities of all the different kinds of political actors who influence policy-making – including their many informal representatives – and hold them all to certain democratic standards, can they hope to secure the proper operation of their democratic institutions. We will begin to get a sense of how citizens can exert this kind of control over their representatives shortly, when I turn to identifying several different sources of authority for democratic representatives as well as different mechanisms of accountability.

But for now, the important point to stress is that there is something troubling about the proliferation of political representatives within contemporary democracies – namely, the extent to which this proliferation disadvantages citizens with scarce political resources. For the increased number of points of access means that those democratic citizens with the resources needed to target a large number of public officials will exercise far more influence, overall, on the public policy-making process than those who lack the requisite resources. In this way, increasing the number of points of access has disadvantaged those with scarce political resources. I contend that it is only by expanding the scope of democratic representation to include both formal and informal representatives that any ethics of democratic representation can hope to address adequately such vulnerabilities on the part of the less privileged members of the democratic polity.[12] For to focus exclusively on formal representation is to ignore how marginalized groups must rely on surrogate representatives; that is, on representatives who have not been directly authorized by democratic citizens yet advocate on behalf of those citizens (Mansbridge, 2002). Such a focus also overlooks the extent to which marginalized groups must rely on social movements and interest groups to advance their causes, as opposed to relying on individual representatives (Weldon, 2002).

Expanding the scope of democratic representation beyond formal political institutions allows one to consider certain ethical constraints that should be placed on all political actors who make demands on public resources and alter the distribution of goods to democratic citizens. Given its focus on formal governmental institutions, current theories of democratic representation cannot, in particular, account for how informal representatives, insofar as they advocate on behalf of democratic citizens, are subject to democratic standards, and thus how they can and should be subject to criticism when they fail to meet those standards. Nor can it account adequately for the multiple and troubling ways in which formal representatives represent democratic citizens. In contrast, in shifting the focus to democratic advocacy, my account of democratic representation has the benefit of clarifying how the activities of all democratic representatives, be they formal or informal, are as democratic representatives properly subject to a single set of specifically democratic standards.

Some may question extending the scope of democratic representation beyond the advocacy work of formal representatives – that is, beyond representatives who have been authorized by governmental procedures such as elections – on the following grounds. In virtue of being elected, such political actors have the authorization of democratic citizens to advance policy preferences on their behalf. And this authority is predicated, in part, on the fact that such elected offices provide institutional incentives to representatives to be responsive and accountable to the preferences of democratic citizens. If, as seems plausible, democratic representation requires some form of authorization by democratic citizens, and some corresponding form of accountability, then it seems that we need to restrict democratic representation to the activity of formal representatives – for it is hard to see how informal representatives can have either this authorization or this accountability.

I want now to counter this objection by identifying sources of authority for engaging in democratic advocacy, and mechanisms for holding democratic representatives accountable, that apply to informal representatives. These sources of authority are not necessarily direct processes of authorization by democratic citizens. Nor are these mechanisms of accountability to which informal representatives are subject necessarily linked to processes of authorization. The objection fails, because democratic representatives can have sources of authority, and be subject to mechanisms of authorization, other than the ballot box. For this reason, democratic representatives are not simply those representatives who have been duly elected to their governmental office.

Sources of Authority for Democratic Representatives

Democratic representatives – both informal and formal ones – can be elected to their particular office. And elections arguably not only authorize such democratic representatives to advocate on behalf of those who elect them, but also make them accountable to those being represented. After all, elections create incentives for representatives to be responsive and thereby accountable to their constituents. Moreover, by being accountable, a representative can acquire the authority necessary for being a fully legitimate democratic advocate.[13] But democratic representatives need not derive this authority from elections. Nor need they be held accountable for their actions through elections.[14] More specifically, there are at least four sources of authority for democratic representatives other than elections: *institutional affiliation, intangible goods, social location*, and *formative experience*. Each of these sources can give a democratic representative the authority to advance public policies on behalf of democratic citizens.

Consider the position of Angelina Jolie, who wants to get the US to fund peacekeepers in Darfur. Over 400,000 civilians have been killed by the Janjaweed militia, which is supported by the Sudanese government. If one were to ask Angelina Jolie why she has the authority to advance public policy positions on behalf of the victims of Darfur, and more generally on behalf of all those who have an interest in seeing human rights protected, she would be likely to appeal to her institutional ties to a particular human rights organization. Her standing as a United Nations goodwill ambassador, say, gives her efforts to lobby, organize, or write media releases about a certain public policy initiative a legitimate claim on the attention and resources of her audience. This authority, however, is not one that she derives from being elected, be it by Darfur's victims, actual or prospective, by members of the UN, or more generally by the public.

Despite the lack of authorization from Darfur's victims, who are arguably most affected by the relevant policies, a policy advocate who is affiliated with a UN organization nonetheless has the authority to act for vulnerable groups. *It is her job.* This response points to the first source of authority for democratic representatives: *their institutional affiliations.* In other words, democratic representatives can derive a legitimate claim that they enjoy on the attention of policy-makers, and the general public of democratic polities, from their affiliation with particular interest groups, associations, or organizations. In an important sense, such democratic representatives rely on the good name of their organizations. Such representatives do not stand simply for themselves; rather, they act as spokespeople, associates, employees, board members, or even volunteers of particular institutions, organizations, and/or associations.[15] The characteristics of the institution, association, or organization, such as its reputation or standing, provide the individual with some authority to act in the name of democratic citizens.

This leads to a second, and higher, source of the authority that democratic representatives can enjoy – namely, *intangible goods.* I borrow this term from Hugo Slim (2002), whose work focuses on the legitimacy of non-governmental organizations (NGOs), not on the authority or legitimacy of democratic representatives. For Slim, NGOs (and thereby the actors who work for those organizations) can derive their legitimacy from what other people consider to be worthwhile and good ends. Similarly, the authority or legitimacy of a democratic representative will depend, to some extent, on what ends democratic citizens consider to be desirable ends. In particular, democratic citizens' recognition of an end in which they have a genuine interest – such as the protection of human rights – coupled with their recognition that particular interest groups, associations, or organizations are valuable advocates of that end, can be a source of authority for those advocacy groups and for advocates affiliated with those groups. The authority of democratic representatives, then, is never completely divorced from public opinion. Unlike rulers who appeal to divine right or rely simply on brute force in laying claim to authority, democratic representatives need to recognize that their authority depends in part on the moral ends they serve and in part on democratic citizens' perceptions of those moral ends.

Third, democratic representatives can derive their authority to advocate from their *social location.* By social location, I mean the various group memberships of the representative; in other words, the different socio-economic, ethnic, religious, and cultural groups to which the representative belongs. As Linda Alcoff argues (1995, 98), "where an individual speaks from affects both the meaning and truth of what she says." For example, having certain experiences – such as having lost a son in a war – can lend authority to one's questioning or advocating for certain policies. Similarly, for better or worse, firsthand experience of war can enhance an elected representative's authority to make decisions about going to war. Being a member of a certain group, or having certain experiences, can give an individual the authority to sit on boards of nonprofits, provide certain testimony in Congressional hearings, or even occupy certain legislative seats. By virtue of having a certain position within a community, a distinctive set of experiences, and particular social connections, a representative may enjoy the authority to serve as the voice of that community.[16] Indeed, the social location of a representative can "authorize" or "de-authorize" that representative by determining the meaning of statements that she makes, or actions that she takes, on behalf of democratic citizens.

Finally, democratic representatives can generate their authority by acquiring certain *formative experiences*, ones through which they prove themselves to be worthy representatives. For example, the Student Non-Violent Coordinating Committee (SNCC) used their members' exposure to racist violence and the enduring jail sentences imposed for their activist work as a weeding out process. Jane Stembridge described SNCC's evaluation process in the following way:

> I think the first thing was "What's this guy been through? Has he really been there? Does he really know what he's talking about?" His jail record; where he's worked; what he's been through; what gives him a right to speak, much more than where he went to school, what he studied, where he comes from. (Stoper, 1989, 252)

Serving jail time for engaging in nonviolent resistance in the service of the US Civil Rights Movement was a test or experiential "hoop" that whites could jump through in order to qualify as legitimate advocates for securing civil rights for blacks.[17] The willingness to put their ideas on the line and to suffer because of those ideas offered some evidence of their devotion to the cause. In this way, what a democratic representative has gone through, endured, or survived can increase his or her authority to act on behalf of certain democratic citizens.[18] Formative experiences provide this authority, in part, by serving as a proxy for a representative's reliability and good intentions.

This brief discussion of the different sources of authority available to democratic representatives is by no means exhaustive. I single out these four sources of authority for two main reasons, each of which highlights why we shouldn't equate democratic representatives with those who have been authorized by formal governmental procedures. First, my discussion reveals that some representatives who perform activities crucial for the proper operation of democratic institutions – for example, advancing human rights or challenging racial discrimination – are unelected. To limit the scope of democratic representation to those representatives who have been elected is to ignore political representation, on the part of informal representatives, that makes vital contributions to the proper operation of democratic institutions.

Second, the multiple sources of authority available to democratic representatives suggest that it is important to understand the authority and legitimacy of a representative as a matter of degree. Even if a given democratic citizen enjoys some degree of authority and legitimacy as a democratic representative, that degree may not be sufficient for her to engage legitimately in a certain act of advocacy. Democratic citizens can justifiably criticize her advocacy. In this respect, there is a parallel between the cases of informal and formal representatives: after all, the manner in which a representative gets elected – for example, the fairness of the formal authorization procedures – can affect the degree of legitimacy that a democratic representative possesses. Moreover, the actual performance of a democratic representative – for example, the extent to which her actions are lawful or morally justifiable – can affect the degree of her authority as a democratic representative, whether she is a formal or an informal representative. My understanding of democratic representation stresses that democratic citizens should not think of the legitimacy of their representatives in "all or nothing" terms.[19]

Holding Democratic Representatives Accountable

An examination of the ways in which democratic representatives can come to enjoy authority alters our understanding of how citizens can hold democratic representatives accountable. The different sources of authority we have distinguished suggest that democratic citizens will have different methods for sanctioning representatives who fail to do their bidding. Moreover, it seems that democratic representatives can be made responsive to democratic citizens' expressed preferences to different degrees, depending on the source of their authority. The various sources of authority for democratic representatives do not necessarily provide citizens with a considerable degree of control over their representatives, as does authorization through elections.[20]

Granted, it is ideal for democratic authority and accountability to be so linked, precisely because such a linkage gives citizens a greater degree of control over their genuinely authoritative representatives. However, it is a mistake to treat authorization and accountability as two sides of a coin, as does Hanna Pitkin.[21] Contemporary practices of democratic representation call into question this assumption that mechanisms of accountability and sources of authority are necessarily linked. In fact, recent theoretical discussions of accountability suggest that democratic theorists need to think "outside of the democratic box" (Mansbridge, 2004a). In their discussion of the accountability of NGOs, states, and multilateral organizations, Ruth Grant and Robert Keohane (2005) identify seven types of accountability mechanisms: hierarchical accountability, supervisory accountability, fiscal accountability, legal accountability, market accountability, peer accountability, and public reputational accountability.[22]

For our purposes, one especially important element of Grant and Keohane's discussion of accountability in the international arena is their recognition that the individuals affected by a policy are not necessarily the ones charged with holding a power-wielder accountable. For example, *fiscal accountability* describes mechanisms of accountability that can be enacted when "funding agencies can demand reports from, and ultimately sanction, agencies that are recipients of funding." In contrast, *peer accountability* occurs when organizations "mutually" evaluate each other.[23] A significant contribution of Grant and Keohane's work is that it provides an understanding of accountability that separates the role of "those who are affected" from the role of "those who authorize a power-wielder."[24] And, in making this contribution, their work shows that political theorists should not confine their understanding of accountability to merely sanctioning political representatives in the voting booth.

Even more importantly, Grant and Keohane's understanding of accountability reveals the importance of *indirect* influence on representatives. Often, democratic citizens only possess indirect and thereby mediated control over the actions of their representatives. To acknowledge the various sources of authority and mechanisms of accountability is to recognize that democratic citizens cannot always choose, let alone directly sanction, those who advocate public policies on their behalf. I want to set aside the question of whether direct forms of accountability are more effective than indirect forms and focus on how indirect forms of accountability reveal the need to examine the norms by which democratic citizens evaluate their representatives. For even though citizens cannot directly sanction or punish those who advance public policies in their name, democratic citizens' understanding of the proper actions of informal and formal representatives can, in part through indirect forms of accountability, shape the behavior of their representatives. This heightens the urgency of developing an ethics of democratic representation that can help inform citizen's understandings of how their representatives ought to advocate on their behalf. In particular, we need an ethics of democratic representation that articulates a framework that citizens can use in developing criteria for determining when political representatives have abused their authority as democratic representatives. Such an ethics needs to identify what it means to excel at representing in a democratic fashion – for in doing so it will be providing the needed framework for going about distinguishing good democratic representatives from bad ones.

We have seen that an adequate ethics of democratic representation cannot simply be an ethics of voting. An examination of the sources of authority and mechanisms of accountability has revealed that democratic citizens come to recognize the authority of their representatives and hold them accountable by means other than the ballot box. This not only shows that informal representatives can have the authority and accountability requisite of any truly democratic representative. It shows that, in order to address these other ways in which citizens relate to their representatives, an adequate ethics of democratic representation needs to provide a framework that citizens can use to assess the advocacy work of all democratic representatives, including informal ones. And, crucially, it must illumine how acts of individual representatives can be profoundly undemocratic, using democratic institutions to oppress and dominate, and thereby undermining the legitimate reasons democratic citizens have for valuing democratic institutions.

To be a democratic representative, I consider it necessary, but not sufficient, that an agent fills a social role, not necessarily a role in a formal institution that has as its function democratic advocacy. Another necessary condition is that the agent has the requisite authority to fill that role.

In light of these conditions, consider first formal representatives. Since to be duly elected to a formal political office is to be properly authorized to fill that office, all duly elected formal representatives are democratic representatives. In being properly authorized, formal democratic representatives are also held accountable by democratic citizens. They can be voted out of office (sanctioned) and thereby given incentives to be accountable (responsiveness). As I mentioned before, such a representative need not engage in democratic advocacy and so actually fulfill the function of a democratic representative in order to count as a democratic representative.

Consider now the case of informal representatives. We have seen that mechanisms of authorization can be decoupled from mechanisms of accountability. For this reason, it is not clear which forms of authorization and which forms of accountability are necessary in order to be an informal democratic representative. First, who needs to carry out the authorization? Second, how are informal representatives to be authorized? Furthermore, it is not clear how responsive and how sanctionable an informal representative needs to be in order to be an informal democratic representative. Nonetheless, the sources of authority and the means of accountability that we have canvassed show that informal representatives can have both the authority and accountability required to qualify as genuine democratic representatives.

Existing Standards for Identifying Bad Representatives

Contemporary political theory has offered at least three different standards for identifying bad representatives – that is, those representatives who engage in morally suspect and undesirable behavior. The first holds that bad representatives are those who violate *the interests of the constituents*. The second maintains that bad representatives are those whose *autonomy* has been compromised. This second standard focuses on evidence that representatives have conflict of interests and that their judgments have been improperly influenced and impaired. On the third standard, bad representatives are those who violate *the professional norms* of their particular offices. Representatives are to be evaluated according to standards that derive from their respective offices. In this section, I contend that although these standards all hold important insights into how political representatives should properly conduct themselves, each of these standards suffers from certain important limitations. Indeed, even taken together, these standards do not suffice for the adequate assessment of democratic representatives.

The interests of the constituents

Perhaps the most common and important standard used to evaluate the behavior of representatives is the standard of constituents' interests. Hanna Pitkin captured the essence of this first standard when she wrote, "the substance of the activity of representing seems to consist in promoting the interest of the represented" (1967, 155). The first standard holds that political representatives should serve their constituents, and that their actions should advance their constituents' well-being.

Within political theory, this standard takes two main forms, each of which associates the proper behavior of a representative with a particular method of identifying constituents' interests. The first form of this standard maintains that representatives should be *good delegates*. According to this form, interests are equated with the expressed preferences of constituents. To be a good representative is to follow the mandate as given by those being represented. The second form of this standard maintains that good representatives should act as *trustees* and thereby use their own assessments to determine the interests of constituents. Hanna Pitkin famously reconciled these competing standards by arguing that good representatives advance the interests of the represented in ways that are responsive to the represented.[25] For Pitkin, good representation can take many forms (e.g., delegate or trustee). What is more important than subscribing to only one form of representation is that when representatives choose to disobey the expressed preferences of those who they represent, they justify their actions. Assessments of political representatives must remain contingent – that is, dependent on the issues and agents involved.

The standard of constituency interests faces two additional complications. First of all, the concept of interests is notoriously ambiguous. People disagree about what should be done to foster their well-being. Brian Barry (1990 [1965]) identifies at least three different meanings of the phrase "x is in A's interests": (1) "A wants x"; (2) "x would be a justifiable claim on the part of A"; and (3) "x will give A more pleasure than any other alternative open to him." One of the reasons why the concept of interests isn't particularly helpful in settling disputes about good representation is because these three meanings of representation can and do conflict. We can want things that don't give us the most pleasure. We can want things to which we don't have a justifiable claim. And, finally, those things to which we do have a justifiable claim don't necessarily give us the most pleasure. Many contemporary theorists forego speaking about interests, because definitions of interests generate different and conflicting solutions for deciding who has the ultimate say in what is an interest. Contrary to those who claim that the concept of interests generates objective criteria for evaluating representatives' behavior (e.g., Pitkin), the concept of interests can shift disagreements about good representatives to disagreements about "what is a legitimate interest."

If that wasn't enough, the standard of constituents' interests faces an additional problem – namely, the difficulty of identifying who is and should be represented by a particular representative. Richard Fenno (2002) famously identified how elected representatives have different and some-times competing constituencies. For instance, formal representatives must owe a certain allegiance to their parties, their particular electoral district, their financial supporters, those who voted for them, their staff, and their nation as a whole. For Fenno, the notion of constituency has different dimensions and is best envisioned as a series of concentric circles.[26] It appears that formal representatives have competing and conflicting con-stituencies, not just one constituency.[27]

Informal representatives can also face competing and conflicting con-stituencies. For example, informal representatives can possess obligations to those affected by policies advanced, those funding their activities, and the well-being of their organization. An informal representative can represent all three "constituencies." Such ambiguous and conflicting boundaries about who is being represented complicate the question of how polit-ical representatives should behave when they advance their constituents' interests, for it requires asking which constituents' interests should take priority over others. If the represented cannot agree on an understand-ing of their interests or on the proper boundaries of a representative's constituency, then the standard of constituents' interests risks becoming merely rhetorical, a way of creating a false sense that the position of a few represents the entire group's position.[28] While the standard of con-stituents' interests focuses one's attention on the potential harms com-mitted by representatives, and on the ways in which representatives can abuse their authority at the expense of those they should be helping, it does not ultimately offer much advice about how to decide who is a good representative, let alone guidelines for identifying a good democratic representative.

Autonomy

The second standard for assessing political representatives maintains the importance of protecting the autonomy of a representative. The autonomy standard focuses on *individual* representatives avoiding improper influence, as opposed to identifying the institutional conditions necessary for autonomous deliberations. For instance, Amy Gutmann and Dennis Thompson (1985) argue that the first duty of a legislator "requires that representative to deliberate and decide free from improper influence" (174). Implicit in this standard is the assumption that representatives should avoid compromising conflicts of interests. John Saxon (1985) put the point this way: "a legislator will not undertake an official act in return for a thing of value which redounds to his personal financial benefit" (201).[29] Saxon's account of conflict of interests points to the fear that representatives who profit from their activities as representatives will be morally corruptible.[30] Their votes can be bought. Their judgment can be clouded by ideology. Corruptibility is identified by financial contributions or ideological commitments playing an excessive and counterproductive influence on the representative's decision-making. Here, the assumption informing this standard is that those who profit unduly have been improperly influenced.

The main problem with this second standard is that there is no consensus about how improper influence is to be understood. Specifically, it is unclear whether representatives should be entirely free of conflicts of interest. After all, representatives should respond to their constituents' preferences. But to the extent that representatives are accountable to their constituents, their interests are tied to their constituents, and they cannot help but benefit themselves when they benefit their constituents. Parallel considerations hold with respect to the authority of democratic representatives: after all, one thing that gives representatives this authority is their sharing similar interests, opinions, and perspectives with their constituents.[31] Enforcing the autonomy standard too zealously could thus actually undercut one important means for achieving accountability and responsiveness in democratic polities and rule out one crucial source of authority for democratic representatives.

Professional norms

The third standard for identifying bad representatives appeals to the professional norms associated with a representative's particular office. The
main virtue of this standard is that it does not adopt a "one size fits all"
approach to political ethics.[32] Rather, it tailors one's political ethics to
a particular office. It requires an ethical division of labor, a kind of political Fordism. Each office demands different forms of behavior. Such
a conception of political morality distributes different aspects of public
morality to different offices.

The reliance on professional norms to evaluate representatives also
reflects the extent to which the business of politics has become profession-
alized.[33] Being an elected representative is a career choice.[34] The expertise
needed to advance public policies means that it is not a job for amateurs
(Johnson, 2001). To function correctly, democratic institutions need
officials with "insider's knowledge" (Shapiro, 2003).

Such an ethical approach toward politics is instructive for articulating
the particular commitments that accompany different roles. Here, the duties
and obligations of senators differ from the duties and obligations of activists
(Sabl, 2002). However, it is less useful for articulating the ways in which
democratic norms can and should condition the actions of different
officeholders. After all, professional norms are not necessarily consistent
with democratic commitments. For instance, professional norms that guarantee confidentiality to one's clients can be in tension with the publicity
needed for democratic deliberations to be transformative and accountable. To emphasize professional norms exclusively is to fail to specify how
those norms should be tempered or modified to encourage representatives
to engage in the kinds of behavior that make it possible for democratic
institutions to function properly.

As can be seen, each of these three standards (constituents' interests,
autonomy, and professional standards) provides some insights into how
representatives can get it wrong. The first standard, that of constituents'
interests, points to the ways in which representatives can betray the trust
of their constituents. It highlights the power that representatives can hold
over their constituents and focuses attention on the irreparable wrongs that
representatives can commit against those whom they claim to be serving.
The focus on interests directs critical attention correctly at the violations
of the basic needs and well-being of those being represented. The second
standard, that of autonomy, emphasizes ways in which representatives can

be unduly influenced. An advantage of the second standard is that citizens are more likely to agree about what undue influence is than they are about what an interest is. Finally, the third standard, that of professional norms, emphasizes the particular duties and obligations required of a particular office. It identifies genuine norms that are generated from one's particular role within governmental institutions.

Despite these contributions, these standards – at least to the extent that they have been developed in the literature – all fail to identify norms that govern the proper behavior distinctive of democratic representatives as *democratic* representatives. For none of these standards have been developed in light of the recognition that democratic commitments generate distinctive constraints on the way citizens are to be represented within a democratic polity. The behavior expected of representatives within democratic polities is more demanding than the behavior expected of representatives in undemocratic regimes. The development of specifically democratic standards for assessing representatives has the added benefit of making some of the problems that plague these standards more tractable.

Consider the first standard, that of constituents' interests. As it stands, it fails to specify how democratic citizens have distinctive interests. For example, democratic citizens, as such, all have an interest in protecting their political liberties – such as their right to run for office – while individuals who belong to a military dictatorship do not. If democratic citizens have distinctive interests, then standards governing democratic representation will differ from those governing political representation in general. Note that, with respect to these interests that democratic citizens have simply as democratic citizens, it is not clear that the first standard is subject to the problems discussed above. These interests clearly have a legitimate claim to being addressed in the course of the operation of democratic institutions. They are common to all of a representative's constituencies. Moreover, the claims that these interests make arguably trump, and set constraints on, the demands that other constituents' interests make on democratic representatives – including interests that are grounded merely in the pleasures of constituents.

Consider now the second standard, that of autonomy. The recognition that democratic commitments set distinctive constraints on the behavior of democratic representatives goes some way to specifying what counts as improper influence on a representative's deliberations and decisions. The key point is that a democratic representative must not allow her own interests to interfere with the proper operation of democratic institutions.

As I will argue in subsequent chapters, this requires that a democratic representative base her advocacy not only on serving the interests particular to the specific constituency that is the source of her authority, but also on commitments she has to all democratic citizens of her polity – including that of realizing equality within the polity as a whole.

Moreover, the recognition that our understanding of a democratic representative's autonomy is subordinate to our understanding of democratic commitments has the virtue of clarifying the importance of a democratic representative's avoiding the perception of improper influence: such a perception is particularly insidious for democratic regimes. After all, the perception that representatives are on the take can have a particularly insidious effect on the legitimacy of democratic institutions. For example, military dictators might require the military's support to continue their rule; but democratic representatives rely on the support of a broader constituency. Consequently, if a majority of democratic citizens view their governments as corrupt, then such a perception can adversely affect democratic institutions in ways that the perceptions of other types of government – for example, military dictatorships – do not. For the perception that corrupt representatives pervade or dominate the political arena can weaken citizens' faith in the ability of democratic institutions to settle political disputes fairly and peacefully.

Finally, the third standard needs to be developed in light of the fact that our understanding of the professional norms governing officeholders needs to be informed by the constraints that a commitment to the proper operation of democratic institutions sets on the behavior of officeholders. Each particular officeholder needs to inform and temper her behavior with the recognition of how her exercise of her office must realize, in some specific fashion, the general function common to all democratic representatives. To the extent that the particular roles within governmental institutions that define particular political offices yield obligations that can and do conflict with the obligations that all democratic citizens as such have to their institutions, the latter obligations override the particular obligations of particular offices. This is what it would mean for democratic norms to condition the choices of political representatives. So the professional norms view cannot, of itself, provide a satisfactory account of the standards to which democratic representatives are subject.

In short, my problem with each of these standards is not that they do not possess genuine insights into the proper conduct of representatives or that they do not apply to democratic representatives. It is, rather, that some additional work is necessary to show how the standards are to be understood and applied within democratic polities. In other words, these standards need to be developed in light of an ethics of democratic representation that applies to all democratic representatives as such.

Why Democratic Standards?

In clarifying the need for democratic standards, looking at an example will help. Consider the performance of Representative Tom DeLay (R-TX) as House Majority Leader.[35] His tenure has certainly been marked by numerous ethical inquiries, questionable financing dealings, and, most recently, an indictment. However, more troubling than any of these particular ethical violations is the impact of his leadership itself on democratic institutions. More specifically, Tom DeLay has consolidated his power as House Majority Leader in ways that limit dissent and prohibit political compromise. To understand why such consolidation would be troubling from a democratic perspective, consider the recent Medicare legislation. Members of Congress were given only one day to study the recent Medicare bill that had more than 1,000 pages, much of it written from scratch in conference. According to Robert Kuttner (2004, 19), "members literally did not know what they were voting for."

Most House members favored amendments allowing drug imports from Canada and empowering the federal government to negotiate wholesale drug prices. Kuttner writes that, "DeLay made sure that the bill passed as written by the leadership, and that members were spared the embarrassment (or accountability) of voting against amendments popular with constituents." In this way, DeLay prevented representatives from having to confront those with whom they disagreed or from having to compromise.[36] In fact, all four House Democratic conferees were excluded from meeting with Senate conferees to reconcile the different versions of the House and Senate bills. Republican House and Senate conferees could work out their intra-party differences and send their nonamendable version of the bill back to each house for a quick up-or-down vote. Such tactics are certainly more efficient and less time-consuming. Deliberations take time. But such measures also curtail an important source of accountability – specifically, preventing representatives from considering those measures in light of their constituents' needs and preferences.

So how should democratic citizens respond to the behavior of Tom DeLay? The issue here is not whether DeLay has engaged in any illegal actions. Rather, the issue is whether his actions in consolidating his power in the House have violated standards governing the proper behavior of democratic representatives. Was Tom DeLay, in engaging in these actions, acting as a bad democratic representative? It seems to me that he was. However, interestingly, none of the three existing standards – not even all three taken together – can fault DeLay's method of consolidating his power in the House. So these standards cannot provide an explanation of why, as seems to me intuitive, DeLay is a bad democratic representative.

Consider the first standard. It would seem that DeLay's actions meet this standard, because these actions are arguably consistent with his constituency's interests – at least, the interests of his diehard partisan supporters. Indeed, the first standard could be understood as suggesting that, to the extent that the Republicans control the House, Senate, and Presidency, DeLay can take some kind of mandate to enact the kinds of policies that he sees fit. Insofar as constraining dissent is how he can be an effective representative and thereby serve his constituents' interests, it is perfectly legitimate, perhaps even appropriate, for him to constrain dissent. To be sure, one could argue that DeLay's constituents would profit if DeLay heard the opinions, perspectives, and values of those with whom he disagrees. Moreover, such conversations, arguably, serve the interests of DeLay's constituents. However, such an argument presumes a certain understanding of interests – one that is distinctive of democratic commitments. But such an understanding of constituency interests – one that would leave DeLay's behavior in violation of the first standard – has not, however, been explicitly developed in the theoretical literature on representation. Articulating such an understanding of constituency interests would amount to a development of the constituent-interest view along just the lines that I am proposing.[37]

Similarly, it is not clear that DeLay's actions violate the autonomy standard, because it is not clear that his autonomy is being compromised by his efforts to squelch dissent and to consolidate his power in the House. In fact, DeLay's autonomy can arguably be seen as increasing as a result of this consolidation of his power. Of course, DeLay has been charged with violating campaign contribution laws in the service of consolidating his power, and these violations are plausibly to be criticized according to the autonomy standard. But this is not to raise a problem with the actions in question – namely, the parliamentary tactics DeLay employed to squelch dissent and consolidate power.[38]

Consider finally whether DeLay's actions violate the third standard, the standard of professional norms. Those who argue that professional norms are sufficient to provide an adequate ethics of democratic representation, and who share my intuition that DeLay conducted himself as a bad democratic representative, need to make the case that DeLay failed to fulfill the obligations of a House Majority Leader. But to the extent that a House Majority Leader is supposed to promote party loyalty and the swift passage of legislation that the party deems fit, DeLay's actions could be justified by appealing to the standard of professional norms. One could, of course, try to make the case that the proper role of a House Majority Leader is, rather, to facilitate fair and productive debate among proponents of differing points of view, regardless of party membership. On such a view, a House Majority Leader should put his loyalty to the House above his loyalty to his party. But to make the case for this understanding of the office of House Majority Leader, and of the professional norms governing its occupant, would again seem to require the development of just the kind of account of the role of democratic representatives that I am proposing.

Thus the three existing standards for evaluating bad representatives do not of themselves offer much guidance for understanding how, as seems intuitive, DeLay's actions pose a problem for the proper operation of democratic institutions. The constituents' interest standard provides the wrong type of guidance, while the autonomy standard and the standard of professional norms are too formal to provide adequate guidance. It is necessary to supplement all three of these existing standards with an ethics of democratic representation – that is, an ethics whose content is informed by a specific and explicit commitment to the proper operation of democratic institutions, where one's understanding of this proper operation is, in turn, informed by a commitment to democratic norms and values.

I am arguing, then, that – contrary to most contemporary discussions of good representation – an understanding of democratic commitments needs to play a central role in evaluating both formal and informal representatives in democracies. Of course, a single understanding of democratic commitments cannot be found etched in stone, there for all to consult. How citizens understand democratic commitments will itself be shaped by democratic practices and by the understandings and preferences of these citizens. I will return to the question of the relationship between democratic standards and democratic preferences below. For now, it will suffice to say that democratic citizens do and should have a significant say in what counts as democratic commitments.

The importance of standards

Before going on to describe my ethics of democratic representation, it is necessary to explain why an accounting of Tom DeLay's behavior according to *democratic* standards is necessary. Not everyone would object to DeLay's behavior. For those who believe that "all's fair in love and politics," DeLay's actions are neither disappointing nor necessarily regrettable. Good representatives should do what it takes to advance the cause of their constituents. Some, such as Joseph Schumpeter (1976) and James Madison (see Madison et al., 1987 [1788]), may recommend zealous competition among advocates as a means for preventing tyranny. These thinkers extol the willingness to do whatever it takes to advance others' policy preferences as animating the electoral mechanisms that keep representatives and thereby democratic institutions accountable.[39]

But it will not do simply to emphasize the importance of representatives advancing the preferences of their constituents. To do so is to overlook both the possibility and the importance of identifying distinctively *democratic* standards for assessing the performance of democratic representatives as *democratic* representatives. Such standards place constraints on the activities of good democratic representatives.

I recognize that any particular standards of this sort that one advances are likely to meet some resistance from some quarters. But that is not necessarily a problem. After all, any adequate ethics of democratic representation cannot require a unanimous consensus among democratic citizens. Democratic citizens should expect conflict about the proper behavior of their representatives. In fact, I would argue that controversy surrounding the proper understanding, and even the existence, of distinctively democratic standards for democratic representation indicates that such standards have some actual substance. It is a sign that one is engaging in democratic politics correctly when certain democratic citizens, specifically those who dominate and oppress other groups, are dissatisfied with how democratic institutions are operating.

So why are democratic standards necessary for evaluating the behavior of political representatives? The first reason is protective. There is simply no guarantee that democratic citizens – let alone a majority of democratic citizens – will seek to preserve the legitimacy of democratic institutions. Either a majority or a powerful minority of citizens can co-opt democratic institutions as a way of dominating certain groups. The injustices committed by democratic regimes are unlikely to be reduced unless democratic norms and values condition the reasons why democratic citizens select their representatives. In particular, democratic citizens need to select their representatives based on the legitimate reasons for choosing democratic institutions over nondemocratic ones.

For example, I take it as self-evident that it is illegitimate to prefer democratic institutions to nondemocratic ones because democratic institutions allow a certain group to dominate another.[40] Democratic citizens who prize democratic institutions not out of a commitment to democratic values but for other and potentially questionable reasons – let's call them "instrumental democrats"[41] – could value the "equality" of elections that follow the "one person, one vote" principle, but also value the unjust outcomes produced by such elections. Democratic citizens need to privilege those democratic norms and values that allow democratic institutions to adjudicate political conflict fairly and peacefully. Democratic representation functions properly only when it stymies instrumental democrats who would use democratic institutions to achieve unjust and oppressive ends. The articulation of democratic standards provides normative tools for identifying instrumental democrats, along with reasons for denouncing their actions.

The second reason I insist upon democratic standards for evaluating political representatives is because democratic ideals are most valuable and needed when there are disagreements in society.[42] Democratic ideals play a vital role in containing political disputes and avoiding violence. Democratic ideals provide sources, albeit limited ones, of hope. Cynicism about democratic ideals can be particularly corrosive to democratic institutions if it stifles the very mechanisms needed to reform and improve those institutions. For this reason, the articulation of democratic standards can help keep alive the reasons why democratic citizens should value democratic institutions as the mechanisms for resolving political conflicts.

Besides, what is most troubling about giving up on holding formal and informal representatives to distinctively democratic standards is that it would entail giving up on those commitments that allow for peaceful resolutions of political disagreements. For constitutive of democratic commitments is the belief that political disputes should be settled by fair deliberations in representative institutions. By prioritizing nonviolent methods in which political actors must justify their actions to citizens, democratic commitments allow for the well-functioning of democratic institutions.

Third, it is important to hold both formal and informal representatives to democratic standards because both formal and informal representatives can play a vital role in the survival of democratic institutions. As Valerie Bunce (2000) noted, "the termination of democracy is very much a matter of what elites choose to do – and not to do." Likewise, Nancy Bermeo (2003) found that political elites played a crucial role in the collapse of democratic institutions in Central America. According to Bermeo, "it seems that democracies do not break down unless political elites deliberately destroy them" (254). Bermeo found that the failure of representatives to distance themselves from anti-democratic and extremist political positions led to the collapse of democratic institutions. It follows from Bermeo's research that having representatives who resist the pull of political extremism – the intense ideological commitments that can justify curtailing democratic practices – can prevent the devastation of democratic institutions.

This leads to the final reason why democratic standards are necessary: articulation of the democratic standards that govern the behavior of democratic representatives can refine and improve citizens' judgments about their representatives. My ethics of democratic representation does not eliminate the need for democratic citizens to exercise their judgment. It specifies certain general standards for democratic representatives that provide a framework within which a fruitful discussion and debate, in which democratic citizens can and must take part, can take place. This debate concerns not only what more particular standards representatives should be held to, but also how these particular standards should be applied in particular cases. The proper role of political theory is to contribute to this discussion and debate by articulating and defending general and particular standards for democratic representation. And in making such contributions, political theory can help democratic citizens make better judgments about their representatives. The fact that some democratic citizens prefer zealous representatives who are not constrained by democratic standards or that some democratic citizens vote according to their checkbooks does not disprove my ethics, any more than the fact that some people shoplift disproves the moral prohibition against stealing.

Besides, the inability to adjudicate between conflicting standards for good democratic representation exacerbates confusion about the proper behavior of democratic representatives and thereby contributes to the paralysis that allows bad representatives to stay in office. Because democratic citizens will sometimes need to defend their democratic institutions, they need democratic standards for evaluating representatives. For example, some democracies – such as Brazil – have collapsed without much of a fight from its citizens. The articulation of clear criteria can be one way for democratic citizens to preserve their institutions and for political representatives to know when they have crossed a line that should not have been crossed. This is especially true given the extent to which democratic citizens rely on their informal representatives to expose and help correct the injustices committed by formal representatives. Because they serve this vital corrective function, it is important that informal representatives also be judged by democratic standards. The function of such representatives within a democratic polity gives them the obligation to act as guardians of the democratic institutions that set the stage for their advocacy. But it is ultimately the responsibility of democratic citizens as a whole to act as guardians of their democratic institutions, by exerting pressure both on their formal and their informal representatives to realize the proper operation of these institutions. Indeed, it is in fulfilling this responsibility that citizens of a representative democracy both rule and are ruled.

If democratic citizens lack an understanding of how democratic representatives can give democracy a bad name, they are not in a position to stop bad democratic representatives. But if democratic citizens achieve a proper understanding of the standards that govern democratic representation, they are more likely to sanction bad democratic representatives and bolster the legitimacy of democratic institutions. The identification of such standards, and the provision of a framework within which democratic citizens can forge a proper collective understanding of these standards, will help democratic citizens select their elected representatives more wisely. The identification of such standards will also help galvanize the political pressure democratic citizens need to exert if those representatives whom they haven't elected are to act as good democratic representatives. In short, our achieving a proper understanding of the norms governing democratic representation is essential to insuring the proper operation of our democratic institutions, and to protecting us from the tyrannical use of these institutions.

The Importance of Function

The identification of a good *democratic* representative requires an understanding of the *function* or *characteristic activity* of democratic representation within a democratic polity. Here I follow Aristotle, who contends that *the good of a thing resides in its function*. In other words, there is a conceptual connection between the function, or characteristic activity, of a thing and its excellence as the thing that it is. The virtues of a thing are to be read off its function. Recall my earlier discussion of a knife's function. If the function of a knife is to cut, then a good knife is a knife that cuts well. The virtue – or excellence – of a knife, then, is sharpness. And, more generally, what it is for a thing to have the virtue or excellence proper to its kind is nothing other than its being disposed, in exercising its characteristic activity, to engage in that activity well (Aristotle, *Nicomachean Ethics*, Book I, Chapter 7, 1097b25–28; see Aristotle, 1970 [1831]). I am proposing that, in parallel fashion, the virtues of democratic representatives are to be read off of the function, or characteristic activity, of democratic representatives.

Contemporary theorists have also recognized the importance of function for identifying good democratic representatives. Most notably, Russell Hardin has recently endorsed assessing representatives by their function. For Hardin, "If we wish to assess the morality of elected officials, we must understand their function as our representatives and then infer how they can fulfill this function" (2004, 76). In pointing to the function of representatives, and deriving their moral assessment from this function, his approach bears an obvious resemblance to mine. However, three important differences between our positions need to be highlighted.

First, Hardin's discussion of representation is limited to elected officials. Mine, in contrast, crucially encompasses the advocacy work of informal, as well as formal, representatives. Moreover, this restriction of Hardin's discussion reflects his treating elected officials as a profession and making any possible ethics of representation derive from the distinctive roles of that profession. My account derives certain highly general standards that govern all democratic representation, regardless of the particular office or role played by different representatives. Second, Hardin draws on David Hume's notion of "artificial duties" in arguing that the duties of a particular elected official are derived from the institutional purposes of her profession as the holder of that office. Such duties are, on Hardin's view, normatively "neutral": they can be specified without appeal to any value claims. On my view, in contrast, the duties that democratic representatives as such stand under are to be specified only by appeal to certain core democratic norms and values. Third, Hardin holds that the assessments of elected officials depend on the citizens' understanding of representation. Hardin is quick to point out, moreover, that citizens' understandings of theories of representation are limited:

[Such limits] makes it difficult for us to assess the quality of the very representatives we elect and in particular to determine whether they live up to
any role morality we might assign to them. In the face of current trends in
electoral motivations, it seems unlikely that the electorate consistently has
in mind any role morality, either conventional or functional, for the media
masters who we put in office. (2004, 99)

Indeed, Hardin concludes from these reflections that it is unlikely that
there is any consensus amongst the electorate about the role morality that
is to be assigned to elected officials and thus that there are no determinate
ethical standards under which elected officials now stand. In contrast, I
do not link the possibility of assessing representatives morally so tightly
to citizen's actual understandings of their representatives' roles. On my
view, there is a proper function that democratic representatives as such
have that is, to a degree, independent of democratic citizens' understanding of this function, and which this understanding ought properly to
register. And, corresponding to this function, there are ethical standards
that govern the conduct of democratic representatives, and these are the
standards that democratic citizens *should* use, regardless of whether or not
they actually do. My project thus is centrally concerned with identifying
normative values that democratic citizens and their representatives are in
fact subject to, that they ought properly to invoke in attempting to settle
their political disputes.[43]

Of course, democratic citizens have some say in the standards governing
democratic representation. For their understanding of, and the intensity
of their commitment to, the standards governing democratic representation determine the specific content of these standards. Democratic citizens'
understanding of who counts as a good democratic representative give
life to these standards, making good democratic representation realizable.
Democratic practices shape citizens' identities and thereby their understanding of the particular ethical standards to which citizens ought to hold
their representatives. Moreover, the activities of representatives, in part,
determine whether democratic citizens have reason to prefer democratic to
nondemocratic practices. Democratic practices can create loyalties toward
democratic institutions, but they can also create aversions. How democracy is practiced can influence the extent to which democratic citizens
are committed to and inspired by democratic ideals. Democratic citizens
will value their political institutions to the extent that the lived realities of
their institutions uphold the promise of democratic ideals.

To recap, my ethics of democratic representation assumes that assessing an individual democratic representative properly requires having some understanding of the function of democratic representatives. It is only once one has identified this function that one is in a position to determine whether an individual democratic representative performs this function well or poorly. I contend, further, that determining what it means to perform the function of democratic representatives well or poorly requires understanding the function in light of certain democratic norms and values. For the function of a democratic representative is to advocate with the aim of realizing these norms and values in her democratic polity. And performing this function well requires that a democratic representative have, and act on, a proper understanding of these norms and values in engaging in democratic advocacy. An articulation of these norms and values, as they ought to inform and guide the characteristic activity of democratic representatives, thus will provide a notion of excellence with some substantive content that can be used in assessing democratic representatives. Moreover, in identifying the excellent activity of democratic representatives, we will be attending to the democratic norms and values that underlie a justified preference for democratic as opposed to nondemocratic institutions. In this way, my account will link the standards governing a democratic representative's performance to our understanding of why democratic institutions matter. Our assessments of representatives will turn out to be inextricably tied to how we find meaning and value both in having democratic institutions and in participating in the operation of those institutions through our democratic representatives.

Identifying the function of democratic representatives

Now, democratic representatives do a lot of things: They bargain and bicker. They give speeches and fundraise. They dull and disillusion. Given the variety of activities performed by representatives, how are we to distinguish incidental activities from their characteristic activity?

To identify *the* characteristic activity of democratic representatives, it is necessary to consider when democratic politics gets hard and messy. In my opinion, how democratic representatives negotiate conflict, not consensus, speaks to their ability to represent in a democratic fashion. For if we ever need good democratic representatives, we need them when we have deep disagreements with fellow democratic citizens. During such times, not only is there something politically at stake in how our representatives act, but the need to reach peaceful resolutions is also the most pressing.

And at such moments, the temptation to stray from democratic representation will be strongest. Just as democratic institutions are necessary under conditions of pluralism, good democratic representation is needed when political representatives confront the fact of pluralism. For this reason, the characteristic activity of democratic representatives and the standards that are derived from this characteristic activity must speak to the need to confront and negotiate pluralism. More specifically, how democratic representatives compete in the political arena marks them as good democratic representatives. And to compete, they must advocate. Good democratic representatives must advocate in a democratic manner – that is, to advance public policies on behalf of their constituents in ways that bolster the legitimate reasons for favoring democratic institutions to nondemocratic ones. The central function of democratic representation is democratic advocacy. Democratic advocacy is what differentiates democratic representatives from being merely political representatives.

My ethics of democratic representation, admittedly, depends on a particular view of democratic representation. More specifically, I contend that democratic representation is indispensable when there are political disagreements – at least, political disagreements about moderately important issues.[44] The reason why democratic representation is vital under conditions of disagreement is that if all citizens agreed with their rules and each other about the proper direction of their political lives, democratic institutions would be superfluous. Consequently, the purpose of democratic representation is inextricably tied to the *negotiation* of political conflicts. More specifically, democratic representatives must negotiate political conflicts in ways that preserve the legitimacy of democratic institutions to resolve political conflict. Preserving that legitimacy requires representatives to act in ways that would justify choosing democratic institutions over nondemocratic ones.

To appreciate the nature of democratic advocacy, it is necessary to briefly examine the meaning of political advocacy. After all, democratic advocacy is a species of political advocacy. Only after discussing the general nature of political advocacy will we be in a better position to understand democratic advocacy.

Political advocacy

Put bluntly, political advocacy is the activity of pleading the cause of others in the public sphere. To be a political advocate is to offer a very necessary and important kind of political assistance. My discussion of political advocacy is framed mainly from within the context of an imperfect representative democracy – specifically, the US. I suspect that my discussion of political advocacy and democratic advocacy will apply to other representative democracies. However, my focus is on how good democratic representatives should behave in the US.[45] The extent to which political advocacy in the US resembles advocacy in other representative democracies and the extent to which the US succeeds in exporting its particular brand of democratic representation will mark the extent to which my ethics is applicable in other contexts.

My understanding of political advocacy is not only limited to the US, it is also limited to a particular location within the US policy-making process. In particular, I understand political advocacy as straddling the governmental and nongovernmental divide.[46] Here, I agree with Nadia Urbinati's understanding of representation as advocacy. According to Urbinati's reading of Mill, representation is a "mediating institution between the state and society, between the general interests of the nation and the particular interests of those who comprised it." The representative "has to have one foot in civil society, and the other in the state" (Urbinati, 2002, 76). Similarly, John Kingdon (1984, 48) describes this location as "outside of government, but not just looking in." Political advocacy exists in a kind of moral no man's land. Advocates are bound by the formal rules of the state *as well as* the informal codes of civic society. Advocates are intermediaries who translate private interests into public policies. By providing such a translation, they literally frame the ways in which problems are understood and dealt with.[47] One can identify those who advocate by their demands on public resources, asking for the governmental institutions to take some kind of action on an issue.

This points to two main components of political advocacy: political advocates *articulate* and *solve* problems that make demands on public resources. Such actors *articulate* problems when they identify the needs of fellow citizens and they *solve* problems when they try to convince others about how the government should respond to those needs.[48] In this way, political advocacy *depends* partially on other agents – for example, members of the bureaucracy or representatives – to determine the outcome of a policy-making decision. Furthermore, political advocates pose solutions in a partisan way, making demands on how social goods are distributed in a society. Such an activity requires appealing to others' understandings of the proper role of government and of what citizens owe each other.

By articulating and solving problems, political advocates can be understood to stitch together a common life within a democratic polity. The actions of advocates provide substantive content to "the lifeworld" shared by democratic citizens. In this way, advocates provide the connective tissue in a democratic polity, binding citizens to the institutions that rule them.

That said, it is important to emphasize that political advocacy advances solutions that advantage some citizens and disadvantage others. To be an advocate is to engage in political competition and to provide political assistance to some citizens at the expense of others. Consequently, political advocacy is an antagonistic business.

Political advocacy is also a privilege, because the act of speaking on another's behalf creates a kind of dependency on the speaker. The act of speaking reflects a kind of political standing. It is to enter the world of the talkers – those who have the capacity and gumption to stand up in the political realm and to demand something. Such an activity is neither desirable nor possible for everyone. To some extent, political advocacy is inherently hierarchical and elitist.[49]

This leads to what can be truly troubling about political advocacy – namely, that the benefits of political advocacy can be cumulative.[50] Political advocacy can exacerbate potentially abusive power relationships between citizens in different social and economic strata. It is because the power of and privileges of advocates can be in tension with democratic norms and the well-functioning of democratic institutions that democratic standards for political advocacy are necessary. Democratic citizens should not reject political advocacy wholesale. Democratic citizens need to attend to the nuances that inform the types of relationships that exist between them and their representatives. The activity of political advocacy is neither "just" an act of power nor "just" a moment of political self-realization; rather, it is a political activity that requires both criticism and affirmation. To see the relationship between representation and advocacy as simply either a threat or a positive political activity is to ignore how democratic citizens need to reflect on and try to improve the behavior of those who advance public policies on their behalf. And paying attention to the nuances of the activity of advocacy offers some important guidelines for evaluating democratic representatives. In my language, they should engage in democratic advocacy. Again, not all advocacy should be understood as consistent with democratic norms and commitments. Political representatives can push it.

Democratic advocacy

Three aspects of democratic advocacy distinguish it from the more generic form of political advocacy. Democratic advocacy, as the function or characteristic activity of democratic representatives, has certain aims, employs certain methods, and establishes certain kinds of relationships. We know that a representative is advocating in a democratic fashion when that representative engages in these three aspects of democratic advocacy. Each aspect identifies a distinctive feature of the function of democratic representatives. I will take each aspect of democratic advocacy in turn.

Consider first the distinctive aim of democratic advocacy. Democratic representatives, like all representatives, seek to advance certain public policies. They advocate. However, the function of democratic representatives is to advance public policies on behalf of their constituents with the governing aim of contributing to the proper functioning, and continuing viability, of democratic institutions. Insofar as a democratic representative does her work, she will thus be concerned about the impact of the policies she advances on democratic institutions. Hence, she will evaluate public policies not simply in terms of the "particularistic" concerns of her own constituents,[51] but also in terms of the effect of those policies on the democratic polity as a whole, and thus on all democratic citizens as citizens. And since the proper functioning of democratic institutions is in fact to provide fair and peaceful resolutions to political conflict, democratic representatives ought, in performing their function, to care about contributing to providing such resolutions. By actually making such a contribution, democratic representatives support the legitimacy of democratic institutions and properly support their continued viability. Moreover – and this point will prove crucial – the first aspect of the function of democratic representation requires democratic representatives to act in light of norms and values that support fair democratic procedures. For example, democratic representatives ought to respect the equality of all races, and in light of this norm, support electoral policies that uphold the principle "one person, one vote." In short, democratic representatives act as democratic representatives – be it well or poorly – only insofar as they try, though perhaps misguidedly, to advance public policies that are consonant with the proper functioning and continued viability of democratic institutions.

Thus, the first aspect of democratic advocacy focuses on how democratic commitments "condition" the types of public policies advanced by representatives. This conditioning would affect not only the justifications for pursuing certain public policies offered by representatives, but also the type of research conducted, as well as the criteria by which democratic representatives evaluate a policy;[52] for representatives who don't care about the impact of their actions on democratic institutions will not try to justify their policies based on their commitment to democracy. They also would avoid certain types of questions by promoting distractions or by downplaying the relevance of certain information for assessing a policy. They will introduce norms that appeal to citizen's public interests as opposed to their merely private ones.

The second aspect of democratic advocacy concerns the methods used by democratic representatives. More specifically, democratic representatives act as democratic representatives when they advance public policies in ways that increase the participation of citizens in the decision-making processes. To advocate in a democratic fashion is to employ the methods of mobilization and deliberation.

The third and final aspect of democratic advocacy refers to the distinctive type of relationship that develops between a democratic representative and those being represented. Democratic representatives aim to develop relationships that promote mutual forms of recognition. When they succeed, democratic citizens correctly understand themselves as "acting in concert" with their democratic representatives, and democratic representatives correctly understand themselves as "acting in concert" with their constituents. In this way, democratic representation facilitates relationships with citizens that increase their sense of ownership of the representative's actions and a feeling of being part of a democratic polity. Democratic representatives understand their activities as a way of serving their constituents, and the constituents of good democratic representatives will in turn recognize their representatives as serving their interests. In this way, democratic advocacy facilitates a kind of identification with democratic institutions.

Taken together, these three aspects of democratic advocacy capture what is distinctive about how democratic representatives advance public policies on behalf of citizens. Democratic advocacy promotes the capacity of citizens to rule themselves by providing information and justifications that strengthen democratic commitments, by adopting methods that create avenues of access, and by fostering relationships that promote identification with democratic processes. To engage in the function, or characteristic activity, of a democratic representative is to advocate in ways that exhibit these three aspects of democratic advocacy.

The Three Virtues

However, to be a *good* democratic representative requires something more. It requires a democratic representative to perform, effectively, all three aspects of democratic advocacy out of a correct understanding of the function of democratic representation. Now this function, as we saw, consists in contributing to the proper functioning of democratic institutions – providing a fair and peaceful resolution to political conflicts. Moreover, I contend that democratic institutions can provide such resolutions only by way of drawing on, and reinforcing, citizens' shared commitment to certain distinctively democratic norms and values, which justify preferring democratic institutions to nondemocratic ones. The good democratic representative is thus one whose advocacy contributes, in and through the proper function of democratic institutions, to the realization in her polity of these norms and values. Good democratic representatives will, in particular, manifest three virtues, corresponding to the three aspects of democratic advocacy just distinguished: the virtue of *fair-mindedness*, through which a representative contributes to the realization of the value of *civic equality*; the virtue of *critical trust building*, through which a representative contributes to the realization of *self-governance*; and, finally, the virtue of *good gatekeeping*, through which a representative contributes to the realization of *inclusion*.

The first virtue of democratic representatives, what I call the virtue of fair-mindedness, requires good democratic representatives to advance public policies that contribute to the proper functioning of democratic institutions, and thereby to the continuing viability of those institutions. This contribution, correctly understood, consists in advancing public policies in ways that are properly sensitive to civic equality. To be properly sensitive to civic equality, in turn, is to further civic equality in light of the ways in which civic equality justifies democratic authority.[53] Good democratic representatives both intend to foster civic equality as a ground of the legitimacy of democratic institutions, and are, in fact, effective in so fostering civic equality. This first virtue reflects the fact that good democratic representatives need to guard against how social and economic privilege can promote unjust inequalities in the political arena. Good democratic representatives seek not only to protect the formal political rights and privileges of all citizens, but also to counterbalance the accumulation of power that, in producing systemic inequalities, undermines the legitimacy of democratic institutions.

The second virtue, the virtue of critical trust building, follows naturally from the first. To advance public policies in line with democratic norms, and in particular that of civic equality, requires that a representative put forward public policies that are recognized by citizens as preferable. Democratic citizens need to recognize that their representatives' advocacy is consonant with democratic values. A good democratic representative, thus, is willing and able to mobilize citizens and engage them in public deliberation of policy alternatives. But there are democratically legitimate and illegitimate methods of doing this. Legitimate methods promote the capacities of citizens to be informed and critical of the actions taken by their representatives. Good democratic representatives do not want citizens to follow their lead blindly (although such a relationship is admittedly more politically expedient). Rather, the second virtue of democratic representation specifies that good democratic representatives are ones who try to develop the capacities of citizens to appreciate and value democratic processes and practices. In particular, citizens will constitute a healthy democratic polity only to the extent that they have developed the critical capacities to be self-governing – the proper functioning of democratic institutions requires what I call *critical trust*. To excel at being a democratic representative is to conduct democratic deliberations and to mobilize citizens to represent themselves in ways consonant with genuinely critical engagement in the political arena.

The third virtue, what I call the virtue of good gatekeeping, in turn follows naturally from the first and the second. In order to be in a position to employ, effectively, the democratically legitimate methods for advancing public policies, a representative must have mutual relations with all her constituents, relations that enable her to mobilize her constituents and help them to engage in public deliberation – all from an informed and critical perspective. Thus good democratic representatives promote and sustain mutual relationships with their constituents. More specifically, the third virtue requires that good democratic representatives promote their relationships with citizens as a way of expanding the inclusive nature of democratic institution. Democratic representatives recognize how democratic processes can exclude as well as include. For this reason, good democratic representatives are ones who seek to redress the ways in which citizens can be unjustly marginalized by democratic processes. And they do so by developing mutual relations with members of marginalized groups. By reaching out and incorporating those who are marginalized by democratic processes, good democratic representatives who exercise the third virtue enable citizens to be and to feel a part of the democratic polity through their political relationships to their representatives.

Together, these three virtues offer a normative framework for determining the extent to which an individual representative excels at representing in a democratic fashion. To be a good democratic representative is to have and exercise all three of these virtues, and to avoid the dangers associated with each of them. Consequently, representatives who advance public policies that undermine civic equality, limit the ability of citizens to govern themselves, or exclude certain groups from participation might be excellent delegates of democratic citizens who hold such preferences. However, such representatives are not to be considered good democratic representatives according to my account. For better or worse, democratic norms and values place certain constraints on the types of behavior that democratic representatives can engage in and still be considered good democratic representatives.

I contend that democratic citizens ought to prefer representatives who exhibit these three virtues over those who do not. And citizens ought to assess criticisms of, and controversies surrounding, representatives in light of the understanding of good democratic representation that a detailed articulation of these three virtues provides. Each of these virtues provides a different focal point for evaluating representatives. Those who are committed to democratic norms and values should look for representatives who not only exhibit these virtues, but who properly negotiate the problems associated with these virtues. In this way the three virtues are normative tools of evaluation, assisting the critical assessments of democratic citizens.

Democracy and Democratic Citizens' Preferences

My ethics of democratic representation has an implication that I would like to draw out explicitly: Polling the preferences of a representative's supporters or those affected by the policies advanced by political representatives is not enough to determine who is a good democratic representative. Being a good democratic representative takes more than winning a popularity contest. And a good democratic representative is not willing to do anything it takes to advance her constituents' policy preferences.

To illustrate why this is so, consider the dispute between Massachusetts Senator Charles Sumner and South Carolina's Representative Preston Brooks in 1856. Their dispute has to be an all time low for democratic

ethics, for it demonstrates how democratic citizens can support a representative who has violated what I take to be a central democratic commitment – namely, the commitment to resolve domestic political conflicts
through nonviolent means. The dispute arose after Senator Sumner had
ridiculed Representative Brooks's cousin, Senator Andrews Butler from
South Carolina, for his pro-slavery stances. Two days later, Representative
Brooks waited for Senator Sumner in the Senate Chamber and physically
assaulted him with a cane. Disturbingly enough, the House was unable to
acquire the two-thirds majority necessary to expel Representative Brooks.
And still more troubling is the fact that even after Representative Brooks
resigned his House seat, his South Carolinian constituents voted him back
into office.[54]

This example might seem extreme – typically, representatives don't use
violence to resolve their conflicts with other representatives – but it usefully
illustrates two points. The first is that democratic citizens can support their
representatives for ethically questionable and democratically problematic
reasons: it is clear enough that Representative Brooks's constituents voted
him back into office because of his support of slavery. Second, democratic
citizens can support their representatives despite, or even for, their engaging in ethically and democratically problematic behavior. I consider it
to be uncontroversial that democratic citizens should spurn, rather than
support, representatives who settle conflicts through violence.

Similar questions about the judgments of democratic citizens arise when
a constituency elects or reelects a representative who is willing to sell his
or her vote to the highest bidder. In his condemnation of the reelection
of Congressman Benjamin Whittemore, a representative who had been
convicted of selling appointments to the military academy, Illinois Congressman John Logan declared that "people do not have the right to
destroy their own liberties by filling Congress with men who, from their
conduct, show themselves capable of the destruction of the Government"
(cited in Baker, 1985, 13). The House supported Logan and voted 130/245
to exclude Congressman Whittemore. This exclusion went against the
expressed preferences of Congressman Whittemore's constituents. For
Logan, men of "infamous character" needed to be prohibited from Congress, despite the support of their constituents. Similar justifications were
invoked for excluding ex-Confederates and rebel sympathizers, despite
their presentation of valid elections certificates.[55]

Logan proposed one plausible ethical restriction on a democratic representative's acceptable behavior: democratic representatives should not

behave in ways that undermine democratic institutions or the democratic commitments of citizens. To the extent that democratic representatives are willing to violate this restriction, even if in doing so they are caving in to their constituents – and so advancing the preferences of their constituents at the expense of the fairness and justice of democratic institutions – they are not acting as good democratic representatives. Good democratic representatives must, even in pursuing preferences of their constituents, exercise some constraint.

Now in saying this, I don't mean to be taking "a top-down" or "aristocratic" approach to democratic representation.[56] Unlike aristocratic ones, my approach requires citizens to take an active role in shaping the policies and institutions that govern them. Democratic citizens play an important role in giving democratic values a determinate meaning. In doing so, democratic citizens also play an important role in providing a determinate understanding of the virtues.

Moreover, citizens' understandings of the virtues are not divorced from existing democratic practices. Their understanding of good democratic representation is shaped by the actions of their representatives. In particular, their understandings of the advantages and disadvantages of good democratic representation, as well as the requirements of democratic norms, will depend on existing democratic practices. As I understand it, democratic practices generate an ethical outlook – that is, a certain way of understanding and seeing the value of democratic institutions, procedures, and norms. Citizens' understandings of democratic institutions are shaped by democratic practices and democratic practices are shaped by citizens' (and their representatives') understandings of democratic institutions and their norms.

For this reason, the meaning of democratic commitments – and consequently the meaning of good democratic representation – must to some extent be open to debate. Consequently, my project is not primarily concerned with providing definitive definitions for democratic values and norms such as equality or inclusion. Rather, it has two more humble purposes. First, it aims to identify the values that democratic citizens will need to negotiate in order to preserve the legitimacy of democratic institutions. Here, I assume that certain norms are more likely to generate fair procedures than others. Democratic commitments are not neutral; rather, they value certain ways of engaging in and resolving political conflicts. Second, my project seeks to provide some helpful guidelines for assessing various interpretations of these values in evaluations of the conduct of representatives. I point to some problems that can arise when we try to develop an adequate understanding of democratic norms and values, but in doing so I do not join those who deny that articulating democratic standards is possible or desirable. My understanding of good democratic representation recognizes that democratic citizens, with their representatives, have to navigate such problems and give life to democratic ideals if there is to be good democratic representation.

The fact that citizens and their representatives jointly give these ideals life also suggests that the understanding of democratic values and democratic institutions in a given polity can change in undesirable ways. My understanding of good democratic representation is therefore consistent with the notion that democratic citizens can make poor choices. To recognize that citizens can get it wrong – that is, prefer certain representatives for the wrong reasons – can easily be understood as simply endorsing an aristocratic vision of democracy. But I hope to make it plausible that, despite their limitations, democratic citizens can, together with capable and responsible representatives, play a quite demanding role in realizing good democratic representation in their polity. Democratic citizens play this role when they understand what good democratic representation requires and insist on good representation. To say that democratic citizens can get it wrong and to say that democratic citizens should have some say in the meaning of democratic commitments provides some – albeit less than is typically assumed – leeway for discussing the proper behavior of democratic representatives. This project is primarily an educational project, one that aims to point out better and less desirable choices that democratic citizens can make, and to examine the role that democratic representatives can play in encouraging better choices even while leaving democratic citizens a crucial role in determining what, exactly, would count as a better choice.

Part of what motivates my view is the thought that democratic commitments and democratic institutions are so important because democratic citizens can get democratic representation wrong. Citizens have bad representatives when their representatives misdiagnose problems, pose the wrong solutions, or misdirect resources. They have bad democratic representatives when their representatives' advocacy work undermines democratic institutions. Of course, democratic citizens can hold their bad formal representatives accountable directly; for example, by voting them out of office. Bad informal representatives of democratic citizens must be taken to task indirectly; for example, by peer accountability and fiscal accountability. In order for both of these self-correcting mechanisms of democratic institutions to operate properly, democratic citizens need to have some say in who rules them. For this reason, opportunities for citizens to evaluate and sanction their representatives lie at the heart of the practices of representative democracies. The articulation of standards for judging representatives contributes to the proper operation of democratic institutions, including this self-correcting mechanism, by aiding the judgments of citizens in selecting their representatives.

In providing democratic standards for evaluating representatives, I contend that it is important to stay focused on the function of democratic institutions and the legitimate reasons that democratic citizens should have for preferring democratic institutions to nondemocratic ones. This position reflects the worry that democratic institutions can lose their appeal to citizens, and thereby their legitimacy, if they simply become systems of oppressing minorities. This appeal of democratic institutions is lost when representatives employ the rhetoric of democratic commitments to justify atrocities, such as human rights abuses, indefinite internments, and the spreading of social chaos. Because the meaning of democratic practices and norms can shift, it is important to condemn publicly acts that undermine the legitimacy of democratic institutions.

I fully expect democratic citizens to disagree about the impact of policies on democratic institutions, about the meaning of democratic commitments, and even about the legitimate reasons for preferring democratic institutions. The extent to which democratic citizens weaken their commitment to settling such disputes in fair and peaceful ways points to an inherent vulnerability of democracy: democratic commitments have the potential to bring about their own demise. An important defense against this vulnerability is to improve citizens' ability to recognize good *democratic* representatives. Democratic citizens also need to recognize the hazards and benefits associated with the virtues of democratic representation.

Irreconcilable differences among democratic citizens, therefore, are not by themselves worrisome: There may be more than one way to get democratic representation right. However, divisions among citizens do become worrisome when judgments about good democratic representation pull citizens toward pursuing unfair, unjust, and even violent methods to settle their disputes. Democratic ideals can be invoked in order to justify endorsing undemocratic ends and methods.[57] The three virtues of democratic representation set up guidelines for determining when a representative violates democratic norms and commitments. In this way, the virtues offer a framework through which conflicts about good democratic representation can be productively settled.

Given the interactive and mutually constituting relationship between representatives and citizens, my current claim that my ethics of democratic representation should inform citizens' choices of their representatives might seem one-sided. For it may seem to leave unanswered important questions about why and how the ethics of democratic representation should directly inform the actions of representatives. Nonetheless, I focus on citizens' choice of their representatives for three reasons.

The first is descriptive: democratic representatives are also democratic citizens. For this reason, my discussion of the guidelines for assessing democratic representatives is a kind of shorthand to refer to both types of actors. This approach assumes that for good democratic representation to take place, there must be some kind of minimal overlap between how democratic citizens evaluate their representatives and how good democratic representatives respond to the criticisms of democratic citizens.

The second reason for focusing on citizens' evaluations of their representatives is based on the belief that democratic citizens are less likely to be disillusioned with democratic commitments and democratic institutions when they have a realistic assessment of political conflicts within a democratic polity. Moreover, for the same reasons, democratic citizens need to have reasonable expectations of democratic practices.[58] An honest assessment of the benefits and drawbacks of democratic representation will help democratic citizens appreciate their political institutions, seeing the need for democratic institutions to reconcile genuine political disagreements among democratic citizens.

Third, my focus on citizens reflects my belief that ultimately representatives should take their cues from their constituents. Because the democratic process must take account of a "rich bundle of substantive goods" (Dahl, 1998), it is important both that democratic citizens' views of these goods influence this process and that democratic citizens learn to appreciate the complex nature of these processes. Surely, democratic citizens can choose to destroy democratic processes. But they cannot rightfully choose to do so. Here I side with Dahl's advocate, who contends that

> the democratic process isn't likely to be preserved for very long unless the people of a country preponderantly believe that it's desirable and unless their belief comes to be embedded in their habits, practices, and culture (1989, 172).

My claim is that democratic processes can function better, and approximate their ideal more closely, when democratic citizens choose their representatives in light of the three virtues of democratic representation. Here, citizens consciously use democratic norms and values in order to fulfill certain functions within the democratic system as a whole. They must in doing so aim to preserve the legitimacy of the democratic process as well as trying to satisfy the rich bundle of substantive goods required for the democratic process to work fairly.

I should emphasize that in focusing on the judgment and actions of citizens, I do not mean to suggest that these actions and judgments should be neatly divorced from the requirements of their democratic representatives. For representatives play a role in developing the capacities of democratic citizens – specifically, in developing their ability to assess their representatives' performance. After all, representatives must not only justify what they advocate, but also examine their advocacy from the perspective of preserving the fairness of democratic institutions. Tom DeLay can contend that shutting up opposition is good for democracy. Moreover, his constituents might endorse his behavior as Majority Whip. However, my ethics of democratic representation points to why they would be wrong to do so from the perspective of democracy.

Two final remarks. First, an ethics of democratic representation requires a certain flexibility to accommodate the challenges facing democratic representatives. The standards for good democratic representation resist codification. That said, it is important to clarify the informal norms that democratic citizens should use for preferring some representatives to others. For such informal norms mark the area of permissible behavior for democratic representatives. Democratic representatives might try to expand that area, by testing what kinds of behavior they can get away with. However, representatives' behavior is influenced by their understanding of how they ought to act. Identifying the informal norms that currently underlie judgments about the undemocratic behavior of representatives not only improves how democratic citizens choose their representatives, but also can indirectly improve the behavior of representatives.

Second, my project assumes an important difference between doing something illegal and doing something undemocratic. To protect democratic institutions, democratic citizens will need to recognize how the undemocratic, as well as the illegal, can weaken the legitimacy of democratic institutions. The undemocratic is tied to the informal norms of democratic citizens, and not just to the boundaries of illegality. Informal norms can therefore directly or indirectly encourage representatives to advocate in an undemocratic fashion, or discourage them from acting in such a fashion. For this reason, identifying the informal norms that should guide good democratic representation can play a crucial role in assisting the proper functioning of democratic institutions.

I have staked out a position on which democratic citizens do and should have some say in the ideals that ought to guide the behavior of their representative. However, political theory can assist the evaluations of democratic citizens by clarifying how democratic representation insures that democratic institutions can function properly in settling political disputes fairly and peacefully. In the following chapters, I articulate the three functions of democratic advocacy and their corresponding virtues. As will be seen, each virtue has its own set of problems. Democratic citizens and their representatives will have to muck through these problems of democratic representation together.

Chapter 4

The Virtue of
Fair-Mindedness

Rabbi Meir Kahane was an Israeli Parliament member who ran on the platform of killing, or at least transferring, all Israeli-Palestinians (those who live within Israel and have Israeli citizenship, as well as those in the occupied territories). His campaign slogan was literally "Give me that power. I will take care of them." Rabbi Kahane won the election fairly and would certainly be considered, by most, a legitimate representative. But was he a good representative? Was he a good *democratic* representative?

In my opinion, Rabbi Kahane might have been a good representative to the extent that he did a good job advancing the positions of those who hold a very bad ideology; however, Rabbi Kahane was a bad democratic representative.[1] Good democratic representatives do not wish their political opponents into extinction. Killing or even exiling a group of citizens in virtue of their religious, ethnic, or racial identity is clearly beyond the pale of acceptable behavior for democratic representatives. This chapter explains why.

Good democratic representatives cannot simply advance whatever public policies they – or even their constituents – want. Good democratic representatives adhere to norms and values distinctive of democratic institutions, and are effective in advancing public policies in line with those norms and values. For it is in advocating in line with these norms and values that good democratic representatives excel at democratic advocacy – that is, at contributing to the proper operation of democratic institutions, in order to settle political conflicts fairly and peacefully, thereby bolstering the legitimacy of those institutions.

In this chapter I focus on how one value distinctive of democratic institutions – namely, civic equality – informs a good democratic representative's aims in democratic advocacy. Good democratic representatives, I contend, successfully advance public policies with the aim of fostering civic equality. By *fostering* civic equality, I mean intentionally protecting and advancing the equal political standing of all qualified citizens.[2] One can foster civic equality directly, by protecting and advancing legal or institutional measures that secure the equal political standing of citizens. But one can also do so indirectly, by protecting and advancing recognition within a polity of the need to secure the equal political standing of all its citizens. In either case, a democratic representative engages in the characteristic activity of democratic representatives, and does so well, insofar as she is effective in fostering civic equality.

Recall, here, that democratic advocacy has as its function contributing to the proper operation, and thereby to the legitimacy, of democratic institutions. One aspect of this function is, in advocating, to negotiate political conflicts with the aim of contributing to the legitimacy of democratic institutions. A democratic representative excels in this aspect of democratic advocacy when, in working to advance public policies, she effectively fosters civic equality in her polity. And in so excelling, the good democratic representative exhibits the first virtue of democratic representation – namely, that of fair-mindedness. Fair-minded representatives are those whose advocacy work is properly sensitive to civic equality. A representative exhibits this sensitivity when she decides on what public policies to back, and to oppose, in light of their effect on civic equality. This sensitivity requires that a representative attend to unjust and oppressive structural inequalities in her society, especially those that adversely impact the ability of citizens to act as democratic citizens. Moreover, a representative also exhibits the requisite sensitivity to civic equality when her advocacy work encourages citizens to appreciate the value of civic equality and to attend, themselves, to unjust and oppressive structural inequalities. In these ways, fair-minded representatives aim to foster civic equality and thereby protect the legitimacy of democratic institutions.

Political Efficacy

Democratic representatives, like all political representatives, are judged by what they accomplish – that is, by their advocating successfully for certain public policies. It follows that no sensible representative aims at being ineffective. To be ineffective in advancing public policies is to fail in one's task as a political representative. To be ineffective is a mark of a loser, someone to be replaced, deadwood.

But what exactly is political efficacy? Political efficacy is the capacity to advance *successfully* the *correct* public policies. Let's begin with what counts as advancing public policies "successfully." Success in the policy-making arena needs to be understood broadly. A representative obviously enjoys such success when she obtains the passage of a desired piece of legislation. However, representatives can also advocate successfully even when they do not succeed in passing legislation that they champion. They can "win" by changing the language of a piece of legislation in order to weaken it. Representatives can be successful when they prevent legislation that they oppose from passing. Getting a certain amount of media attention or improving one's negotiating positions can also count as a success. Representatives can furthermore "win" by preventing the funding of a piece of legislation that they cannot defeat, or even by preventing legislation that was passed from being properly implemented. All of these different understandings of political efficacy suggest that political efficacy can be a matter of degree: representatives can be more or less successful in advancing certain public policies. They also suggest that a wide range of possible outcomes can indicate a representative "successfully" advancing public policies.

However, political efficacy, as I define it, does not only require advancing public policies successfully. It also requires advancing the "correct" policies, the policies that a political representative ought to advance. But what counts as the "correct" policies? Here, both the theoretical and empirical literature on representation has remained silent, unable to resolve disagreements about the proper way to identify "correct" policies.

Hanna Pitkin (1967) famously identified two conflicting schools of thought about the proper way to identify the policies that representatives should advance. The first, known as the delegate conception of representation, claims that representatives should be judged by success in achieving what their constituents want. Correct policies correspond to the preferences of those being represented. The second school of thought is the trustee conception of representation. This school of thought maintains that representatives should advance those policies that they consider to be in the best interest of the represented. Correct policies are those policies that the representative identifies as being in the best interests of the represented.

According to Pitkin, both schools of thought are right, for both representatives and their constituents can be wrong about whether a public policy is in the best interests of the constituents. Consequently, good representatives sometimes follow their own judgment about the proper course of action, and they sometimes obey the preferences of their constituents. Moreover, the concept of representation is, according to Pitkin, best understood as paradoxical – representatives can be subject, in a given circumstance, both to the requirement to follow their own judgment and to that of obeying their constituents' preferences, so that they will violate the norms of being a good representative no matter what they do. Pitkin recommends, further, that we should try to preserve, as opposed to eliminating, the paradoxical nature of representation. That is to say, good representatives should try to preserve both the autonomy of the represented and their own authority as trustees. Finally, Pitkin recommends that those who sit in judgment of representatives evaluate the reasons that the representative adduces for not following the preferences of the represented. In particular, evaluations of representatives depend on whether the actions of a representative violate the "objective interests" of constituents.

Unfortunately, Pitkin does not discuss what she means by objective interests, let alone how the objective interests of a given constituency are to be specified. Nor does she address how conceptions of interest vary with different kinds of government: the interests we have as democratic citizens differ, for example, from those we have as citizens of a country ruled by a military dictatorship. It is, after all, in the interest of democratic citizens, as such, to have their rights as democratic citizens – such as the right to vote – upheld. This point raises a possibility that Pitkin does not consider, a possibility I will explore: namely, that the paradox of representation might take a specific form for *democratic* representation.[3]

Pitkin is right on many points. Standards for evaluating representatives can be contradictory, so that representatives can find themselves in the unfortunate position of violating some standard no matter how they act. It is also important to preserve the autonomy of the representative as well as the autonomy of the represented. Furthermore, the reasons given by a representative for disobeying the preferences of their constituents certainly do matter.

However, Pitkin attends only to political efficacy, and not to democratic efficacy – that is, to the political efficacy characteristic of democratic representatives. And, in doing so, she overlooks a distinctive set of standards that are to be used for evaluating the political efficacy of democratic representatives, as such. Granted, appeal to these standards will not settle every disagreement about the proper course of action that a democratic representative should pursue. However, just as political theory can provide some general guidelines about which institutional designs for political institutions are preferable to others, political theory can provide some general guidelines for identifying preferable representatives. To do this, political theory needs to attend to the distinctive function of democratic representatives – namely, how democratic advocacy allows for the fair and peaceful resolution of conflicts within a pluralist society.

Good democratic representatives do not aim only at advancing the policy preferences of their constituents. Rather, their advocacy is properly constrained, and informed, by their commitment to the legitimacy of democratic institutions. As I argued in Chapter 3, democratic representatives engage in their characteristic activity only insofar as they aim, in advancing public policies, to protect the well-functioning of democratic institutions. Democratic representatives, then, should as democratic representatives seek to guarantee that democratic institutions can peacefully and fairly reconcile conflicts within society. They should not merely advance the opinions, interests, and perspectives of the people who they claim to represent. Good democratic representatives, then, will excel at securing the proper functioning of democratic institutions. And, as such, they need to possess and exhibit not just any political efficacy, but democratic efficacy.

Democratic Efficacy

Let me begin by stating how democratic efficacy should *not* be understood. Democratic efficacy should not be understood as simply obeying the policy preferences of those citizens whom a democratic representative claims to represent.[4] Nor should democratic efficacy be understood as political efficacy that is consistent with the preferences of the majority of citizens. Indeed, it is necessary to move beyond the trustee–delegate debate. What is relevant to evaluating a particular policy from the perspective of democratic norms and values is not *who* endorses that policy, but *the effect* of that policy on civic equality, and thereby on the legitimacy of democratic institutions. Moreover, good democratic representatives aim to advance public policies that further the cause of civic equality in particular ways. Their advocacy aims to vindicate and strengthen citizens' faith in democratic institutions as institutions that provide fair methods of settling political conflicts. Good democratic representatives want to win, but they also want to make sure that citizens recognize the preferability of democratic forms of government to nondemocratic ones. Good democratic representatives need to have (at least minimally) a certain loyalty to democratic institutions.

Of course, some citizens might not appreciate the value of democratic institutions as institutions that provide fair ways of settling political conflict. Indeed, some democratic citizens might reject democratic institutions outright. Others might value democratic institutions only as instruments to their own particular ends – that is, they might support democratic institutions only to the degree that doing so advances their particular policy preferences. Representatives who, in line with the preferences of such citizens, value democratic institutions only instrumentally might be very good representatives of those citizens. But they are not, on my view, good *democratic* representatives. To recognize the diverse attitudes that democratic citizens can possess toward democratic institutions is to recognize why standards for identifying good democratic representatives should not be tied simply to satisfying the policy preferences of citizens. Good democratic representatives must educate citizens about the value of democratic institutions, encouraging them to support democratic institutions even when doing so can require sacrificing their own public policy preferences. Good democratic representatives must thus preserve the fairness of democratic institutions, and thereby encourage democratic citizens to continue to resolve their conflicts through democratic institutions. In order, in these ways, to support the proper functioning of democratic institutions, the advocacy work of good democratic representatives must be sensitive to civic equality. A democratic representative shows this sensitivity to civic equality when she intentionally, and publicly, advances public policies in ways that protect the capacities of citizens to interact as equals and thereby protect their shared political status and standing.

Why Civic Equality?

A fundamental characteristic of democratic institutions is that they bestow voting equality at the decisive stage of collective decisions (e.g., Dahl, 1989). Citizens who have an equal say in the outcomes of the public policy-making process have some – albeit minimal – control over those outcomes. Having an equal say in the public policy-making process provides a justifiable reason for thinking that democratic procedures are fair. Civic equality is therefore central to the legitimacy of democratic institutions. While political theorists might define civic equality differently,[5] there exists a consensus that civic equality is the democratic value that underlies and legitimates democratic authority. For example, Joshua Cohen and Joel Rogers (1995) contend that "An outcome is legitimate only if it emerges from a process of representation and bargaining in which all interests have substantively equal chances of being heard and influencing outcomes (28). Charles Beitz (1989, 22–3) goes further, claiming that the only thing that those who support procedural methods for determining democratic authority can agree upon is the idea that those procedures should "represent a division of political influence that would appropriate among persons regarded as equal citizens." Thus, my emphasis on civic equality reflects the general agreement among political theorists that the fairness of democratic processes is strongly tied to their providing equitable ways in which democratic citizens can express their preferences and impact the public policy-making process.

Now not everyone agrees that civic equality is a desirable feature of democratic institutions. Alexis De Tocqueville (2003 [1835]) famously attributed the spread of equality as responsible for the leveling down of society as well as the tyranny of the majority. But most theorists would agree that civic equality is at least one important value. My focus on civic equality does not presume that every democratic citizen (or theorist) prioritizes equality over other values. Civic equality is only one crucial democratic value – one that is crucial insofar as it permits resolving disagreements among democratic citizens fairly and peacefully.

Here, Jane Mansbridge is instructive. Mansbridge (1983, 5) persuasively argues that "when citizens have the same interests, as they do in unitary democracies, they do not need equal power to protect their interests against one another since each will promote the interests of others." Mansbridge maintains that equal power in the political arena is necessary when citizens' interests conflict. For if citizens agree about the proper course of action, then it doesn't matter whether citizens have an equal political standing. The outcome would be the same regardless of the level of civic equality.

On the present view, the fact that democratic citizens disagree about the importance of various political values, far from telling against my championing of civic equality, bolsters my claims about the importance of civic equality. For the norm of civic equality also provides grounds for the fair resolution of conflicts among democratic citizens over the question of which values ought to be privileged.

My focus on civic equality is also justified given current social, economic and political realities within the United States. Joseph Carens (2000) has argued that it is important to consider the meaning of certain ideas in relationship to their particular political context. I agree. Given recent empirical evidence of growing economic inequalities within the US (cf., Neckerman, 2004), it is important to consider the meaning of civic equality for good democratic representation. My focus on civic equality is justified to the extent that these economic inequalities impact the capacities of citizens to fully participate in politics. In particular, such inequalities are troublesome from the perspective of democratic theory to the extent that they keep the voices of the worst off from being heard. Sidney Verba, Kay Schlozman, and Henry Brady (1995, 11) found that "Disparities in political activity parallel the fault lines of significant political and social division in American Society." They go on to conclude that "any system that denies equal participatory rights violates a fundamental principle of democracy."

My emphasis on civic equality gains some further justification from reflections on the possible impact that the growing socioeconomic gap in the US might have on how democratic citizens perceive the legitimacy of the public policy-making process. One concern is that this gap could lead many US citizens, not unreasonably, to perceive their government as captured by the wealthy, or at least under the sway of corporate interests. Such perceptions would undermine further the legitimacy of the authority claimed by US democratic institutions. These reflections suggest that, to the extent that democratic representatives aim to preserve the legitimacy of democratic institutions, they need to be concerned with socioeconomic disparities that impact on the perceived, as well as real, ability of citizens to exercise influence on public policy-making.

Finally, my emphasis on civic equality is justified because economic disparities can promote anti-democratic tendencies among citizens. As Simone Chambers and Jeffrey Kopstein (2001) contend, economic disparities promote "bad civil society" – that is, civic associations that embrace hate, bigotry, racism, anti-Semitism, and aggressive xenophobia. In promoting such bad civil society, social and economic inequalities erode citizens' commitment to reciprocity and thereby their commitment to democratic institutions. Political theorists cannot ignore economic disparities.

Democratic representatives and democratic citizens need to understand how democratic values and norms should constrain, and inform, political advocacy. Democratic representatives cannot ignore how their advocacy work can undermine civic equality. Moreover, democratic citizens need to value (and choose when possible) those representatives whose advocacy exhibits proper sensitivity toward civic equality. Moreover, a democratic representative shows the requisite sensitivity to civic equality, in part, in encouraging the citizenry to value civic equality, and to engage in the political process with the aim of furthering civic equality. There is thus a virtuous cycle between good democratic representation and good democratic engagement on the part of citizens. In short, good democratic representatives are effective in advancing public policies in ways that they understand will preserve and further the civic equality of citizens, for it is in doing so that they contribute to the fairness and the legitimacy of democratic institutions.

Of course, not all representatives will engage in advocacy out of a sensitivity to civic equality. My point is that they should. The reason that representatives who advance racist, sexist, or xenophobic public policies – for example, Rabbi Meir Kahane – are bad democratic representatives is simple: such representatives violate the demands set by the democratic value of civic equality. And they thwart the realization of a value that makes democratic institutions worthy of our support.

The Meaning of Civic Equality

Let me recap. To exercise the virtue of fair-mindedness is to advocate in ways that are properly sensitive to civic equality. More specifically, the virtue of fair-mindedness requires good democratic representatives to attend to the ways in which civic equality legitimates democratic authority. Fair-minded representatives are, thus, indispensable to democratic institutions. For democratic institutions are less likely to settle conflicts of interests fairly and peacefully when democratic representatives lack the virtue of fair-mindedness.[6]

My contention that democratic institutions need democratic representatives who advocate in light of their understanding of civic equality may seem problematic in light of the fact that there are apt to be disagreements within any given polity over the meaning of civic equality. Consider, for example, how Americans possess, and have possessed, different conceptions of civic equality. In the past, both formal representatives and informal representatives endorsed policies that supported and sustained slavery in the US. And they did so on the grounds that civic equality did not extend to all members of society – just to the freemen. A similarly restrictive view of the scope of civic equality, espoused by women as well as by men, has disenfranchised women. Some women's groups have maintained that formal civic equality undermines a desirable status that women have traditionally enjoyed in society. Indeed, in the 1970s, Phyllis Schaffly successfully led the organization STOP-ERA, in its quest to prevent a constitutional amendment that explicitly recognized the equal status of women in the US. Conceptions of civic equality that extended the scope of civic equality to poor whites refused to extend the rights and privileges of equal citizenship to blacks.[7] To endorse a conception of civic equality, then, is not necessarily to commit to the equality of all members of a society, or even of all citizens. Another moral of these observations is that democratic citizens often disagree about the best way to understand the scope, nature, and value of civic equality.

However, the fact that democratic citizens possess different under-standings of civic equality does not entail that democratic representatives cannot be evaluated by their ability to advance public policies in ways that foster civic equality. To see this, we need to consider the ways in which certain general conceptions of civic equality, or what I call "approaches" to civic equality, provide citizens with genuine reasons for obeying the authority of democratic institutions. I claim that there are at least three different legitimate approaches to civic equality: the *formal approach*, the *gap approach*, and the *threshold approach*.[8] To possess the virtue of fair-mindedness, democratic representatives need to balance all three of these approaches to civic equality. For each of these approaches appeals to a distinctive understanding of fairness that plays an important role in justifying democratic political institutions. To ignore, let alone to act in ways that seriously undermine, any one of these approaches to civic equality is to weaken the legitimacy of democratic institutions.

Let's begin with the *formal approach*. This approach equates civic equality with providing all citizens as citizens with the same rights and entitlements. On this approach, civic equality is realized when everyone has the same entitlements (e.g., the right to vote), the same civic duties (e.g., following the law and paying taxes), and the same standing (e.g., a common status before the law). These rights and entitlements, when designated as shared features of citizenship, allow citizens to flourish as equals. According to this first approach to civic equality, the legitimacy of democratic processes is achieved when citizens are, through these rights and entitlements, given the *same* political standing.

The formal equality approach certainly enjoys considerable appeal.[9] However, it has its limitations. The most basic problem with the formal equality approach is that to bestow the same entitlements, standing, and privileges to all qualified citizens can advantage some citizens at the expense of others. Martha Minow (1991) has famously articulated this problem, which she calls the "dilemma of difference." Minow notes that in a polity with significant differences among citizens, either ignoring these differences or incorporating them within the general scheme of entitlements can be counterproductive to (or even dangerous for) vulnerable groups in representative democracies.

For example, consider Minow's discussion of problems with formal equality as it applies to one dilemma of difference – namely, the provision of pregnancy benefits. Of course, not all women have the ability or desire to become pregnant; however, one salient difference among women and men is the ability to become pregnant. To incorporate this difference in the scheme of formal entitlements – so as to require employers to provide maternity leave to pregnant employees – encourages discrimination against women (e.g., refusal to hire women). But to ignore this difference is to fail to provide needed protection to the distinctive interests that women have, in virtue of their ability to become pregnant. Ignoring differences among citizens or recognizing these differences can have drawbacks from the perspective of certain groups. Minow's discussion suggests that conceiving civic equality simply as a matter of treating all qualified citizens the same can bar some citizens from securing the full benefits and protections of citizenship. In the process, she reveals a problem with adopting only one approach to civic equality.

This leads to the second approach to civic equality, the *gap approach*. This approach conceives of civic equality as achieved by minimizing differences among groups of citizens in respect of the different amounts of political resources they command. Here, I adopt Robert Dahl's notion of political resources, on which such resources are "whatever can be used among a specific collection of people to influence the decisions of a government, particularly the government of a state" (1998, 639). Examples of political resources include "money, wealth, social standing, honor, reputation, legal status, knowledge, cognitive ability, information, coercive capacities, organizations, means of communication and 'connections'" (ibid.).

Put simply, the gap approach identifies the degree of civil equality within any given democratic society by comparing the political resources of one group to those of another. Inequalities of political resources that arise from unjust sources – such as slavery – are particularly troubling for the legitimacy of democratic institutions, for such inequalities lead democratic citizens to perceive democratic institutions as the tools of oppression. Good democratic representatives who pursue the gap approach to civic equality advance public policies in ways that try to reduce and compensate for inequalities in the holdings of political resources, especially those that have unjust sources.

The third and final approach to civic equality is *the threshold approach*. According to this approach, fairness is achieved only when all citizens possess the minimal political resources necessary for exercising their rights and privileges as citizens. The threshold approach focuses on the resources that are vital for citizens to possess the capacity to rule and be ruled. On the threshold approach it is not simply the relative amounts of resources possessed by different groups that matters; rather, fairness is achieved only when all citizens have enough of the relevant resources. Proponents of the threshold approach contend, against proponents of the formal approach, that having the same status or political standing as other citizens is meaningless if citizens do not also possess the minimal resources required to exercise that status or standing. So, for example, freedom of the press becomes meaningless if citizens can't afford a printing press (or a television commercial). Dr. Martin Luther King Jr. made a similar point when he observed that desegregating restaurants isn't worth much if citizens can't afford to eat in those restaurants.

As we have just seen, representatives who pursue a threshold approach to civic equality focus on the resources necessary to be politically effective. Those who pursue the gap approach to civic equality, in contrast, worry about relative disparities of resources, even among groups that all possess the minimal resources necessary for political efficacy. Proponents of the gap approach, therefore, might consider civic equality to be sufficiently achieved when the different amounts of resources possessed by citizens have been reduced, while those who adopt a threshold approach would focus on whether all citizens possess the minimal amount of resources necessary to be effective (regardless of whether some citizens possess more or less resources). Those who use a threshold approach might be satisfied when everyone is above the threshold and ignore the fact that a huge gap still exists between different groups of citizens. And those who pursue the threshold approach would worry that disadvantages are precluding the achievement of civic equality even if all citizens have the same level of political resources, if that level is insufficient for enjoying genuine political efficacy, and so for enjoying genuine political standing.[10]

A fully adequate approach to civic equality needs to incorporate all three of these approaches. We have already seen that, even if a society achieves formal equality, it does not achieve meaningful civic equality among its citizens unless all its citizens have the resources to impact the outcomes of public policies at the final decision stage and thereby to protect their equal standing. Formal equality can become meaningless if the gap between the worst off and the better off in a democratic polity grows too large. Consider, again, the plight of African-Americans during Reconstruction. After the passage of the Fourteenth Amendment, which gave African-Americans citizenship rights, and the passage of the Fifteenth Amendment, which gave African-Americans the right to vote (although this right was weakened by the fact that states set qualifications for voters), African-Americans were legally allowed to vote and in fact, elected black legislators to the state assemblies. However, blacks in the South faced serious economic problems, lynchings, and intimidation from white supremacy groups – all of which impeded their exercise of their citizenship rights. And the fact that African-Americans did not have the real standing in Southern society required even to retain their formal equality is evident from the fact that the political gains they had made were soon lost after the federal withdrawal of troops. The experience of African-Americans in the South during Reconstruction reveals that formal equality is not always sufficient for achieving and preserving the equal political standing of citizens.[11]

The moral is that good democratic representatives must, in developing and pursuing their political agendas, bear in mind the effect that the public policies they champion are likely to have on civic equality, on a conception of civic equality that incorporates all three approaches to civic equality. These different approaches to civic equality suggest that good democratic representatives cannot be too narrowly or exclusively focused on the needs of the groups they purport to represent. Good democratic representatives need to attend to the effects of their actions not just on their constituents, but on other democratic citizens as well. In particular, they need to attend to the good of the democratic citizenry as a whole, in respect of its realizing civic equality. Each of the three different approaches to civic equality contributes to the understanding of civic equality that should inform the advocacy of a good democratic representative. For each approach provides a genuine standard in light of which the fairness of democratic institutions can be assessed.[12] And to the extent to which a democratic process of policy-making respects one of these conceptions of how civic equality is to be structured, it provides democratic citizens with moral reasons for considering the outcomes of that process to be legitimate.

Let me summarize. The three different approaches to civic equality provide reasons for considering a political outcome legitimate. Each approach captures a different and sometimes competing sense of fairness. An outcome is unfair when someone is not treated the same as others. An outcome is unfair when some people get more goods than others. An outcome is unfair when it does not provide someone with enough goods. Good democratic representatives try to balance all three approaches to civic equality.

However, a problem arises, for each approach to civic equality can place different, and sometimes incompatible, demands on the types of policies that democratic representatives should pursue. Each of these different senses of unfairness justifies and inspires different ways to pursue public policies. The formal approach emphasizes the rights and duties of representatives to advocate zealously for their clients (whether these clients are corporations, teacher unions, or poor Appalachians) – for this approach grants all citizens a similar political standing regardless of their ideological positions, their interests, or their group membership. The gap approach to civic equality stresses the need to consider how public policies comparatively affect different citizens. On this approach, one cannot simply advocate zealously on behalf of one's constituents in a manner oblivious to the distribution of political resources in one's polity, and still respect the demands of civic equality. For instance, advocates who argue for tax cuts and less government regulation need to consider the impact on the least well off. And, on the threshold approach, good democratic representatives need also to evaluate public policies based on the effect of those policies on the minimal threshold needed by democratic citizens to enjoy political influence. For instance, good democratic representatives might have to supplement the political resources available to worst off citizens to make sure they have an equal opportunity to be heard.

The tensions among these three approaches to civic equality suggest that to restrict oneself to any one approach to civic equality would be to overlook a range of genuine normative reasons that ground a preference for democratic ways of organizing one's political life. For this reason, the advocacy work of good democratic representatives should balance all three approaches to civic equality. Correspondingly, democratic citizens should not simply identify good democratic representatives by appealing to just one of the approaches to civic equality. Rather, they ought to assess a representative in terms of the impact of the policies she advances in accordance with all three approaches to civic equality.

To recap, good democratic representatives need to think about the impact certain public policies have on the common political standing that should extend to all members of a democratic society. In doing so, they need to understand how some minimal level of political resources is necessary for exercising one's formal political standing. And democratic representatives need, further, to think about comparative problems: that is, about the political obstacles created by the gap between privileged and disadvantaged citizens. For a full commitment to democracy requires us to worry not just about protecting the equal formal standing of all members of society, but also about the particular problems facing certain citizens that prevent them from participating fully in a democracy's political life.

Using the First Virtue to Evaluate Representatives

So what, exactly, is it to exhibit fair-mindedness, the first virtue of democratic representatives? And, correspondingly, how should democratic citizens identify good democratic representatives in light of the first virtue of democratic representation? I have given initial answers to these questions. The virtue of fair-mindedness requires a democratic representative, in advancing public policies, to attend to civic equality, specifically by balancing all three approaches. Democratic citizens ought to select representatives who excel at advocating in this way. In the present section, I elaborate these answers, drawing out what considerations should inform the evaluation of representatives.

Consider, to begin with, whether, to be a good democratic representative, one must be successful in advancing public policies. In a very simplistic way, the answer is, of course, yes. Those who have little or no impact on public policy, even if through no fault of their own – for example, they lack the resources to do any better – are less efficacious than those who do make a significant impact. And since efficaciousness is a cardinal virtue of good democratic representation, such representatives are not in fact good democratic representatives, even if they have a deep commitment to democratic values and thus a tremendous *potential* to be good democratic representatives. So representatives who live under conditions of fundamental inequality – for example, South African Apartheid – and who are deeply committed to racial equality, can only fully realize the first virtue to the degree that they can successfully advance the cause of oppressed groups.

It would, of course, be unreasonable to make it a condition of being a good representative that one be successful in implementing every public policy one seeks. Recall, in this connection, that in characterizing political efficacy I employed a broad understanding of "success" according to which hindering the passage, or even the effective implementation, of legislation that one opposes counts as success. Consequently, a good democratic representative must have some significant degree of success in influencing the public policy-making process. Moreover, such success must be consonant with the legitimacy of democratic institutions.[13]

However, once we have distinguished the three approaches to civic equality, it becomes evident that political efficacy of any stripe is not sufficient for good democratic representation. The point is not merely that the first virtue specifies that there is more to being a good democratic representative than simply enjoying success in advancing and implementing policy goals, whatever those goals might be. The crucial point is that a good democratic representative does not engage in no-holds-barred advocacy on behalf of one's own constituents. Those representatives who insist on *doing nothing but* helping particularistic interests – whether they are lobbyists for corporate interests or activists for historically disadvantaged groups – violate, in two ways, the demands of the first virtue of democratic representation.[14] First, a commitment to formal equality, even in grounding a duty on the part of every democratic representative to advocate zealously on behalf of his or her own constituents, also grounds a constraint on such advocacy: such advocacy must respect the equal formal political standing of all democratic citizens. Second, the gap and threshold approaches set a further constraint on how a good democratic representative advocates on behalf of her constituents. These approaches require good democratic representatives to be concerned with the access that citizens have to decision-makers. In other words, they require good representatives to be concerned with a problem that David Truman describes:

> The problem is that all groups do not have equal access. Some groups are more likely to be heard than others. In a system that is biased toward those groups that have access, the question is how to gain it. (1951, 506)

Good democratic representatives are alarmed by chronic patterns of injustice that prevent certain groups from gaining access and exercising political influence. Symbiotic relationships among government officials and interest groups that preclude the access of relevant citizen groups violate the norm of civic equality to the extent that they deny sufficient access to certain citizens. In these ways, good democratic representatives constrain their advocacy on behalf of their constituents by their commitment to fostering civic equality – where that includes minimizing the negative impact that bad public policies can have on civic equality.

I am arguing, then, that one must attend to a representative's actions – which policy preferences they endorse, ignore, or fight against – in assessing whether her performance is consonant with democratic norms and values. This insight reflects a recent trend in political theory to insist on what Charles Beitz aptly called "complex proceduralism," which offers a much more demanding vision of civic equality than does simple proceduralism. It requires not only that certain procedures be employed in reaching political decisions, but also that these decisions lead to fair outcomes. My discussion of the first virtue suggests that there are at least three different grounds for criticizing the fairness of outcomes. Each approach to civic equality provides a valid reason for questioning the fairness of an outcome of the public policy-making process. Thus, articulating the first virtue improves our understanding of how to evaluate democratic representatives by identifying three different approaches to fairness that democratic citizens should use in assessing the performance of individual representatives.

But, one might well ask, what is the proper balance among the three approaches to civic equality in light of which a good representative properly constrains her advocacy work? Here I am inclined toward a particularism concerning the proper balance that is to be struck. How a democratic representative should go about balancing these approaches to civic equality in a given case will depend on both the particular issue at hand and the particular context in question. So what can be said in general about how these approaches are to be balanced is limited. But we can say something about the proper method citizens should use for evaluating the fair-mindedness of their representatives. First, democratic citizens should pay attention to whose interests representatives claim to advance (and whose interests they are willing to sacrifice, ignore or even denounce). The fair-minded representative will claim to serve the interests not just of his constituents, but of all democratic citizens.[15] Second, good democratic representatives will offer justifications for their policies in terms of all three approaches to civic equality and thus in terms of the effects that these policies will have – not just on their own constituents, but also on other citizens. Good democratic representatives should not hide the costs of their policies on their constituents or on other citizens. The kinds of justifications required of good democratic representatives allow democratic citizens to assess their representatives' activities and thereby hold them accountable for those activities.

Indeed, the nature of the tensions among the three approaches to civic equality raises the possibility that there might not, even in a particular case, be one right answer to the question of how these approaches are to be balanced. For equal formal standing and the political resources required to exercise one's rights are arguably incommensurable goods. Consider a case in which a representative must choose whether to strengthen the formal standing of all citizens or to secure for a significant portion of citizens the political goods required to get them over the minimum threshold required for exercising their formal standing. Perhaps there is no right answer about which course she should take. Good democratic representation might well be a kind of *tekhne* that allows for a range of different possible approaches to the same problem.

What is more, there seem to be conceivable circumstances in which the three approaches to civic equality conflict in a stronger sense than merely that of providing different and incompatible forms of guidance to a representative. The pursuit of one approach to fostering civic equality might require weakening civic equality, understood according to a different approach. And, it would seem, if the policies endorsed by a representative weaken civic equality in any one of those three ways, then that political representative is not being a good democratic representative. Indeed, a democratic representative could conceivably face a dilemma of sorts, facing a set of options any one of which would result in weakening civic equality in respect of one of the three approaches. A given representative may, through no fault of her own, be unable to meet the demands that the first virtue sets on good democratic representation, on account of such conflicts among the three approaches to civic equality. Here, degree matters – for democratic citizens need to consider the extent to which democratic representatives are forced to sacrifice one approach to civic equality in order to bolster another approach to civic equality. Degree also matters because democratic politics requires compromise and, thereby, forces democratic representatives to sacrifice their regulative ideals.

Tensions among the three different approaches to civic equality suggest that certain disagreements about good democratic representation will persist even after extensive public debate about the nature of good representation within the framework of an ethics of democratic representation. Representatives who insist that democratic citizens only endorse certain policies or who question the commitment of democratic citizens to democratic institutions simply in virtue of their support of certain public policies do not fully appreciate the meaning of democratic representation. In particular, they fail to see that the distinctive function of democratic representation is to provide the means for settling political disagreements fairly and peacefully. Excelling at their characteristic activity thus requires democratic representatives to mediate, and thus to some extent to accommodate, disagreements among citizens. Good democratic representation does not require loyalty oaths. Good democratic representatives will thus recognize and respond to the diversity of legitimate public policy preferences held by their constituents that are consistent with the three different approaches to civic equality. By the same token, democratic citizens should be suspicious of those who assert that all citizens or groups do or must share the same views on particular public policies. And they should not identify a good democratic representative simply by the extent to which he or she endorses particular policy preferences or claims to have a single authoritative account of a group's interest.

To acknowledge that good democratic representation is not always self-evident is not to say that a citizen should endorse a representative simply to the extent that he or she advances what that citizen takes to be the right outcome. Rather, one's assessment of a democratic representative ought to be sensitive to how that representative responds to the uncertainties of democratic advocacy. By "uncertainties of democratic advocacy," I am referring to the conflicting or unclear obligations that the virtues can impose on democratic representatives. Sometimes, it is difficult to discern the proper way of advancing public policies in light of democratic norms and commitments. This is true because representatives can be uncertain about the impact of public policies on democratic citizens. But it can also be true because citizens can understand democratic norms and commitments in such drastically opposed ways that democratic representatives are unable to accommodate disagreements among citizens.

Such uncertainties do not mean that democratic representatives can do whatever they want. Rather, their existence suggests that democratic citizens should evaluate their representatives by their ability to respond to conflicts among their constituents about the best policy to pursue. My discussion of the first virtue thus suggests a fourth way to identify good democratic representatives – namely, by their ability to remain open-minded about the proper ways of balancing the three approaches to civic equality. Moreover, they should remain open-minded about how their constituencies are defined. Good democratic representatives should try to expand their constituencies, reaching out to those who have been marginalized by political processes. Good representatives will, in deliberating about what public policies to advance, consider all the legitimate policy preferences of their constituents. And, after they have made up their minds, they will, in light of the possibility that they have made a mistake, maintain their right to change their minds, and citizens should respect this right. Good democratic representatives will thus continue to be sensitive to their constituents' competing policy preferences, and be willing to revisit public policy issues. This openness means that all those responsible for advancing public policy, and not just those who hold the office of Senate (Sabl, 2002), must sometimes moderate the passions of democratic citizens. Moreover, democratic citizens also need to tolerate the uncertainties of democratic advocacy, allowing their representatives to revise their opinions about public policies.

Thus, the virtue of fair-mindedness requires good democratic representatives to pursue democratic efficacy – that is, a political efficacy that attends to how civic equality legitimates democratic authority. More specifically, my discussion reveals that several factors are relevant for identifying good democratic representatives. First, good democratic representatives need to balance all three approaches to civic equality. Second, the tensions between these different approaches to civic equality suggest that those who assess representatives need to attend to the justifications that a representative gives for privileging, on a given occasion, one approach to civic equality over another. Third, good democratic representatives should preserve the access of fellow citizens to government officials. Fourth, good democratic representatives should remain open-minded, aware of the uncertainties that surround good democratic representation. There is one further, and final, consequence that my discussion of the virtue of fair-mindedness has for the proper evaluation of good democratic representatives. Such evaluations cannot be reached through some straightforward formula: one cannot simply plug in certain values and calculate the virtuous way of being a good democratic representative. One reason for this is that democratic representatives, like all political representatives, face paradoxical standards rooted in the fact that they need to act both as delegates and as trustees. Both the delegate and trustee conception ground genuine, and sometimes conflicting, standards of good democratic representation. The first virtue of democratic representation suggests that democratic representatives should, in negotiating between these two competing conceptions, attend to the effects that their actions have on democratic institutions. The objective interests that Pitkin never articulates, but which ground the demands of both the delegate and the trustee conceptions of democratic representation, include the interests that all democratic citizens have as democratic citizens. Most crucially, all democratic citizens, as such, have an objective interest in democratic institutions settling political conflicts justly and peacefully. A good democratic representative, both as delegate and as trustee, works to protect and advance this objective interest. The first virtue, in laying down this demand, does not specify particular policy preferences (such as supporting affirmative action) as ones that good democratic representative must support. But the first virtue does provide citizens some very good reasons for objecting to, and opposing, representatives who endorse certain proposals, such as disenfranchising certain groups, as profoundly undemocratic. For example, Rabbi Kahane's willingness to "take care" of Israeli-Palestinians by exiling or eliminating them clearly violates the first virtue. In this way, the first virtue of democratic representation identifies some general guidelines for judging the performance of particular representatives. It partially constitutes the normative framework within which, drawing on fundamental democratic norms and values, democratic citizens evaluate their representatives. And, in doing so, the first virtue provides democratic citizens genuine normative reasons for preferring some representatives to others.

Two Problems with the First Virtue

The first virtue does suffer from two problems. Both of these problems derive from the fact that the requirements of political efficacy and those of civic equality are apt to come in conflict with each other. Since the virtue of fair-mindedness is one of democratic efficacy, and democratic efficacy is a species of political efficacy, these conflicts pose problems for this virtue.

The first problem of democratic efficacy derives from the fact that political efficacy requires political resources, so that those who are in a position to succeed in advocacy work are those who already possess the political resources to be successful at advocacy work. Steven Rosenstone and John Hansen make this point well:

> Because neither resources nor interests are distributed evenly across the population, some people find the costs [of participation] less burdensome and the benefits [of the same] more attractive than others do. The wealthy, the educated, the experienced and the efficacious can more easily afford the demands [of political activity] on their money, time, skill and self-confidence. (1993, 6)

To advance political efficacy, even where this efficacy is constrained by a sensibility to civic equality, as a standard for evaluating democratic representatives is thus to recommend for political office those with the socioeconomic resources and political experience to be effective in the political arena. To endorse the first virtue of democratic representation is thus to endorse the hierarchical relations of the status quo that civic equality requires us to challenge. It is to endorse, among others, established representatives, and to place newcomers – who after all have not proven their effectiveness, or had the opportunities to develop political clout – at a severe disadvantage.

The first problem with the virtue of fair-mindedness is tied to a problem with descriptive representation of historically disadvantaged groups.[16] After all, such representatives (take, for example, female representatives) are apt to be newcomers to the political arena. And those women who possess the socioeconomic resources necessary for running for office (let alone for being effective in those offices) may, for that very reason, be ill suited to speak for the socioeconomically worst off and so for some of the most politically marginalized women. The worry, then, is that widespread endorsement of the first virtue will disadvantage those most suited to being good descriptive representatives of historically disadvantaged groups.

A second problem for the first virtue deriving from the conditions of political efficacy will confront representatives who seek to exhibit the virtue of fair-mindedness. As David Easton and Jack Dennis (1967, 25) argue, the ability of political actors to gain policy influence cannot be neatly divorced from the political context in which they act. And there are contexts in which pursuing civic equality properly will conflict with enjoying success in advancing public policies. A commitment to civic equality might render a representative politically irrelevant, especially in a political climate rife with racism or xenophobia. Worse, in some political climates, advocating out of a commitment to civic equality is tantamount to political suicide. Racists and bigots will turn up at the polls to punish representatives who speak out in support of racial equality. Some democratic citizens endorse ethnic cleansing. Powerful corporate interests are apt to reward representatives willing to turn a blind eye to the cause of civic equality, and to punish those who do. And if a representative refuses, out of a concern for civic equality, to "bring home the bacon" for her constituency, she might be punished by being turned out of office in the next election. Good democratic representatives understand, and are sometimes willing to endure, such repercussions in order to preserve the legitimacy of democratic institutions. How high such costs become – indeed, whether good democratic representatives can enjoy any success at all – will depend on a society's political system as a whole. The degree to which the political system rewards or punishes those who pursue political advocacy in a fair-minded way will, in short, influence the extent to which that system promotes good democratic representation. Moreover, the ability to be a good democratic representative is not strictly within the control of individual representatives.

Democratic citizens thus share the responsibility for creating the conditions that allow democratic institutions to function properly. Particularly crucial is the extent to which citizens are willing to tolerate, or even reward, their representatives when they sacrifice their constituents' narrow self-interests for the sake of democratic institutions. Citizens need to provide incentives, or at least political cover, for their representatives to be good democratic representatives. And good democratic representation is bolstered when citizens recognize that protecting the civic equality of all citizens is in their own interests as democratic citizens. Such citizens would be less likely to punish representatives whose advocacy is constrained by the requirements of civic equality. And they are apt to resist the efforts of powerful corporate interests to punish representatives who do not cater to their demands. But if democratic citizens do punish representatives who safeguard civic equality, or fail to provide political cover for them, it is possible that democratic ideals might be too good for a democratic polity.

As we will see, the second problem with democratic efficacy suggests that the first virtue of democratic representation depends in an important way on the second virtue, the virtue of critical trust building. Good democratic representatives excel at improving the capacities of democratic citizens as such, and so develop citizens' capacities to engage critically in the democratic process. A democratic representative exhibits the second virtue, then, when she enables citizens to evaluate public policies, and the activity of their representatives, in light of the requirements of the virtues of democratic representation. It follows that a good critical trust builder helps citizens properly evaluate competing rationales for adopting public policies – by, among other things, encouraging them to prize the end of furthering civic equality in the polity. The ability of democratic representatives to advocate effectively for civic equality, and exhibit the virtue of fair-mindedness, will depend in part on democratic representatives developing citizens' capacities as democratic citizens and, thereby, exhibiting the second virtue of democratic representatives.

Chapter 5

The Virtue of Critical Trust Building

Democratic representatives can use questionable methods. Consider the following examples:

In 1988, James Roosevelt, a former congressman and founder of the National Committee to Preserve Social Security and Medicare, issued a political call to arms. In a direct mailing to senior citizens, he wrote, "Never in the 45 years since my father, Franklin Delano Roosevelt, started the Social Security system has there been such a severe threat to Social Security and Medicare benefits." What was peculiar about Roosevelt's mailing is that he was describing a proposal to expand, not cut, benefits to Medicare. In particular, Roosevelt's mailing referred to the Catastrophic Act of 1988, a bill that introduced benefits such as long term care and prescription drugs into Medicare coverage. What concerned Roosevelt was the surtax that came with these increased benefits. Seniors who paid at least $150 in income taxes had a 15 percent surcharged added to their bill. The surcharge was capped at $800. Roosevelt denounced this surtax as an "elderly surcharge." In his mailing, Roosevelt presented this surcharge as requiring all senior citizens to pay an additional $800 a year. (Later, officials from the National Committee to Preserve Social Security and Medicare admitted that they had misrepresented the tax as being placed on all elderly.) The outrage was immediate. Senator Daniel Patrick Moynihan received nearly 37,000 letters protesting the proposed cuts in a ten-day period. Busloads of old people showed up on the steps of American Association of Retired People's headquarters in Florida. The American Association of Retired People (AARP) had been one of the few advocacy organizations for the elderly that had supported the surtax. In response to the outrage of its membership, AARP changed its position. In 1989, the proposal to include Catastrophic Care coverage was defeated in the House by 360 to 66. Three hundred and twenty eight congressmen who had previously voted for the Catastrophic Act in 1988 switched their votes, partially as a result of Roosevelt's misleading letter.

In 1989, Vertac, Inc. held a raffle with prizes in Jacksonville, Arkansas. Taking the names and addresses of those who signed up for the raffle, they listed those people who signed up for the raffle as members of the Jacksonville People with Pride Cleanup Coalition. This organization then applied for an Environmental Protection Agency (EPA) grant under a program designed to assist citizens' groups that wished to monitor Superfund site cleanups. Although it claimed to represent the people of Jacksonville, this organization was really a political front for a Superfund polluter. The grant that was designed to give local citizens more input into the environmental regulatory process had been co-opted by the company that was supposed to be being monitored. Only after local environmentalists pointed out this misleading raffle did the EPA withdraw the grant.

In *Losing Ground: American Environmentalism at the Close of the Twentieth Century* (1995), Mark Dowie pronounced that the national environmental movement is "courting irrelevance." For Dowie, the leaders of the environmental movement are "too white, too male, too elite, too polite and too involved with Washington." While previous generations of environmental activists gained political influence by rousing the grassroots, the current movement is led by "bland lawyers and M.B.A.'s" whose primary interest is "developing entrepreneurial skills and organizational enhancement skills" designed to collect money from big business and industrial foundations.

How should good democratic representatives go about advocating on behalf of their constituents? In particular, are the methods employed by democratic representatives relevant to the question of whether they are representing in a *democratic* fashion? And if they are relevant, what methods ought they to be using? Are good democratic representatives, for instance, those who advocate by employing methods that increase the civic participation of democratic citizens – that is, by encouraging democratic citizens to write letters to elected officials, deliberate, and mobilize? If so, then Dowie would be correct to chide the current heads of environmental movements. However, if good democratic representatives are ones who simply increase participation, does that mean that James Roosevelt is a good democratic representative? Given the manipulative practices of organizations such as Vertac and of individuals such as Roosevelt, it would seem that we should not identify good democratic representatives simply by their employing the method of generating civic participation, regardless of how they do so.

Although I agree that political participation of citizens is vital to the well-functioning of democratic institutions, I contend that one should not identify *good* democratic representatives simply by their promoting the participation of citizens. The participation of the represented is a necessary, but not a sufficient, indicator of good democratic representation. Instead, good democratic representatives need to be assessed according to whether they exhibit the virtue of *critical trust building* – that is, whether they develop and protect the capacities of democratic citizens to be self-governing. Thus, the second virtue of democratic representation provides a general standard for evaluating democratic representatives by the extent to which their methods in advocating maintain and improve citizens' abilities to rule themselves. More specifically, good democratic representatives must employ methods of advocacy that promote what I call *critical trust*. To maintain that representatives are to be assessed by their ability to promote critical trust is to rule out the possibility that good democratic representatives use "any means necessary" to increase participation. Hence, the issue is not simply whether the environmental leaders or James Roosevelt promoted participation; it is, rather, whether they increased the critical trust of democratic citizens.

This chapter begins by examining the relationship between participation and democratic representation. More specifically, I identify four functions attributed to civic participation and demonstrate how these functions often rely on the activities of representatives. It is wrong to understand civic participation as independent from the actions of representatives. Next, I consider what is wrong with identifying good democratic representatives simply by whether they promote the political participation of citizens. I then explicate my understanding of the virtue of critical trust building, arguing that good democratic representatives increase the participation of citizens in ways that foster self-governance. More specifically, I argue that the methods of good democratic representatives foster critical trust. After describing how democratic representatives can employ methods of advocacy that promote critical trust, I conclude by examining several obstacles faced by good democratic representatives who try to foster critical trust.

Democratic Representation and Participation

There is an extensive and growing theoretical and empirical literature on the relationship between democracy and participation (e.g., Pateman, 1970; Barber, 1984; Verba and Nie, 1987; Rosenstone and Hansen, 1993). Most would agree that participation in the decision-making processes is constitutive of democratic citizenship. Democratic theorists, however, disagree about the proper manner in which democratic citizens should participate. Some emphasize the importance of voting and protesting; others maintain the importance of deliberating. Nonetheless, most democratic theorists treat participation – be it voting, mobilization, or deliberating – as the main stuff of which democracies are made. According to this understanding of the relationship between democracy and participation, citizens act as *democratic* citizens only when they participate.

Dennis Thompson (1970) has very helpfully identified the main functions of political participation found in citizenship theories. First, the participation of citizens protects them against *sinister interests*. Citizens need to be self-protecting. Relying on others to advance one's interests is fraught with risks. The participation of citizens in the political arena is vital for constraining the malfeasance committed by public officials. In this way, participation is inextricably tied to democratic accountability. The second function of participation, that of avoiding what Thompson calls *excluded interests*, is based on the thought that "extensive participation is necessary so that all interests are considered and expressed by those who know them best" (1970, 56). Third, civic participation has the function of providing *political knowledge*. Through political participation, democratic citizens gain competency and improve their understanding of their own and other citizens' needs, desires, and interests. Participation can thereby improve political outcomes by helping citizens and their representatives to base decisions on better information. Fourth, citizen participation has the function of improving the *legitimacy* of democratic institutions. Here, active participation indicates the consent of citizens to the political institutions and, thereby, to the decision-making authority of political institutions. Conversely, citizens' refusing to participate in political institutions is evidence of their disapproval. (Such thinking drives those who worry about decreasing rates of voter participation and civic volunteerism.) The fifth function of participation is *self-realization*. Democratic citizens shape themselves and the laws that govern them through their participation.

Thus, if citizens are to be self-governing and autonomous, they must participate.

Thompson's discussion of the functions of civic participation is important for my project to the extent that it brings to light how the realization of these functions can depend on the activities of representatives. Consider, for instance, that both formal and informal representatives play crucial roles in the gathering and distribution of information necessary for improving democratic citizens' political knowledge. Similarly, Thompson's discussion of the function of avoiding excluded interests shows how fulfilling this function depends not simply on citizens expressing their views, but also on representatives agreeing to meet with those citizens and seriously considering the preferences that those citizens express. So when the National Association for the Advancement of Colored People (NAACP) refused to meet with and accept a donation from the D.C. Coalition of Black Lesbians, Gay Men, and Bisexuals, this group blocked certain excluded interests from accessing the traditional avenues of participation (Cohen, 1997). And, when President George W. Bush refused to meet with the NAACP, his actions also prevented certain citizens' interests from being expressed and heard. At the very least, some functions of civic participation depend on the actions of representatives. Consequently, the functions of civic participation should not be understood as completely distinct from the functions of democratic representatives.

The functions of civic participation and the functions of democratic representation are crucially linked in another respect: democratic representatives create incentives and disincentives for civic participation. Jack Nagel contends that

> While spontaneous popular action warms the heart of any good democrat, a moment's reflection shows that the people initiate little of what we normally call participation. . . . Acts of participation are stimulated by elites. (1983, 3–4)

Steven Rosenstone and John Hansen concur, noting that "People participate in politics not so much because of who they are but because of the political choices and incentives they are offered" (1993, 50). Formal representatives, like the president, in Samuel Kernel's terminology, "go public" (Kernel, 1986) by asking democratic citizens directly to contact public officials and thereby to pressure those officials to adopt certain public policies. Kenneth Kollman (1998) points out that informal representatives can employ the strategy of lobbying the public, what he calls "outside lobbying."[1] What is important about "outside lobbying" is that it accomplishes two tasks: signaling aspects of public opinion to public policy-makers and changing how selected constituents consider and respond to policy issues.

For my purposes, it is also important to see that through the use of phone banks, faxes, and email, representatives can, and routinely do, make outside lobbying more effective by targeting particular groups that would be impacted by the relevant legislation. Because of this selective lobbying, American politics is, according to Steven Schier, a "politics of exclusive invitations." More specifically, political parties, organized interests, and candidates "carefully [target] segments of the public to vote or press demands upon elected officials. In the process, a large segment of the public – about half – receive little invitation or inducement to participate in our politics" (2000, 1). But representatives do not only extend invitations to participate in the policy-making process. Representatives also discourage the participation of citizens; for example, when their use of negative advertising drives down voter turnout. By framing the issues to be deliberated, offering incentives to participate, and avoiding strategies that discourage participation, democratic representatives can play an important role in enabling the functions of civic participation – specifically, those of safeguarding the mechanisms of accountability, and preserving the access of all citizens to governmental bodies.

Given the importance of citizen participation and given the role that both formal and informal representatives play in promoting that participation, it might be tempting to conclude that good democratic representatives are simply representatives who create opportunities for participation. According to this line of thinking, when party organizers turned to mass communications – pamphlets, public letters, and newspapers – as a way of exciting the voters to participate using emotional appeals, one could say that those party organizers were acting as good democratic representatives. Furthermore, such a line of thinking would hold that good democratic representatives are simply those actors who preserve the avenues of access available to democratic citizens; for example, safeguarding democratic citizens' voting rights and civic liberties, such as the freedom of speech and the freedom of association. This line of thinking would further hold that good democratic representatives would also create opportunities for deliberation, such as enacting citizens' juries or deliberative polls.[2] In order for the functions of civic participation to be realized, representatives simply need to increase citizen participation and safeguard citizens' formal rights to participate. And good democratic representatives are simply those representatives who increase civic participation and safeguard citizens' formal rights to participate.

Problems with Evaluating Representatives by Citizen Participation

However, in simply increasing civic participation, a representative does not necessarily exhibit a virtue, for attempts to increase civic participation can work against the proper operation of democratic institutions. Conversely, a representative may develop citizens' capacities to rule themselves even when she does not increase opportunities for civic participation. For these two reasons, democratic representatives should not be judged as satisfying the second virtue when they merely increase participation. Rather, they should be judged by whether they encourage forms of participation that further the well-functioning of democratic institutions, and foster democratic citizens' capacities and opportunities for such civic participation.

The first reason to resist simply equating the second virtue with increasing civic participation is that even when they increase civic participation, far from contributing to the well-functioning of democratic institutions, some methods of advocacy actually impede this well-functioning.

A good example of such a method is the practice of push-polling, which does motivate some citizens to vote, but by spreading false information and corrupting the electoral process. In push-polling, a representative (via her advisors) ostensibly polls citizens regarding their preferences, but with the aim of manipulating their preferences. For example, during the 2000 Republican presidential primary race, Karl Rove, one of President Bush's campaign advisors, devised and executed a particularly effective push poll against Senator John McCain (R-AZ). In particular, before their primary election, South Carolina voters were asked, "Would you be more likely or less likely to vote for John McCain for president if you knew he had fathered an illegitimate black child?" By raising this question, the poll was able to create the impression that McCain did have a black child. Voters were especially prone to have this impression because McCain had campaigned in this state with his adopted Bangladeshi daughter. Senator McCain lost South Carolina, effectively ending his run for the presidency (Morrow, 2003).

Informal representatives have also adopted similarly manipulative strategies with the express aim of mobilizing democratic citizens in support of their causes. Recall James Roosevelt's letter to the elderly or Vertac's fake raffle to enlist citizens as members of its organization. Informal representatives can also "mobilize" citizens through the creation of political fronts, misinformation, and deceptive campaign tactics. It seems plausible that informal representatives' use of such methods, especially insofar as it manipulates citizens into misidentifying the political issues that are in fact at stake, undermines the proper operation of democratic institutions. And to that extent, the evaluation of informal representatives' performance as good democratize representatives simply in terms of their increasing civic participation is also inadequate.

To get a full sense of the degree to which democratic citizens are vulnerable to being manipulated by their representatives, it is useful to attend to the different forms that manipulative practices can take in contemporary representative democracies. In his analysis of manipulation, Robert Goodin (1980) identifies four distinct strategies that are used by political manipulators, all of which may potentially be used by representatives.[3] The first is lying, or the "deliberate dissemination of untrue information." The second strategy is secrecy, "the deliberate withholding of information that tends to undermine official policy." Propaganda is the third strategy, one that may disseminate true, albeit biased, information. Finally, manipulators can overload by releasing "so much information that citizens will have trouble assimilating it all" (Goodin, 1980, 39). This variety of manipulative strategies, each of which could be used by representatives to boost participation in the service of certain policy aims, underscores the importance of basing the evaluation of a democratic representative on more than her ability to get citizens to participate.[4]

In short, it is important not to assume that all methods of increasing civic participation support the capacities of democratic citizens to participate in the political process properly. In evaluating a democratic representative as a critical trust builder, one needs to attend to whether a representative's methods of advocacy support or undermine civic participation that contributes to the proper operation of democratic institutions. In doing so, one will be considering whether the participation fostered by a representative results in the desired effect – that is, satisfying the functions of civic participation described by Thompson.

I turn now to the second reason for not basing the evaluation of democratic representatives simply on their ability to increase civic participation.

Equating good critical trust building simply with increasing civic participation reflects a mistaken demand for citizens to be constantly actively engaged in politics. And this mistake, in turn, can rest on the failure to recognize the unavoidably episodic nature of democratic representation and the fact that this episodic character is proper because of the passive aspects of democratic citizenship.[5]

It is not realistic to expect all democratic citizens to be engaged, let alone highly engaged, in politics all of the time. Not every democratic citizen will have the desire to make such a commitment to politics. Moreover, even the most committed will find that at times they are unable to maintain such a commitment: people get sick, they grieve, they have babies. Nonetheless, the thought that good democratic representation requires that citizens be so engaged in politics may be tempting, because it can seem that citizens must be so engaged if they are to be self-governing.

We can see, however, that self-governance does not require constant engagement with politics. Self-governance requires that democratic citizens both rule and be ruled. And provided that citizens are not always, and entirely, passive – so as to be exclusively being ruled – they may be fulfilling all that democratic representation can and does require of them. In particular, for some periods at least, some democratic citizens may be fulfilling these requirements without being actively engaged in politics, provided that they, perhaps only indirectly through the agency of other citizens or their representatives, monitor the political process, so as to be able and willing to engage actively in that process when they really need to.

In order to see what is actually required, both of citizens and of critical trust builders, for self-governance, we need to attend to the active and passive aspects of democratic citizenship. I begin with the active. Now, admittedly, it is natural to distinguish between active and passive participation, as Iris Marion Young (1997, 352–3) does, when she describes how "in assemblies of a few hundred people, most people will be passive participants who listen to a few people speak for a few positions, then think and vote."[6] Citizens who show up to town meetings, yet refrain from speaking, are indeed naturally said to be passive participants. But, for my purposes, such citizens are still relatively active: they headed out to the town hall, listened somewhat attentively to the discussion, thought for themselves about what position they should take, then voted for that position. We might say that such participation is not as assertive as that in which citizens express their opinions, values, and perspectives with an aim toward shaping and directing public deliberation. Nonetheless, for my purposes, it is still to be classified as an active aspect of citizenship.

Consider now the passive aspects of democratic citizenship. Democratic citizenship requires passivity of citizens, and not just activity. And it requires this passivity, insofar as democratic citizens need to acknowledge the authority of democratic institutions to enact public policies in their name. Democratic citizens need to acknowledge this authority even when they do not participate in the polity's democratic policy-making processes. And in giving this acknowledgment they are being passive, consenting to being ruled.

Of course, if they are to be truly self-governing, democratic citizens need to monitor their representatives. Indeed, without some degree of monitoring, democratic institutions will not function properly. This requirement, admittedly, can seem overwhelming. Recall that William Greider (1993) estimates that Americans collectively elect over 500,000 formal representatives (cf., Chapter 3). In 2000, *Washington Representatives*, a directory of lobbyists and interest groups, had approximately 17,000 entries, including lawyers registered as lobbyists, think tank staff, corporations, and labor unions. Moreover, by some estimates, there are now approximately 40,000 international nongovernmental organizations (INGOs) (Kovach, Neligan, and Burall, 2003, iv). And the United States is purported to have at least two million nongovernmental organizations (NGOs) (Zadek, 2003, 34). Given the sheer number of the formal and informal representatives who work the many points of access in modern democracies,[7] any effective monitoring of the political process would, it seems, require constant vigilance. However, citizens can fulfill the requirement to monitor their representatives without themselves being constantly highly engaged in policing their representatives. For citizens can properly rely on intermediate agents – fellow citizens or watchdog agencies – to do much of the required monitoring. Douglas Arnold (1990) shows how potential challengers can draw voters' attention to politicians' unpopular actions. Such dependence on intermediaries, such as political parties and other representatives, is not in and of itself "anti-democratic," because it still requires citizens to be committed to maintaining the health of democratic institutions and to be ready to address the demands that this commitment places on them, when necessary. Here, democratic citizenship is understood as a latent condition, one that can be triggered by invitations to participate from representatives. On the view I am advancing, then, the participation properly required by democratic citizenship is episodic.

Democratic representation is best understood as an episodic process – sometimes requiring active participation, sometimes tolerating passivity and disengagement. At times, democratic citizens need, and may, "check out." In any case, democratic representation is not simply the processes of authorization – that is, of the activities that happen on election day (d'Entreves, 1992, 161).[8] Democratic representation should not be identified as only those political moments, be it a revolution or a town hall meeting, in which citizens are active. Democratic representation allows citizens to be passive, sometimes to a considerable degree, and still retain control over the public policy-making process.[9]

However, for my purposes, there is a further point that is important to see; namely, that democratic representatives play a crucial role in allowing citizens to preserve the capacity for self-governance. Central to this capacity is the ability to make sound judgments both about those who issue invitations to participate and those who monitor government. If one fully appreciates how some democratic citizens are political "free-riders," relying on the active engagement of others, one can see that evaluations of democratic representatives are vital to citizens' capacity to be self-ruling. All democratic citizens (but especially those who free-ride) need to be able to evaluate the reliability of those who monitor and those who advance policy preferences on behalf of democratic citizens. Moreover, democratic citizens, even when they are not actively engaged, must retain the capacity to determine when it is necessary for them to get involved. Part of the job of a democratic representative is to foster this capacity for self-governance in democratic citizens.

To recap, democratic representatives must do something more than increase citizens' active participation in the political process. Proper evaluation of democratic representatives should attend not so much to a representative's impact on rates of civic participation, but to her promoting throughout the polity the capacity of citizens to be self-ruling. Democratic representatives will provide citizens occasions for active participation that contribute to the proper operation of democratic institutions.

The Virtue of Critical Trust Building

Good democratic representatives exhibit the virtue of critical trust building when they employ methods of advocacy that create opportunities for proper civic participation and foster citizens' capacity for self-governance.

One fosters citizens' capacity for self-governance not only in providing them with all the resources they need for full citizenship in a democratic polity, but also in nurturing in them the qualities, talents, and skills necessary for this full citizenship.

The virtue of critical trust building, as I understand it, thus ascribes an educative function to democratic representatives. The characteristic work of democratic representatives includes "teaching" citizens through deliberating on their behalf, offering descriptions of, and prescriptions regarding, political issues. In this way, representatives properly help citizens frame important policy issues. In shaping how democratic citizens understand an issue, politicians need not pander to citizens; rather, they can and should craft their policy talks so that citizens can understand policy issues and respond adequately to these issues (Jacobs and Shapiro, 2000). Representatives also "teach" citizens when they inspire democratic citizens, perhaps by example or by expanding the scope of a conflict in which they are already engaged, to get involved in a given political issue. Representatives also educate citizens about self-governance, and teach them the skills required for self-governance, by bringing citizens into the public policy-making process. Democratic representatives establish committee hearings, town hall meetings, teach-ins, and other forums that allow testimonials. Increasingly, democratic representatives justify their policy preferences by invoking the experiences of their constituents.

Through these pedagogic functions, good democratic representatives can preserve and develop the capacities of citizens to be self-governing. Moreover, when citizens are self-governing, literally becoming part of democratic decision-making, democratic institutions and the people who occupy roles in those institutions play a vital role in shaping the identities of citizens (Bickford, 1999).

A democratic polity can enjoy good democratic representation in respect of all three of the virtues only if its democratic representatives exhibit the second virtue of democratic representation. For the ability of a representative to excel at representing in a democratic fashion depends importantly on those she represents having and exercising the capacity of self-governance. The more democratic representatives foster this capacity in their constituents, the more their constituents will give them the political cover needed to exhibit the three virtues of democratic representation. Good democratic representatives must seek to safeguard those capacities democratic citizens need in order to determine when and how they should participate.[10] Preserving such capacities is also important, in part because citizens must decide the appropriate degree of participation or passivity in light of particular circumstances. And, in particular, democratic citizens need in making this decision to recognize how their nonparticipation can constrain the ability of a good democratic representative to perform her characteristic activity and thereby weaken the legitimacy of democratic institutions.

For democratic representation to be more than the coercive exercise of authority – for example, ruling by controlling citizens' choices – democratic representatives must safeguard citizens' capacities to assess when invitations to participate are manipulative and to determine when it is necessary for them to participate. Otherwise, democratic institutions can become mere tools of domination. The operation of those institutions can reify certain citizens' inferior status even as those institutions espouse norms and values that favor civic equality (Smith, 1997). The exhibition of the second virtue by democratic representatives is essential to counteracting oppressive biases that can develop within democratic institutions and that prevent democratic citizens from governing themselves.

Note that so far I have said little about what the capacity for self-governance, the capacity necessary for full democratic citizenship, amounts to. And I will offer no definitive list of the resources, skills, talents and dispositions that a citizen needs for full citizenship. Indeed, I think the project of supplying such a list is misguided, because what belongs to the capacity necessary for full citizenship is contingent. This contingency is twofold.

First, the capacities necessary for full citizenship have varied, and will continue to vary, over time.[11] During the colonial era, full citizenship in the US depended on one's property status or a religious identity. During McCarthyism, US citizens' ability to participate required avoiding being affiliated with socialist or communist organizations. In recent years, a different "bundle" of qualifications has come to be required for full citizenship.[12] One dimension of this change regards developments in the resources and technology that political processes employ. When the resources and technology available to democratic citizens for exercising influence on the political process change, the capacities that citizens require to utilize those resources and technology also change. While previous generations might have relied on patronage and later making petitions or canvassing door-to-door, modern technology seems to demand access to public relations firms, fax machines, and email. Corporations can use "advertorials" – that is, paid or sponsored messages on the editorial pages that aim to create a favorable climate of opinion (Brown and Waltzer, 2004). These examples should suffice to make clear that the capacities for full democratic citizenship are not static.

The second way in which democratic citizens' capacities for full citizenship are contingent results from the fact that these capacities may properly be latent ones, exercised only in times of crisis. As discussed earlier, democratic institutions do not need all citizens to be participating fully, and such participation is neither possible nor desirable. Indeed, any adequate ethics of democratic representation must recognize the episodic nature of citizen participation. More specifically, it must recognize that democratic representatives play a crucial role in sustaining citizens' capacities for self-governance even when these citizens are not actively engaged in politics and thus are relying on others to advocate public policies on their behalf. And what is required in order to safeguard these citizens' ability to actualize their latent capacity for full citizenship, and so to actually be in a position to fulfill the functions of civic participation (e.g., accountability, excluded interests, and political knowledge), will vary in different circumstances.

Instead of merely listing all of the possible resources necessary for full citizenship, I focus on a "meta-capacity" or a "second-order capacity" – that is, a capacity necessary for discerning what, in given circumstances, is necessary in order to retain and to develop the capacity for self-governance. This meta-capacity is concerned crucially with the question of when representatives and fellow citizens can be relied upon to use democratic institutions fairly and responsibly, as well as the question of whether the system is failing to provide the requisite information and resources for genuine self-governance on the part of its citizens. I thus call this capacity one for *critical trust*. The need for critical trust arises *because* the exercise of full citizenship can require such a wide variety of skills and talents. Critical trust allows citizens to discern when their active participation is necessary and when they can be passive. Democratic citizens' ability to balance properly their ruling and being ruled, the active and passive aspects of democratic citizenship, requires that they correctly determine under what conditions their participation is vital to the survival of democratic institutions. Citizens must trust the working of government enough to accept the legitimacy of democratic institutions and yet retain a critical attitude toward the actions of their representatives, always being on the alert for ways in which they may be misled or manipulated. They must be critical, on pain of being vulnerable to being manipulated by their representatives.[13]

The term "critical trust" might strike some as an oxymoron for the simple reason that being "critical" of one's representatives is not necessarily compatible with "trusting" them. I wholeheartedly agree that these attitudes are in tension. To recognize the importance of critical trust is to recognize that democratic institutions require citizens to exhibit both of these contradictory attitudes in a certain balance in order to sustain those institutions. The issue, then, is not simply whether democratic citizens trust or do not trust democratic representatives and democratic institutions. The trust that democratic citizens need to have in their government should not be understood as simply being in a binary opposition with distrust.[14]

Critical trust pulls democratic citizens in two diametrically opposed directions. On the one hand, democratic citizens need the desire to get involved, and this desire presupposes that citizens have some degree of faith in democratic institutions as appropriate means for settling political conflicts. Moreover, democratic citizens need to trust that democratic institutions are in fact appropriate means for settling political conflict: After all, their acceptance of democratic institutions is necessary for preserving the legitimacy of those institutions. Cynics will lack such faith and trust. However, democratic citizens also need to be critical of democratic institutions. After all, the fact of pluralism requires that democratic citizens take sides and be able to assess competing claims to truth from different sources of information. To make such assessments properly, they need to be able to recognize the limitations of democratic institutions and the limitations of representatives who occupy those institutions. Democratic citizens will need a certain amount of critical distance from their representatives in order assess the performance of their representatives. A degree of separation from democratic institutions (and their representatives) is crucial for preserving the critical capacities of democratic citizens.[15]

Critical trust is especially important given the manipulative strategies employed by all too many contemporary representatives (Page and Shapiro, 1992). The extent to which contemporary representatives employ various manipulative strategies – that is, lie, disguise, employ propaganda, and overload citizens with information – is the extent to which they can weaken democratic citizens' capacity to act autonomously and to rule themselves. For such practices can have real costs for democratic institutions. Too much manipulation can encourage democratic citizens to become cynical, perceiving democratic representation as a façade for power relations. And sustained and pervasive cynicism about the value of civic participation, in turn, can undercut the legitimacy of democratic institutions.

To summarize, the methods of good democratic representatives will promote participation *and* critical trust among democratic citizens. I recognize that democratic citizens are likely to disagree about the amount of statistical knowledge or social capital needed to be full democratic citizens. Without entering disputes about what resources democratic representatives should provide their constituents, I want to make a more general claim: assessments of good democratic representatives should center on whether their methods develop democratic citizens' critical trust. Good democratic representatives are those who aim to foster, and succeed in fostering, critical trust.

Promoting Critical Trust

Now, in emphasizing the importance of critical trust, I do not mean to imply that democratic representatives can simply distribute or implant critical trust in democratic citizens. Nor can they "command" citizens to have critical trust. To think otherwise is to ignore the important role that civil society, comprised of families, schools, religious organizations, and so forth, has in training citizens.

However, the fact that the capacities of democratic representatives and those of democratic citizens are inextricably linked does not entail that democratic representatives are unable to promote critical trust. Democratic representatives can promote critical trust in three ways. First, they can provide reliable information about their advocacy work, for democratic citizens depend to some degree on the information provided by representatives – both formal and informal ones. Good representatives, then, do not try to deceive the public about the substance of legislation, either by providing misinformation regarding legislation (as James Roosevelt did) or by giving legislation a misleading name (as legislators recently did in naming legislation that would substantially increase air pollution and mercury contamination the "Clean Skies Act"). Good democratic representatives are upfront about the benefits and drawbacks of the policies they pursue. More generally, democratic representatives will make available to citizens (or at least their intermediaries) information that allows them to assess public policies accurately. As Ruth Grant and Robert Keohane (2005, 3) noted, information is "necessary but not sufficient" for accountability. Moreover, crucial to citizens' assessing information adequately is their knowing who funds the relevant research, or what organization is disseminating the information. In this respect, the need for some level of transparency about the nature and source of the information is also crucial to supporting democratic citizens' competency to evaluate public policy proposals. In particular, democratic representatives need to disclose potential conflicts of interest so that citizens can realize when certain information should be treated more suspiciously. Of course, some secrecy regarding information, or its source, may be necessary for the security of democratic states (see Thompson, 1999). Nonetheless, the point holds that democratic representatives need to be judged by the degree to which they provide citizens with adequate opportunities and resources for evaluating their policies.

Second, democratic representatives can promote critical trust by helping to keep their fellow representatives accountable. They can provide "horizontal accountability", to borrow Guillermo O'Donnell's (1998) terminology, or "peer accountability", to use the language of Grant and Keohane (2005). Part of the function of democratic representatives is to monitor the behavior of others who advance public policy on the behalf of democratic citizens. Good democratic representatives, then, are able watchdogs. They expose and denounce dishonesty, manipulation, or incompetence on the part of their peers, be they opponents or allies.

Third, democratic representatives can promote critical trust by being good role models.[16] In being good role models, democratic representatives can give substance to democratic values and inspire others to live up to certain democratic commitments.[17] As Patrick Dobel notes, "The power of example and purity of commitment inspires others to take their views seriously. . . . Public action and even suffering demonstrate the power of a cause" (1992, 1). It is thus doubly important that, in engaging in the political process, democratic representatives defy the pressure to compromise on and erode democratic norms and values. Good democratic representatives, then, lead by example, embodying commitment to democratic ideals so as to serve as good role models. Their example can, in giving life to those commitments, help restore citizens' trust in democratic processes. Good democratic representatives also inspire imitation, encouraging other representatives to excel at representing. And when good democratic representatives succeed in realizing good democratic representation, democratic citizens and representatives alike can discern concretely the value of having democratic commitments. Finally, in leading by example, good democratic representatives improve the political arena not least by showing others the importance of leading by example.

Attending to the importance of leading by example brings to light a constraint on the practices of democratic representatives: democratic representatives need to be sensitive to the growing cynicism of democratic citizens. One of the main dangers of manipulative political tactics – especially those that appeal to citizens' commitment to democratic ideals – is that such tactics can lead to cynicism about professions of democratic ideals. William Miller notes the more general point that those who deceive us by appealing to our morals "impose vices on us: distrustfulness, cynicism, and paranoia. They make all virtue suspect" (1997, 187). The harm caused by manipulation – making fools of people who hold moral principles – is suspicion toward all professions of moral principles. Such cynicism, when it concerns the profession of democratic ideals, is harmful both because it can lead citizens to withdraw from the political arena and because it can promote a "no-holds-barred" approach to politics. Neither result is conducive to the proper functioning of democratic institutions. Moreover, in weakening commitments to democratic ideals, manipulative tactics make democratic citizens and representatives less likely to believe that it matters whether their institutions are democratic, undermining the legitimacy of democratic institutions.

Good democratic representatives, then, will excel at all three ways of fostering critical trust that I have distinguished. Good democratic representatives will not merely increase participation, but in their advocacy work will use methods of increasing participation that promote critical trust, thereby enhancing the capacity of democratic institutions to resolve conflicts fairly and peacefully. Democratic representatives' responsibility to promote critical trust is, moreover, grounded in their having the function of enabling the autonomy, or self-rule, of democratic citizens, to the greatest extent possible. The importance of critical trust stems from the function that democratic representatives have in promoting the ability of citizens to be self-governing when possible. One crucial feature of critical trust is that it allows for citizens to be self-governing without being entirely consumed by politics, by allowing them to assess when and how they need to become actively engaged.

Problems with the Second Virtue

Endorsing the virtue of critical trust building assumes that democratic citizens, at least to some degree, can and want to engage in politics. Indeed, my account of this virtue assumes that the capacity of democratic citizens for critical trust and the capacity of democratic representatives to realize the virtue of critical trust building are mutually interdependent. In light of these assumptions, four problems regarding the tenability of the second virtue immediately spring to mind.

The first problem centers on the extent to which democratic citizens (let alone those who are impacted by democratic public policies[18]) have the capacity to engage in the operation of democratic institutions. I call this problem *the capacity problem*. Of course, certain citizens are, or are particularly vulnerable to becoming, temporarily or permanently unable to participate. Consider the positions of children (especially infants), the severely mentally disabled, the sick, and convicted felons.[19] The apathetic, the tired, and the despairing also lack the capacity for self-governance. However, political scientists have raised serious doubts about the meaningfulness of participation when US citizens are so woefully ignorant of the issues and institutions (e.g., Campbell, Converse, Miller, and Stokes, 1960; Converse, 1964; Miller and Shanks, 1996).[20] The value of democratic methods – let alone those methods that develop critical trust – decreases with the level of citizens' competence for valuable participation.

The fact that citizens have different levels of capacities for valuable participation has an important implication: vulnerable citizens might not always be able to have good democratic representation. Their capacity for self-governance depends partially on the actions of democratic representatives. The capacity problem thus points to a limitation of good democratic representation. As John Stuart Mill (1991 [1861]) points out, the well-functioning of representation depends on the capacities of citizens. Despite the best intentions and actions of democratic representatives, if certain citizens cannot or will not participate, that sets a limit on how well these representatives can do their job.

This leads to the second problem, what I call *the dependency problem*. If some democratic citizens do not have the desire or the ability to assess those who advocate public policies in their name, then those citizens must rely on others to interpret and explain their needs and preferences. Under such circumstances, even good democratic representatives are apt to become overly dependent on elites of groups in trying to understand the needs and preferences of those groups. Such a situation is ripe for abuse. The problem is not simply with relying on representatives; the problem, rather, is that such a reliance on representatives can inadvertently support "secondary marginalization" – that is, that the regulation and policing of certain members of a marginalized group by relatively privileged members of that group (Cohen, 1999).[21]

The third problem with the virtue of critical trust building is *the problem of participation burdens*. Participation has personal costs, ones that vulnerable citizens are less likely to be able to afford. Put bluntly, it is expensive to get one's voice heard. This is especially true given contemporary advocacy practices: public relations firms, public opinion surveys, and think tanks are all expensive. Writing a letter requires verbal acuity. The money and time necessary for participation can be prohibitive to certain groups. As Steven Rosenstone and John Hansen point out, political participation puts unacceptable demands on citizens with already scarce resources:

> Because neither resources nor interests are distributed evenly across the population, some people find the costs less burdensome and the benefits more attractive than others do. The wealthy, the educated, the experienced and the efficacious can more easily afford the demands on their money, time, skill and self-confidence. (1993, 6)

The requirements for full citizenship thus seem to disadvantage the vulnerable, making standards of good democratic representation easier to achieve for more privileged, or at least financially better off, groups.

The fourth and final problem with the virtue of critical trust building is *the viciousness problem*. Put bluntly, it is not clear whether good democratic representatives can compete successfully with representatives who increase participation through vicious and less democratic methods. After all, racist campaign strategies might mobilize citizens more effectively than a strategy of appealing to citizens' commitment to fair democratic procedures. In other words, when citizens are not adequately informed or adequately committed to democratic ideals, good democratic representatives who excel at promoting critical trust via participation must compete against those who antagonize divisions among citizens. If citizens are unable to assess the methods of representatives adequately in light of democratic commitments, then it is possible that democratic representatives will not be able to adopt democratic methods effectively when competing against those who are willing to win at any cost.

These four problems associated with the second virtue reveal a genuine worry – namely, that the second virtue expects too much of democratic citizens and their representatives. This worry grows deeper when one recognizes the extent to which citizens fail to meet even minimal requirements for participating in ways that further the proper operation of democratic institutions: consider here the work of Walter Lippmann (1922), Joseph Schumpeter (1976), Bernard Berelson, Paul Lazarsfeld, and William McPhee (1954), and Philip Converse (1964). If democratic citizens are unable, or unwilling, to support representatives who exhibit the second virtue of democratic representation, and if they allow a political culture of pursuing policy preferences "by any method necessary," then those citizens are not ready for good democratic representation. When democratic citizens do not press for good critical trust building, representatives are apt to employ methods that, while they are formally democratic, in that they work by mobilizing citizens, nonetheless support political corruption and end up promoting disillusion with democratic institutions. Under such circumstances, the task of a good democratic representative is difficult indeed. She must continue to work to develop citizens' critical trust, sensitive to the four problems just canvassed. She must wait for circumstances that allow for some success, and hope that her success will build on itself, gradually improving the citizenry's capacity for good representation. On a related point, citizens' assessments of representatives who strive to realize the virtue of critical trust building need to take into account the difficult circumstances under which they operate, and resist the temptation to succumb to political disillusionment.

Chapter 6

The Virtue of Good Gatekeeping

In 1995, leading Republican activists began what was called the "K Street Project."[1] This project tracked the political donations of Washington lobbyists. Based on this information, Republicans created a list to be used in controlling access to the White House, Congress, and federal agencies. More specifically, they created this list to deny, or to threaten to deny, access to those lobbyists who donated to Democrats. In connection with this list, the chairman of the National Republican Congressional Committee, Representative Thomas M. Davis III (R-VA), commented that contributions to the wrong party "can buy you enemies. People don't remember who gave them contributions. But they remember who gave to their opponents" (see VanderHei, 2002a,b). The Senate Minority Whip Harry Reid (D-NV) called upon President Bush to denounce the K Street Project. President Bush refused, arguing that it was not his project.

Bush's rationale for refusing to denounce the K Street Project rings hollow. Democratic representation is not a solitary activity. It is a political activity that is done *with* others – that is, with other representatives and with democratic citizens. As a consequence, democratic representatives should be judged by the company they keep. It matters with whom they meet and make contact, and from whom they accept funding. It also matters who they denounce and from whom they distance themselves. Moreover, it matters not only with whom democratic representatives associate, but also what kinds of relationships democratic representatives possess and foster with these associates. Good democratic representatives foster – to whatever extent possible – mutual relations with *all* democratic citizens. Of course, good democratic representatives will face conflicting obligations to different groups of democratic citizens. Bush cannot accommodate the demands both of the Republican activists spearheading the K Street Project and those of the lobbyists that these activists worked to exclude. Consequently, good democratic representatives face hard decisions about who should be included. Good democratic representatives are those who, in facing these decisions, exercise what I will term *the virtue of good gatekeeping*.

In insisting that good democratic representatives should be assessed by the extent to which they promote the political inclusion of all citizens, I go against a dominant trend in political science. Most political scientists assess representatives primarily in terms of their relationship to a particular subset of democratic citizens, namely, their constituents. In particular, political science tends to emphasize the importance of "policy linkages" or "policy congruence" – that is, the sharing of public policy preferences by representatives and constituents. Indeed, most contemporary empirical research is predicated on the assumption that the performance of representatives should be assessed in terms of representatives' furthering fundamental policy interests and preferences that they share with their constituents.[2] Of course, political scientists recognize that representatives can develop different kinds of relationships with different constituencies (Fenno, 2002). And they recognize that the constituents of representatives can have different, and incompatible, policy preferences (e.g., Pitkin, 1967, ch. 10). However, when it comes right down to it, most contemporary writings on representation treat the role of democratic representatives as simply that of serving the interests of those citizens who authorized them. Amy Gutmann and Dennis Thompson (1985) summarize this perspective when they write that

> A legislator is sometimes expected to vote in the interest of his constituents even if the vote is contrary to the public interest. The justification for such permission is a moral one: a system in which individual representatives advocate the interests of their constituents is more likely to yield the general interest in the long run. Furthermore, given such a system, a legislator who always neglects his constituents to serve nobler causes may actually betray his trust; after all, he promised to look after their interests. (168)

According to this perspective, representatives are (at least some of the time) obligated to put their constituents' expressed preferences first, since articulating the interests, opinions, and perspectives of their constituents is essential to representatives' aggregating those interests, opinions, and perspectives to determine the best approximation of the common good.

Articulating and defending particularistic interests, opinions, and perspectives is certainly vital to democratic institutions; however, it is important to develop this way of understanding democratic representation further and to qualify its particularistic emphasis. The key point to see is that a democratic representative's proper function includes the cultivation of a particular kind of relationship with democratic citizens. More specifically, this relation requires that both parties to it – the representative and the represented – recognize themselves as engaged in a joint project. This recognition creates a political partnership and serves as the glue that binds citizens not only to their groups but also to democratic institutions. I term such a relation between two parties a *mutual relation*. A large part of this chapter will be devoted to explaining what specific sort of mutual relation between representative and represented constitutes democratic representation. On the position I develop, democratic representation essentially requires that representatives foster certain mutual relations with their constituents – that is, with those citizens whose support serves as a source of authority for the representative. But attending only to these mutual relations is insufficient for identifying *good* democratic representatives. A good democratic representative will develop mutual relations in ways that realize democratic values and norms in her polity. And this requires that she develop mutual relations, to the greatest extent possible, with all democratic citizens, and not just with her constituents. Indeed, this requires that she seek to develop mutual relations even with her political opponents, as well as with the dispossessed and the marginalized within her polity.

The idea of mutual relations is thus crucial to an adequate understanding of the distinctive function of democratic representatives. The distinctive function of democratic representatives includes advancing their constituents' policy preferences in ways that make those constituents feel part of the political life of the polity. On this understanding of democratic representation, representation is distinctively democratic to the extent that both democratic citizens and their representatives recognize themselves as engaged in a joint project, one that requires each party to fulfill distinctive functions for the sake of realizing a healthy democratic polity. Democratic representation is not only about the distribution of public resources, but also about a form of recognition,[3] one that links the fate of democratic citizens. In order for democratic institutions to function properly, democratic citizens need to recognize the ways in which their fates are linked with those of other citizens, as well as the value of such connections for the well-functioning of their institutions. It follows that democratic representatives ought to work to link the fates of their constituents both to the fate of democratic institutions and to the fates of their fellow democratic citizens. Put bluntly, a democratic representative who fosters mutual relations exclusively with her own constituents cannot be a good democratic representative.

The good democratic representative, moreover, will excel at linking the fates of her constituency with those of fellow citizens in a well-functioning democratic polity. And in doing so, a good democratic representative will help foster mutual relations in the polity in ways that exercise what I term "the virtue of good gatekeeping." Good democratic representatives will open doors as much as possible, thereby maximizing the political arena's potential to be inclusive. But in doing so, the good democratic representative will not simply let everyone in. Good democratic representation can require limiting and constraining the influence of some citizens. For example, good democratic representatives will need to limit and constrain the influence of those who exclude unjustly: good democratic representatives will exclude the unjust excluders. Good democratic representatives must also be willing to create space for underrepresented groups that have a legitimate claim, based on considerations of justice, to more representation. These points reflect a general guiding principle of good democratic representation: considerations of justice should determine how a representative fosters mutual relations. Considerations of justice should not only inform a democratic representative's decisions about with whom she will develop mutual relations. They should also inform how she goes about developing such relations. Good democratic representatives will develop mutual relations that promote the proper understanding of political inclusion within her polity.

Developing the Right Relationships

The claim that representation, generally, and democratic representation, specifically, require certain kinds of relationships between constituents and representatives is certainly not a new one. Much of the theoretical debate about representation has focused on a particular question: What is the proper relationship that should exist between constituents and their representatives? Recall Pitkin's earlier discussion of two schools of thought – those, such as James Madison, who endorse *a delegate conception* of representation and those who, with Edmund Burke, endorse *a trustee conception*.

On the delegate conception, representatives need to be *responsive* to the preferences of those being represented. In contrast, on the trustee conception of representation, representatives need to resist undue and undesirable pressure from those they represent. Representatives are the guardians of their constituents, watching over their best interests: the relationship between representatives and constituents is thus properly paternalistic, not responsive. What matters in this delegate versus trustee debate is the reason that a representative gives for choosing a particular course of action. The main difference between the delegate school and the trustee school concerns who has the ultimate control over what gets done.

Political scientists tend to side with the delegate school, arguing that democratic citizens should have the ultimate say in the laws that govern them.[4] Democratic citizens get the last word, so to speak, because they are the ones who authorized the representative and because democratic citizens are the ones affected by the policy decisions made by representatives. Hence, having responsive representatives (delegates) is often equated with having democratic ones.[5]

However, the adoption of responsiveness as the standard for democratic representation is troubling both from an empirical and from a theoretical perspective. Examining roll call voting and district interests, an extensive literature has developed showing that US representatives are not very conscientious about advancing their district's interests (e.g., MacRae, 1958; Stokes and Miller, 1962; Miller and Stokes, 1963; Jacobs and Shapiro, 2000). Moreover, democratic citizens in the United States are remarkably ignorant about the issues at stake and their representatives' positions on those issues (Campbell, Converse, Miller, and Stokes, 1960; Converse, 1964; Popkin, 1991; Miller and Shanks, 1996).[6] Moreover, they have proven to be fickle (Zaller, 1992) and manipulable (Page and Shapiro, 1992). These, and other, empirical findings lead Russell Hardin (2004) to conclude that

> we have representatives who cannot know much about their constituents trying to represent constituents who do not even know their interests in many areas and who, in any case, know very little about their government, its policies, and its officials. (95)

Given these empirical findings, it is tempting to reject out of hand equating a conception of democratic representation with a delegate one.

Several empirical studies have examined other ways in which democratic institutions are responsive to citizens, thereby identifying alternative ways in which democratic representatives could serve as delegates. For example, some have responded to this empirical evidence pointing to a dearth of policy responsiveness by stressing the importance of personal relationships with constituents; for example, the importance of constituency service. For Bruce Cain, John Ferejohn, and Morris Fiorina (1987), personal relationships are favored by citizens as the criteria for choosing representatives and therefore are more relevant than law-making in determining who gets reelected. Other political scientists have responded to the public policy gap by arguing that representation should be examined collectively (Weissberg, 1978). In other words, political scientists should examine the degree to which citizens' preferences are represented in the legislature as a whole, instead of the policies advanced by their particular representatives.

Political theory has also offered some important insights into problems with simply equating good democratic representation with a delegate conception of representation. Recall Hanna Pitkin's observation that although representatives should *sometimes* be responsive to their constituents, at other times they should *not* be responsive to their constituents. For Pitkin, the standards for good representation depend on which view of representation is used. The standards for being a good delegate (responsiveness) contradict the standards for being a good trustee (the interests of the represented). Because both the represented and the representative can be wrong about which policies are preferable – that is, which policies advance the interests of the represented – Pitkin contends that responsiveness alone is insufficient for identifying good representatives. Thus, Pitkin resolves the debate between the delegate and trustee conceptions by maintaining that both sides have some insight into good representation.

Ian Shapiro (2003) provides a different perspective on the question of the responsiveness of democratic institutions and thereby on the responsiveness of democratic representatives. Shapiro recommends adopting a modified Schumpeterian vision of democracy; that is, an aggregative vision of democracy supplemented by a commitment to preventing domination. Shapiro's "anti-domination" conception of democracy holds that democratic institutions need to intervene into the Schumpeterian workings of democracy – but only under certain limited conditions, namely when citizens' basic interests are at stake and when the affected citizens have no exit rights. It would follow that democratic representatives should be responsive not just to their own constituents, but also to citizens whose basic interests are not adequately addressed and who face high exit costs. Shapiro is right to suggest that the crucial question is not "Should democratic representatives be responsive to their constituents?" The crucial question, rather, is "What is the appropriate level of responsiveness depending on the interests at stake and the political context?"

The literature on descriptive representation – that is, the representation of historically disadvantaged groups by members of those groups – has taken a somewhat different approach to identifying the proper relationship between representatives and constituents. According to this literature, representatives for historically disadvantaged groups should "look like" and/or "share certain experiences with" their constituents. In other words, certain salient characteristics of representatives should *correspond* with the characteristics of their constituents.[7] Why does this literature identify shared characteristics as necessary (albeit not sufficient) for good democratic representation of historically disadvantaged groups? One main reason is that, in the case of historically disadvantaged groups, a relationship of well-grounded trust can exist between the representative and the represented only when they share the characteristics that are distinctive of members of historically disadvantaged groups. In support of this line of argument, Jane Mansbridge (1986) recounts how Equal Rights Amendment activists did not heed the good advice of Senator Birch Bayh concerning the wording of the ERA Amendment because, being male, he was not regarded as trustworthy. The distrust of the female activists was compounded by a "young, male, Ivy Leaguer" staffer who reportedly described the ERA proponents as "hysterical" (643). Along similar lines, Melissa Williams (1998) notes how past and persistent betrayals of historically disadvantaged groups render it impossible for these groups to trust those who are not members of the group. Such distrust justifies why these groups need descriptive representation. Virginia Sapiro (1981) also endorses this line of reasoning when she discusses how women need descriptive representatives, because men have not adequately protected their wives', daughters', mothers', and sisters' interests. All of these theorists, then, emphasize the importance of having a relationship of deserved trust between representatives and constituents. Thus, one way in which political theory has posed an alternative relationship between representatives and democratic citizens is to emphasize the importance of trust.[8]

The literature on descriptive representation reflects a broader tendency, within the more general literature on representation, to understand the relationship between representatives and their constituents in terms of trust.[9]

Recently, there has been an explosion in the literature that addresses the function of trust in democratic institutions (e.g., Putnam, 1993; Warren, 1999; Uslaner, 2002). Trust provides a variety of benefits, ranging from improving the quality of deliberations to increasing the participation of democratic citizens. Implicit in this literature is the assumption that democratic institutions are not functioning properly if democratic citizens do not trust their representatives. Diminishing trust in governmental institutions among democratic citizens signals a problem for democratic institutions. Indeed, one approach to assessing democratic representatives common in this literature is to determine whether these representatives enjoy citizens' trust (e.g., Gay, 2002).

The main problem with using trust to identify good democratic representatives (or a lack of trust to identify bad democratic representatives) is that thinking of paradigmatic democratic representation in terms of trust casts it as a one-sided relationship. It downplays the importance of how the representative recognizes democratic citizens; for example, whether the representative trusts democratic citizens. Granted, any defensible trust-based analysis of good democratic representation will attend to the difference between representatives who are trustworthy and those who are not. And it will encourage the represented to adopt a stance of critical trust, one that demands representatives to earn their trust, by exhibiting trustworthiness. Nonetheless, to think of the relationship between representatives and their constituents primarily in terms of trust focuses on the actions of representatives, and – if it does so at all – attends to the represented only insofar as they evaluate whether they should trust representatives to act as they ought.

But democratic citizens only truly rule themselves insofar as they themselves take an active role in determining public policy through the relationships that they have with their representatives. Democratic representation should be understood as placing demands on citizens *as well as* on representatives. It is a mutual and reciprocated activity – something that democratic citizens do *with* their representatives. This conception of democratic representation, moreover, implies that the function of democratic representatives, in turn, includes soliciting active input from democratic citizens, and encouraging their active participation in the political process. And to think of democratic relations only in terms of the way in which citizens recognize their representatives as worthy of trust is to ignore the ways in which democratic representatives must, as such, recognize their constituents as democratic citizens.

But my point is not merely that to think of democratic representation solely in terms of trust is to overlook an important dimension of representation. Trust in democratic representatives can be less than benign (cf., Chapter 5). Such trust can be counterproductive to the health of democratic institutions, and not merely to the degree that trust can keep citizens from vigilantly monitoring the activity of their representatives. More generally, trust can promote the passivity of the represented. If a citizen trusts her representative, she will tend to pay less attention than she otherwise would to the actions of that representative. And, as the experiences of historically disadvantaged groups suggest, democratic citizens need to monitor their representatives. Moreover, if a citizen trusts her representative, she will also tend to rely on the advocacy of her representative and take a less active role herself in the political process. Such an effect runs counter to what I have just claimed is central to any adequate understanding of good democratic representation – namely, that good democratic representation demands and facilitates the active participation of citizens.

My criticism of adopting the trust paradigm for democratic representation draws on David Plotke's important contention that indirect, as well as direct, democracy requires the active participation of citizens.[10] For Plotke (1997), "if x represents y, y is guiding and constraining x, enabling and authorizing her or him" (28). On Plotke's view, the relations between representatives and their constituents are properly ones "in which both parties are active" (29).

Indeed, I would add that, in democratic representation, the activities of the representative and citizens are mutually interdependent and to some degree mutually reinforcing. In order for democratic representatives to fulfill their function as democratic representatives, citizens must be willing and able to play their active role in this mutual relation. And in order for democratic citizens to fulfill their function as citizens, representatives must in turn play theirs. For the interests of citizens come to be articulated and placed on the political agenda in such a way that representatives can serve them only in and through citizens and their representatives interacting with one another in a manner that enables and realizes a specific sort of mutual recognition. As we will see in the following section, this is a mutual recognition that properly informs and shapes the identities of democratic citizens. Representatives play their role in this mutual recognition by engaging in the activity of critical trust building (cf., Chapter 5) – facilitating citizens' participating in the political process by educating citizens about the public policy issues at stake and encouraging them to press their representatives to serve those interests – in a way that properly shapes and informs the identities of citizens. Notice how, on my account, democratic representation can require that the mutual recognition between democratic representatives and democratic citizens include the recognition of each other's actions as desirable for democracy.[11] This recognition is especially important for the kinds of mutual recognition necessary for binding citizens to democratic institutions, and thereby for any mutual relations between representatives and citizens that can properly constitute the identity of democratic citizens as such. And representatives can only represent in a democratic fashion to the extent that the polity contains the right kinds of citizens, and representatives foster the right kinds of relationships with those citizens.[12]

Following Richard Fenno, we can put my – admittedly as yet still somewhat schematic – characterization of democratic representation usefully in terms of the idea of connection. Having invoked the thought, common to most political theorists, that democratic representation is a process, Fenno argues that "the idea that best conveys process is the idea of *connections*. Representation is about connecting" (2003, 5). Observing representatives in their districts, Fenno found that the traditional formulation of the relationship between representatives and constituents – that is, as descriptive representation or substantive representation – was inadequate, too broad to capture the fluid relationships that develop between representatives and their constituents. In his account of this relationship, Fenno identifies five different types of connections between representative and constituents: symbolic connections, policy connections, personal connections, electoral connections, and organizational connections. For Fenno, these connections between representatives and constituents need to be constantly worked on to the provisional satisfaction of both parties.

Fenno's research provides an empirical description of the kinds of activities that representatives and constituents engage in together in realizing a mutual relationship. However, Fenno's work is focused on explaining the representative's behavior when he or she goes home to the electoral district. In contrast, I am primarily concerned with how mutual relations constitute democratic representation. On my account, democratic representation requires that representatives and citizens "connect" in a particular way: both democratic representatives and the represented must mutually recognize each other as "ruling and being ruled" in the manner distinctive of democratic representation.

The Scope of Mutual Relations

But exactly how should democratic citizens and their representatives recognize each other? Democratic representatives and their constituents must recognize each other as having linked fates.[13] For my purposes, I will focus on the linked fates that citizens have with each other as members of a democratic polity, either simply as democratic citizens who belong to the same polity, or as members of a particular group that properly makes up a well-functioning democratic polity. The former connections constitute the identity common to all democratic citizens simply as such. The latter constitutes the identities different citizens have as members of particular groups that have a legitimate claim to recognition in the functioning of the democratic polity as a whole. In constituting these identities, the linked fates of democratic citizens give determinate form to the interests of democratic citizens who make legitimate demands on democratic policy-making. Indeed, it is insofar as these connections make up, and ground the interests recognized in, a healthy and well-functioning democratic polity that they are connections that democratic representatives ought properly to foster.

Democratic representatives do not merely recognize, and prompt their constituents to recognize, linked fates that these citizens already have. They can interact with democratic citizens to facilitate their political participation in ways that help shape, or even generate, a sense of linked fates. Indeed, they act as democratic representatives when they play an active role of this sort in linking citizens' fates as members of the democratic polity. Moreover, they play this role in three different ways: (1) they help to consolidate their constituents' particular identities; (2) they promote their constituents' identification with the representative, and thereby with the democratic polity as a whole; and (3) they bind their constituents to democratic institutions. I will take each of these three ways in which democratic representation links fate in turn.

First, democratic representatives consolidate the identity of the group they represent by articulating that group's interests, opinions, and perspectives. They create the public face for their constituents. Consider, for instance, the role that Boston's Mayor James Curley played in shaping his Irish constituencies' identities as Americans in the early 1990s. Mayor Curley was famous for attributing all of Boston's progress to the hard work of the Irish, claiming that "At the bottom of every American is an

Irishman." As can be seen in Mayor Curley's statement, a representative's interpretations of a group's interests, opinions, and perspectives not only shape what other citizens know about that group, it but also influences how the group understands its own identity.[14] By providing an interpretation of a group's interests, opinions, and perspectives, democratic representatives help create a shared history. In this way, representatives play a crucial role in regulating the boundaries of a group as well as in influencing how other democratic citizens recognize that group.

The fact that representatives play an important role in shaping a group's identity is one reason why descriptive representation is necessary. This last point is made by both Iris Marion Young (2000) and Melissa Williams (1998). Here, I am generalizing their insight that democratic citizens need to retain control over the shaping of their identities. This "shaping" is a process by which representatives articulate the perspectives, opinions, and interests that citizens have – not simply as citizens of the polity as a whole, but distinctively as members of different particular groups, insofar as they make up the democratic polity as a whole.

For example, consider Nelson Mandela's reaction to the assassination of Chris Hani.[15] A popular leader among young black militants in South Africa, Hani was killed on April 10, 1993, by a Polish immigrant linked to an extremist right-wing group opposed to black majority rule in South Africa. The murder had the potential to destroy the Multi Party Negotiating Process (MPNP) that had only days before restarted after a ten-month break. In his "Televised Address," Mandela was able both to express the grief and anger at the assassination felt by black South Africans and to call for a transformation of the group's identity away from Apartheid's violent past. Mandela denounced the assassination as a "national tragedy that has touched millions of people, across the political and colour divide,"[16] and he articulated an understanding of black South Africans' identity as consistent with the principle of "nonracialism" established in the Freedom Charter of 1955. More specifically, he portrayed Hani's followers as "newly transformed radicals following liberal norms of deliberative democracy." According to Kenneth Zagacki (2003, 716), incorporating elements of traditional eulogies, Mandela both acknowledged the group's anger and grief and "elevated the survivors above the divisive partisan struggles." Mandela thereby played a crucial role in shaping the group's response to a tragic death. Zagacki maintains that "by most accounts, Mandela's speech helped to dissipate black frustration and anger across South Africa, thereby preempting a bloody catastrophe and paving the way for democratic change" (ibid.). Mandela's speech demonstrates how good democratic representatives can play a crucial role in shaping the identity of groups in ways that make democracy possible.

Second, a democratic representative links the fates of his constituents in his person by encouraging his constituents to identify with him. Richard Fenno (2003) describes this identification between the representative and his constituents in his analysis of what he calls a representative's "homestyle."[17] By dressing in a certain way – for example, donning a cowboy hat, or talking in a local dialect – democratic representatives encourage constituents to see their representatives as "one of us." In this way, democratic citizens see themselves *in* their representatives. Having a representative who "looks, thinks, and feels" like them allows democratic citizens to feel present in the democratic polity. The kind of mutual identification between representative and represented in question is well illustrated in Fenno's account of Louis Stokes, a black politician from Cleveland, Ohio:

> He is sensitive to all the common experiences and common aspirations that bind black people one to the other. The term he uses is "the black community." And he works, every chance he gets, to deepen the sense of community among blacks. His own identification with the black community is obvious and total. Every expression he gives or gives off conveys the idea that "I am one of you." His view of "me-in-the-district" begins, then, with a feeling of total immersion in the black community. (2003, 17)

Provided that, in publicly identifying with his community in this way, a democratic representative sets an appropriate political agenda for that community, he can thereby enhance the extent to which citizens "own" the actions of their representatives. By promoting the identification between representatives and their constituents, mutual relations have the potential to increase citizens' sense of responsibility for what occurs in their political institutions.

This second way of linking fates reflects the extent to which all democratic citizens, and not just members of historically disadvantaged groups, have a legitimate interest in having representatives who look, think, and feel like them. This point has been treated insightfully by Jane Mansbridge (2002) in her recent account of representation. Mansbridge proposes updating our understanding of representation by recognizing a new form of democratic representation, that she calls "gyroscopic representation." This form reflects citizens' desire to have representatives who, in virtue of bearing certain similarities to them, possess an internal gyroscope – that is, are guided internally to do their constituents' bidding. Gyroscopic representation is "internal" because it operates through the representative's looking inward to determine the proper course of action (as opposed to consulting her constituents or responding to the pressure exerted on her by her constituents). By selecting a representative who resembles them, who feels to them like "one of us," democratic citizens are able to influence the political arena, not through advising or lobbying, but by introducing someone "like them" into the political arena.

In introducing the notion of a gyroscopic form of representation, Mansbridge modernizes and democratizes the traditional concept of trusteeship. And she does so in a way that accounts for the importance that citizens place on moral character.[18] Democratic citizens prefer representatives with a certain moral character because this character serves as a proxy for the represented's interests, opinions, and perspectives. The fact that a representative has the desired moral character assures the represented that the representative will act as those constituents would want her to act. In this way, the possession of moral character by their gyroscopic representatives allows citizens to trust these representatives. Implicit in Mansbridge's description of gyroscopic representation is the idea that gyroscopic representation is appealing because it allows democratic citizens to have a sense of ownership of their political lives, even when they are not directly involved in the democratic processes. In my terminology, gyroscopic representation is a form of representation that a democratic representative can adopt in order to strengthen the sense of shared fate in the democratic polity that is crucial to the health of that polity.

However, in one important respect, my account of democratic representation, and the distinctive role that descriptive representatives play in linking fate, is more demanding than the account that Mansbridge gives in terms of gyroscopic representation. Mansbridge does require, as a condition of its providing good democratic representation, that gyroscopic representation be accompanied by good democratic deliberation (e.g., one that is informed by adequate information about the candidate's personal history) regarding the representative's character prior to voters' authorization of the representative. But this requirement does not, in my view, go far enough. One does not secure good democratic representation if one simply lets one's representative, once vetted, loose in the political arena, to be guided only by her internal resources. For one thing, a representative who relies too heavily on her gyroscope is all too apt to isolate herself from those citizens who hold dissenting views. But, more fundamentally, to think that a purely gyroscopic representative could be a good democratic representative is to fail to recognize that democratic representation is not a solitary activity.

Formal representatives must negotiate and compromise with each other, as well as with other branches of government. The legislative process does not allow effective representatives to stand alone – in isolation from other public officials or from informal representatives. That democratic representatives can advance constituents' policy preferences only by forming coalitions, building bipartisan alliances, or negotiating with business interests or with leaders of social movements suggests that Mansbridge's account of gyroscopic representation does not adequately capture the activities of democratic representatives, at least ones who want to be effective.

Besides, democratic representation is an activity that representatives properly engage in together with the citizens whom they represent. Democratic representation requires that truly mutual relations between the representative and the represented guide that representative's advocacy work. On this central point, my account of linked fate, and the distinctive role that descriptive representatives play in linking fate, differs from the account of democratic representation that Mansbridge offers in terms of gyroscopic representation.

Third, democratic representatives link fates with democratic citizens when, in their activity as advocates, they create mutual relations with their constituents that link those constituents to their democratic institutions. As Stuart Hampshire (2000, 79) reminds us, "the fair procedures, political and legal, constitute the cement that holds the state together, and supply a common ground of loyalty shared by the citizens who recognize this institutional bond between them." Democratic representatives can serve to further citizens' recognition of the institutional bond that unites them as members of the same state.[19] They do so when they educate constituents about the proper functioning of democratic institutions and when they frame deliberations of public policies in terms of their impact on democratic institutions. Indeed, democratic representatives link fates when their advocacy work teaches their constituents about the needs and desires of other citizens, especially how such needs and desires impact democratic institutions. Moreover, through their representatives, democratic citizens cannot only come to understand their own needs and desires better; they can also come to better identify how democratic institutions safeguard their well-being. But democratic representatives fulfill these functions only in and through interactions that promote the mutual recognition that links the fates of democratic citizens in the three ways I have outlined. In promoting this mutual recognition, they inspire and render more concrete the sense of shared loyalty grounded in democratic institutions that Hampshire describes. In particular, democratic representatives, when they act in their positions to promote this mutual recognition, thereby personalize fair democratic procedures. And when this mutual recognition inspires citizens' loyalty to their democratic representative, it inspires their loyalty to the democratic institutions that bind citizens to each other as members of the same state. And through this mutual recognition, democratic representatives serve as trustees of democratic institutions in a distinctive and crucial fashion.

By creating mutual relations with citizens that connect them in the three ways I have described, democratic representatives instill in their constituents a sense of shared fate as members of the same democratic polity. Their advocacy work helps shape, and regulate, the boundaries of the communities they represent and this shaping, in turn, frames the interests of their constituents in such a way that good democratic representatives can serve those interests. Moreover, the mutual relations promoted by democratic representatives allow constituents to identify with their representatives and to feel a sense of loyalty to democratic institutions. These mutual relations give democratic citizens a sense that they are present via their representatives in the political process. Their representatives allow them to have a stake in the process and play a real role in affecting the means and outcomes of this process. All three of these mutual relations collectively serve not only to give representatives and the represented an experience of their political life as a communal activity, but also to promote the sensibility that "we are in this together." And in promoting this sense of sharing a common fate as members of the same democratic polity, even in the face of conflict and disagreement, democratic representatives help to provide legitimacy to democratic institutions.

Furthermore, all three ways of linking fate can account for the importance that democratic citizens place on moral character in choosing their representatives – a representative's moral failings, when they come to light, can weaken the community's identification with her, and thereby the community's sense of linked fate with and within the democratic polity. With moral failings, representatives lose the moral authority required to articulate effectively the group's interests, opinions, and perspectives, and they lose the ability to inspire the loyalty that binds their constituents with democratic institutions. Such moral failings therefore undermine a representative's ability to perform the functions necessary of democratic representatives.

The Virtue of Good Gatekeeping

I have sketched how developing mutual relations with constituents is essential to the function of a democratic representative. However, if a representative is to excel at representing in a democratic fashion, having such mutual relations is not enough. Good democratic representatives will develop these mutual relations with their constituents wisely, in light of a correctly understood commitment to political inclusion. By developing mutual relations with all citizens in ways that promote inclusion, good democratic representatives satisfy the function of democratic representation of promoting citizens' sense of belonging to a political community. Good democratic representatives exercise the virtue of good gatekeeping.

To engage in the activity of good gatekeeping, a representative must open doors. But that alone is not enough. To be a good gatekeeper, a representative must expand the scope of her mutual relations beyond her supporters or political base, with the aim of encompassing all democratic citizens, so as to provide all citizens entry to the political arena.[20] She must even strive to develop mutual relations with her political enemies. And, crucially, she must strive to develop mutual relations with the dispossessed and the marginalized within her polity. For her aim, as a good democratic representative, is to realize democratic norms and values – including the core value of inclusion – within her polity to the greatest degree possible. And the health of a democratic polity requires that all citizens be included in the polity (or at least that factions not be polarized to the point that a faction pursues its own issues using violence). To be sure, as I stressed at the outset of this chapter, there will be circumstances in which a representative cannot maintain mutual relations with all political groups, but must choose with whom she will associate. And, confronted with such situations, a good gatekeeper must base her choices of associations in light of excelling at the function of democratic representation. This will require choosing with whom to associate out of a sensitivity to what is required in order to realize democratic values in the democratic polity to the greatest extent possible. For example, all things being equal, good democratic representatives who have to choose between associating with unjust excluders or with other democratic citizens will choose to exclude the unjust excluders. Similarly, good democratic representatives might need to exclude some legal "persons" – for example, multinational corporations – from decisions about the use of natural resources.[21] Sometimes, considerations of justice dictate that a representative needs to exclude those who have the wrong kind, or simply too much, influence in a democratic state.

In developing this account of good gatekeeping, I will begin by expanding on my claim that good democratic representatives seek to develop mutual relations with (1) their political opponents, (2) the dispossessed, and (3) the marginalized. These three groups are not necessarily distinct from each other. For instance, a representative's political opponents might be dispossessed and marginalized. Moreover, a representative's supporters might be marginalized but not dispossessed. And, finally, there might be some significant overlap between a representative's constituency and any of these three groups. The crucial point is that a good democratic representative will seek to develop mutual relations, to the greatest extent possible, with all three of these groups. Democratic advocacy of any kind requires that a democratic representative be committed to preserving democratic institutions, but this commitment may not lead her to do the difficult, and sometimes politically costly, work of reaching out to these groups. Only a commitment to advocating in a democratic fashion that is informed by the values distinctive of democratic institutions, coupled with a proper understanding of what such values require, dictates that a democratic representative seek mutual relations with these groups. I will now consider each of these groups in turn.

Political opponents

Democratic representation is an antagonistic business. Democratic representatives advocate on behalf of some citizens and against other citizens. Consequently, democratic representatives, and even good democratic representatives, have political opponents. Nonetheless, a sign of a good democratic representative is that he does not isolate himself from those with whom he disagrees, let alone polarize the polity by demonizing his opponents.

The natural temptation to allow political disagreements to become excessively antagonistic is one to which Representative Thomas Davis III (R-VA) succumbed when he characterized Democrats as his enemies. Good democratic representatives strive to avoid creating political enemies. They do so because they realize that preserving democratic authority requires that political power be shared and that different political factions can take turns ruling. Michael Walzer (1996) aptly characterizes how regarding one's political opponents as enemies precludes the possibility of sharing power with them:

> When we turn opponents into criminals and enemies, we no longer look to compromise with them or to win some temporary victory over them; our goal is to drive them out of politics entirely, ban them from office-holding, lock them up. (7)

When he casts his political opponents as evil, even if he does so in the service of advocating effectively on behalf of his constituency, a representative is not acting as a democratic representative should.[22]

It is also worth noting that good democratic representatives avoid humiliating their political opponents. It matters how good democratic representatives compete.[23] For example, President Reagan failed to act as a good democratic representative when he made a joking reference to a media rumor that Michael Dukakis, his political opponent, suffered from mental health problems. Reagan had joked, "I'm not going to pick on an invalid." Such an attack on one's opponent does not promote the kind of mutual recognition needed for citizens – either Dukakis's supporters or those suffering from disabilities – to feel included in a democratic polity.

For similar reasons, good democratic representatives will refrain from using false and misleading campaigns to achieve certain public policy preferences or to win a political campaign. For example, in a recent Virginian election for governor, the Republican candidate's advertisement claimed that his Democratic opponent, Tim Kaine, "says that Adolf Hitler doesn't qualify for the death penalty." Yet Kaine had said repeatedly that, despite his religious objection to the death penalty, he would carry out the death penalty if elected governor. The use of false and misleading advertisement campaigns can have a number of bad effects on the democratic polity, in addition to that of polarizing the polity: these effects include keeping citizens away from politics or distracting citizens from substantive issues.[24] Moreover, deceitful attack campaigns undermine the legitimacy of the electoral process. Indeed, when a candidate is elected by "deceiving the public about his opponent's character or qualifications for office, a mockery is made of the public's right to exercise a meaningful franchise" (Houston, 1985, 68).

Refraining from demonizing, slandering, and humiliating one's opponents is not, however, enough. In the service of guarding the polity from
political extremism and dangerous forms of polarization, a good democratic representative will reach out to her political opponents and strive to
develop and maintain mutual relations with them.[25] Moreover, interactions
with her opponents should foster a sense that although they are political competitors, they still share a political life, namely, the common democratic processes
that aim to resolve disagreements fairly and peacefully. For example, consider
how President Lincoln successfully persuaded his political opponents in
the Republican Party to join his administration – William H. Seward as
Secretary of State, Salmon P. Chase as Secretary of the Treasury, and
Edward Bates as Attorney General (Goodwin, 2005). Lincoln's skill in turning these rivals into allies arguably allowed him to win a war and preserve
democratic institutions. This case illustrates, in dramatic fashion, how
mutual recognition among political opponents contributes to the proper
functioning of democratic institutions. Indeed, democratic representatives
inevitably face situations in which they can govern the polity properly only
if they bargain and compromise with people whose values, perspectives,
and policy preferences radically differ from their own.

To shirk the hard work of reaching out to one's political opponents,
and thereby to run the risk of allowing one's polity to grow polarized, is
to ignore the extent to which democratic politics relies, not only for its
legitimacy but also for its very preservation, on bargaining and compromise.
Democratic representatives must, as Madison warned, avoid creating per-
manent faction. To borrow language from Just War theory (Walzer, 2000),
good democratic representatives need to develop mutual relations with
their political opponents that allow not just for victory, but for "a livable
peace." It is the willingness to forgo polarizing the polity, and to seek out
possible compromise, and to do so out of an acknowledgment of the
possibility of one's own political defeat, that allows us to live together in a
democratic polity. For these reasons, good democratic representatives do
not presume that they will always be ruling and that their opponents will
always be ruled. Rather, they act as if they will rule and be ruled.

The dispossessed

Good democratic representatives will also seek and establish mutual relations with the dispossessed. By "the dispossessed," I mean those citizens
who lack the political resources necessary for being full democratic citizens.

It is not simply being recognized as having the status of a citizen that allows a person to be a full citizen. Democratic citizens need political resources to exercise the rights they have as citizens. Moreover, here I adopt Robert Dahl's account of political resources. As noted in Chapter 4, Dahl (1998, 639) characterizes such resources as "whatever can be used among a specific collection of people to influence the decisions of a government, particularly the government of a state." And he offers, as examples of political resources, "money, wealth, social standing, honor, reputation, legal status, knowledge, cognitive ability, information, coercive capacities, organizations, means of communication and 'connections'" (ibid.). I would add that this list of resources needs to be expanded to include all those capacities vital for acting as a full citizen. As David Held (1995) notes,

> If people are to be equally free, they must enjoy rights which safeguard their capacities, that is, which shape and facilitate a common structure of political action. These rights must demarcate the minimal rules and resources necessary for participation, in principle, in the determination of the conditions of their own association. (201–2)

My definition of the dispossessed is therefore a contingent one: what counts as being dispossessed will depend on the ways in which a democratic polity can marginalize and prevent citizens from fully exercising their capacities as democratic citizens. Here I follow Russell Hardin (2004), who states that

> Exactly what it takes to make individuals politically equal is not easily determined, but some elements seem clear enough. Anything that is an obstacle to political participation, such as extremely poor education, and that might be affected by public policy is an issue that we might expect our representatives to take on, even though it goes beyond our own interests and beyond their representation of our interests. (95–6)

What it is to be dispossessed is contingent on the kinds of political resources that are necessary for full citizenship in a given democratic polity. My contention, then, is that the legitimacy of democratic institutions requires that representatives in democratic institutions seek mutual relations with the dispossessed, where the dispossessed are so characterized.

To demonstrate why good democratic representatives need to develop mutual relations with the dispossessed, consider one particularly salient group of citizens who are dispossessed – namely, the poor.[26] By the poor, I do not mean citizens who have a certain income or SES score; rather, I mean those who, through class relations that are produced and main- tained through political institutions (Acker, 2000), lack the relative level of crucial political resources, such as time and money, required to exercise the rights that they have as citizens. Their lack of sufficient levels of such resources is thus reflected in their lower levels of participation. The poor might not be legally prohibited from participating, but they face certain structural obstacles to being full citizens. With E. E. Schattschneider (1960, 35), who proclaimed that "the flaw in the pluralist heaven is that the heavenly chorus sings with a strong upper-class accent," we need to recognize that democratic institutions favor the better off. The traditional means for getting preferences onto the policy agenda – studies, public relations campaigns, and lobbying efforts – advantage citizens who are financially better off and resource rich.[27] Even to be able to stay informed about political issues, let alone to participate effectively, requires time and economic resources. And the fact that these political resources are needed to monitor and influence government obviously places poor citizens at a severe disadvantage.

Such a disadvantage can be overcome partially if poor citizens have mutual relations with democratic representatives. For such relations can be vital to getting preferences on the policy agenda. Typically, citizens who lack financial resources need to register their preferences through noninstitutional and confrontational tactics. As Frances Fox Piven and Richard Cloward (1979, 3) put the point, "protest tactics which defied political norms were not simply the recourse of troublemakers and fools. For the poor, they were the only recourse." Piven and Cloward's position reflects the common belief in the literature on social movements that disruptive tactics are more likely to be successful than those that are not (McAdam, 1983; Tarrow, 1994). But disruptive tactics depend, for their efficacy, on numbers and relationships. The poor are in the unfortunate position that even the effectiveness of disruptive tactics they may take up will depend on the cultivation of mutual relations – and not only mutual relations between the poor and their representatives, but also mutual rela- tions between the poor and other democratic citizens.[28] A representative of the poor who acts as a good gatekeeper will cultivate all these mutual relations. And, in doing so, such a representative will be developing the political resources she needs to be in a position to advance the interests of the poor.[29]

The experiences of the poor reveal why mutual relations with the dispossessed are crucial for preserving the legitimacy of democratic institutions. The poor know, from first hand experience, that – absent the intervention of democratic representatives who cultivate the requisite mutual relations with them – their lack of money leaves them unable to influence the operation of democratic institutions. And their perception that money rules democracy rightly erodes their faith in democratic institutions. As Andrew Sabl (2002, 152) writes, "if elections and decisions are determined by wealth more than by the influence of ordinary voters, the regime is an oligarchy rather than a democracy." Good democratic representatives need to work to preserve citizens' faith in democracy by giving them a credible case for thinking that their democratic institutions are not for hire.[30] Indeed, the belief that money rules democracy undermines democratic citizens' sense of identification with their representatives as well as with their democratic institutions. More insidiously, the belief that democratic representatives are for hire promotes the sense that democratic norms and values are simply rhetoric, empty words used by the powerful to justify their wishes.

The marginalized

To the degree that democratic politics is fueled by competition, democratic politics will have winners and losers. The competitive nature of democratic politics guarantees that some citizens' preferences, opinions, and perspectives will be satisfied only by marginalizing other citizens' preferences, opinions and perspectives. Viewed from a particular perspective, a representative's job is to advocate effectively on behalf of certain positions and thus to marginalize those democratic citizens who do not share those positions as much as possible.[31] After all, those who understand being a good representative as nothing more than being a zealous advocate think that obtaining a particular outcome is more important to a good representative than any marginalization of opposing perspectives, interests, and opinions. From this viewpoint, marginalization by itself is not necessarily opposed to democratic representation, or even good democratic representation.

But if we note that democratic citizens can adopt behavior or political views that contribute to their marginalization, we can see that a good democratic representative will care about minimizing the marginalization of democratic citizens. Some citizens may be marginalized because they don't care for politics, preferring to spend the time and money on fun and family. Others, such as convicted felons, may have engaged in behavior that has led to their being formally banned from voting or running for political office. A high degree of such marginalization, insofar as it leaves a large portion of the population disengaged from politics, threatens the legitimacy of democratic institutions. And the formal barring of citizens from political participation should be of special concern to a democratic polity to the extent that such citizens will be inclined to pursue their political ends by other means. Regardless of the cause of the marginalization, good democratic representatives will seek to develop mutual relations with the marginalized, and thereby to mitigate their marginalization, because doing so is crucial to democratic citizens' having, and recognizing their having, a continuing interest in playing the democratic game. Good democratic representatives are committed *to some extent* to preventing the political isolation of citizens.

These reflections on the dangers of marginalization to the well-functioning of democratic institutions suggest that good democratic representatives need to counterbalance the cumulative effect on certain citizens that can occur through their constantly losing political battles. As a result of losing too often, citizens can learn helplessness, refusing even to try to advance their policy preferences (Gaventa, 1982). Indeed, as Lani Guinier (1994) warns, democratic institutions that don't provide ways of allowing different constituencies to take turns ruling are unfair and thereby illegitimate. My point is simply that democratic representatives need to do the work that is required for democratic institutions to work properly. If they will not act to counteract marginalization, who will? If democratic institutions are to maintain their legitimacy, representatives must reach out to, and develop mutual relations with, marginalized citizens; for those who have little or no chance of winning in the political arena will have little stake in supporting democratic institutions. Such citizens, even if they are not formally barred from participating in the political process, will have strong motivation to pursue their political ends by other means.

The development of mutual relations with political opponents, the dispossessed, and the marginalized can, to the extent that it gives some voice to the legitimate concerns of these groups, help prevent them from giving up on democratic institutions. For relationships with representatives can give members of these groups some connection to governmental institutions even when the everyday practices of politics fail them.

In developing mutual relations with their political opponents, the dispossessed, and the marginalized, good democratic representatives promote the value of political inclusion. They engage in the virtue of good gatekeeping when they open doors to those who need access and those who should have access in virtue of being democratic citizens. Up to this point, then, my discussion has followed a current trend among most theorists writing about political inclusion – namely, that of envisioning democratic politics as requiring political acts to simply let more voices in. For the main question that has preoccupied contemporary theorists has been "Whose interests, opinions, and perspectives need to brought into the political arena in order for democratic institutions to function fairly and justly?" According to this understanding of inclusion, democratic representation is a process by which democratic citizens (or at least their voices, opinions, perspectives, and interests) are made present via their representatives in governmental processes. Such an understanding of inclusion starts from the assumption that democratic representation requires that more and more different perspectives, interests, and opinions of citizens be expressed and integrated into the decision-making processes of a democratic politics.[32] My treatment of the first part of the virtue of good gatekeeping – maximizing the access of all democratic citizens – draws on the insights of this existing literature on political inclusion.

However, once we have identified the three groups with whom good democratic representatives should seek to establish mutual relations, a puzzle emerges: When should good democratic representatives privilege developing mutual relations with their constituents over their opponents, the marginalized, or the dispossessed? When should the dispossessed be prioritized over the marginalized? Should one ever seek mutual relations with one's political opponents at the expense of the marginalized? Such questions reveal that good democratic representatives do not only let people in. They must sometimes choose to develop mutual relations with some citizens at the expense of developing mutual relations with other citizens. Sometimes, increasing the access of some democratic citizens to democratic decision-making will be inextricably tied to decreasing other citizens' sense as belonging or "owning" the polity. To identify the competing obligations of a good democratic representative, as I have done, is to recognize that good democratic representatives will face hard choices about how they should include democratic citizens into public policy-making processes. And sometimes, they will need to limit the participation of certain actors in order to preserve the legitimacy of democratic institutions. To exercise the virtue of good gatekeeping, good democratic representatives need an adequate understanding of political inclusion, one that recognizes these complexities.

A Perspective of Exclusion

To determine how good democratic representatives are to prioritize with whom they should build mutual relations, it is necessary to move beyond the just "open the door" approach. More specifically, good democratic representatives need to adopt what I call *a perspective of exclusion.*

A perspective of exclusion has two components. First, such a perspective recognizes that politics can be a zero-sum game: inclusion of the preferences, interests, and perspectives of some citizens can come only at the expense of the exclusion of other citizens' preferences, interests, and perspectives. When democratic politics is a zero-sum game, it becomes vital to view democratic representation from the perspective of exclusion. But the perspective of exclusion has a second component: a perspective of exclusion recognizes how good democratic representation can require limiting, constraining, and even marginalizing the profoundly anti-democratic perspectives, interests, and opinions of some democratic citizens. In other words, to adopt the perspective of exclusion is to ask the question "How should democratic citizens and democratic representatives limit the perniciously anti-democratic influence of certain citizens and their representatives?" Good democratic representatives must also confront this question in order to promote the value of political inclusion properly. Good democratic representatives will recognize when they need to marginalize, and thereby seek to isolate politically, those citizens (and their representatives) who seek to destroy democratic institutions or who support democratic institutions only insofar as these institutions allow them to dominate other citizens.

To illustrate the importance of the perspective of exclusion for understanding inclusion properly, consider the question of descriptive representation from the perspective of exclusion. Typically, descriptive representation is understood as the representation of historically disadvantaged groups by members of those groups. Often, political scientists measure descriptive representation by the number of representatives from historically disadvantaged groups in formal or informal institutions and the resulting effect on substantive outcomes. According to this thinking, the more blacks, the better is the representation of blacks. However, increasing the number of black representatives can require decreasing the number of white or Latino representatives. Consider the decision of a formal representative to make a political appointment, or the decision of an informal representative to appoint a new member to his supervisory board. If the number of political appointments or advisory board members is fixed, in making these choices these representatives will sometimes need to make choices that will decrease another group's representation in the political arena. A parallel point holds for the hiring of staff and the designing of electoral districts. Democratic representatives can make choices about which groups of citizens will have representatives, or citizens working in government, that "look, think, and feel" like them. What these examples reveal is that democratic representatives will often be called on to make decisions about how the presence of historically disadvantaged groups (groups that are often currently marginalized and dispossessed) in the political arena is increased. In performing their function well, good democratic representatives might have to limit, constrain, and marginalize the perspectives, interests, and opinions of other citizens – most clearly those who have too much or the wrong kind of influence.

It is beyond the purview of the present work to give a full account of how democratic representatives ought to handle their obligations to different groups – say to different historically disadvantaged groups – when those obligations conflict. I will have to rest content simply with proposing one principle that, I contend, should guide democratic representatives when they adopt the perspective of exclusion. The guiding principle is that good democratic representatives need to exclude the unjust excluders. Of course, one's conception of justice will make a difference to how one interprets this principle and so to how one determines the proper actions of a good democratic representative. The approach I favor understands the relevant sorts of injustice in terms of patterns of social inequality that constitute forms of oppression and domination of certain groups of citizens. On this understanding of injustice, it is natural to interpret my guiding principle as directing democratic representatives in their gatekeeping to marginalize and even isolate those citizens who aim to dominate and oppress other groups of citizens. Note here that I take *intentional* acts of domination and oppression to be the proper targets of political exclusion. Citizens who consciously advance policies with the aim of keeping certain groups, simply in virtue of a characteristic of those groups (as opposed to the views they hold) marginalized, are ones whose influence within a democratic polity needs to be constrained. So I am proposing, for example, that good democratic representatives, and democratic citizens more generally, ought to try to restrict the influence of racist, sexist, anti-Semitic, or anti-Muslim groups within their polity.

That said, I do not wish to restrict democratic representatives' responsibility for fighting oppression and domination simply to excluding the unjust excluders. Contemporary acts of oppression and domination are often subtle, and not driven simply by agents' racist or sexist views. For example, individuals who are driven simply by profit can, in a society that suffers strains of racism or sexism, play an integral role in the oppression and domination of a particular group. Indeed, a wanton disregard for vulnerable citizens can, even independently of any racist or sexist views, have the effect of pushing out of the political arena the interests, opinions, and perspectives of dispossessed and marginalized citizens. Acts of domination, be they intentional or unintentional, therefore need to be "defaced," as Clarissa Hayward (2000) recommends. For Hayward, power relations are defaced when one focuses on how institutional norms and processes constrain the choices of democratic citizens. It is important for good democratic representatives to look out for systemic obstacles that contribute to citizens' being unjustly excluded from democratic processes. Increasing the number of access points to these processes is not enough. For, as I argued in Chapter 3, while democratic representation is a process with multiple points of access (Cohen, 1997, 575), the proliferation of access can favor those groups with more resources and thereby the ability to monitor that growing number of points of access.

Good democratic representatives, then, will need to be vigilant in guarding against power within democratic institutions being produced, shifted, and accumulated in subtle ways that exclude unjustly. They will need to take precautions against the cumulative benefits bestowed on those who participate. Hence, good democratic representatives should resist the development of symbiotic relations between governmental officials and interest groups that deny access to relevant citizens.

But democratic processes are also not static. Good democratic representatives must remain open to the appeals of all those who society excludes and stigmatizes. Moreover, good democratic representatives must recognize that not all members of disadvantaged groups are powerless and not all members of advantaged groups are powerful. For this reason, the third virtue requires democratic representatives to determine when a member of a marginalized group polices and regulates other members of a historically disadvantaged group in ways that promote unjust inclusion. Good democratic representatives need to guard against mutual relations with democratic citizens that contribute to the isolation of those citizens who suffer most acutely under the current distribution of social, economic, and political goods.

To do this, good democratic representatives must be sensitive toward multiple forms of oppression (e.g., Collins, 1990; Higginbotham, 1992; hooks, 2000). They will need to attend to the different faces of oppression (Young, 1990) – that is, the ways in which citizens can be victims of exploitation, marginalization, powerlessness, cultural imperialism, and violence. Young's discussion of the faces of oppression suggests that democratic representatives will need to avoid overly simplistic understandings of the processes that can de-legitimize democratic processes. Keeping in mind these complexities, good democratic representatives who face choices between conflicting obligations to different groups of democratic citizens, where one group dominates and oppresses others, will favor those who do not dominate.

The reason that I require good democratic representatives to exclude the unjust excluders is simple. Political inclusion fosters the legitimacy of democratic institutions to the extent that it provides ways of resisting and counteracting political injustices. As Iris Marion Young (2000) contends, the value of political inclusion is inextricably tied to the value of fighting injustice. More political inclusion is needed when injustices occur. Consequently, the scope of a democratic representative's proper concern in developing mutual relations most urgently needs to be expanded beyond the realm of her own constituents when political conflicts are generated by injustices. Moreover, this scope may be contracted to a considerable degree when a democratic polity does not suffer from these forms of injustice. Democratic representatives can focus on developing mutual relations with their own constituents when forms of systemic injustice have been sufficiently alleviated. Exactly with whom good democratic representatives need to establish mutual relations will be determined by the extent to which citizens suffer from injustice. However, in a world rife with injustices, the performance of democratic representatives should be judged by how they handle the disagreements and conflicts that emerge from political injustices.

The virtue of good gatekeeping therefore requires democratic representatives to attend to unjust and oppressive structural inequalities, especially ones that adversely impact the ability of citizens to exercise fully their rights as democratic citizens. Good representatives recognize that some degree of marginalization is part of the democratic process; however, unlike representatives more generally, good democratic representatives keep an eye out for perennial losers, with the aim of preventing their sense of political alienation and resentment from growing too large. Democratic representatives will preemptively tend to the needs and interests of those whose marginalization might turn them against democratic commitments and institutions.

To recognize these complexities regarding how democratic citizens can be marginalized is to recognize just how much work is required in order to apply the third virtue as I have characterized it in general terms to particular real-world cases. I certainly do not want to pretend that simply invoking the third virtue suffices to settle all questions about with whom a good democratic representative should establish mutual relations. In an important sense, answers to such questions must be determined in light of the particular issues facing a democratic representative and the specific context of the polity in which the representative is working.

Problems with the Third Virtue

The idea that good democratic representatives should develop mutual relations to the maximum extent possible with all democratic citizens certainly sets a lofty goal. After all, promoting mutual relations with those citizens who agree with and support a democratic representative is hard enough. To seek mutual recognition that binds one's fate with that of one's opponents, or even with that of those who don't care about politics, is surely unrealistic. Why make the job of a good democratic representative that hard?

I fully admit that the third virtue is highly demanding. It is, perhaps, the most difficult of the three virtues to obtain. For it requires good democratic representatives to confront head on the messy nature of democratic politics, and to confront the limitations of their fellow citizens. It requires reaching out to the disgruntled and the bitter. The third virtue asks good democratic representatives to serve as peacemakers, a truly thankless task. Such a task is likely to be interpreted by those who understand political compromise as "selling out," as "flip-flopping," or as a detour from the real task of representatives – advancing supporters' policy preferences.

The difficulty of achieving the third virtue is exacerbated further by five different problems associated with this virtue: the *sycophant problem*, the *problem of vicious divisiveness*, the *paralysis problem*, the *misdiagnosis problem*, and the *co-option problem*. A good democratic representative will be sensitive to all of these problems, and use good judgment in negotiating them to the greatest extent possible.

Democratic politics can blur the line between political opponents and political supporters: on a given issue, dissent can come from one's political base and support can come from one's opponents. When these lines blur, the temptation on the part of democratic representatives to associate only with those citizens who agree with them increases. In other words, the difficulty of differentiating constituency lines contributes to the sycophant problem. The practice of democratic representatives surrounding themselves with yes-men and flatterers undermines good democratic representation for two reasons. First, when democratic representatives do not associate with those with whom they disagree, they are isolated from a crucial source of information and political feedback. Second, and more fundamentally, a democratic representative who is insulated by sycophants cannot, as the third virtue requires, develop mutual relations with democratic citizens and thereby cannot link the fates of all democratic citizens both to each other and to their institutions.

This leads to the second problem associated with the virtue of good gatekeeping: the problem of vicious divisiveness. Democratic representatives need to resist consolidating their constituencies by stoking paranoia and fostering xenophobic feelings toward those outside of their political base. Hatred and intolerance of dissension can be used to consolidate one's political base, but only at the cost of forgoing the task, required by the third virtue, of linking the democratic citizens in the three specified ways. Fostering vicious divisiveness is diametrically opposed to fostering in citizens the honesty, courage, and mutual understanding required for them, despite their differences, to form a single, tolerant democratic polity. This is why Representative Thomas Davis's remark that campaign contributions to the wrong party can "buy you enemies" is unacceptable: good democratic representatives do not cast opponents as enemies. And it is also why the K Street Project marks a low point for democratic representation: good democratic representatives do not deny access based on past campaign contributions.

The third problem is the paralysis problem. I have argued that good democratic representatives need to include the marginalized. However, this sensitivity to the marginalized can open a good democratic representative to being inundated with competing and incommensurable demands for mutual relations on the part of citizens who claim to be marginalized. As Bernard Berelson, Paul Lazarsfeld, and William McPhee (1954) contend, democratic institutions can be overloaded. One can even imagine a cacophony of such demands paralyzing democratic politics. After all, it is difficult to prioritize among different forms of marginalization, especially when marginalization arises from social and political injustices. Indeed, too many demands for mutual recognition can dull the sympathies of democratic citizens for each other, leaving those democratic representatives committed to linking fate with an impossible task.

This leads to the misdiagnosis problem: the desire to develop mutual relations can prevent democratic citizens and democratic representatives from recognizing sources of subordination. In his insightful discussion of mutual recognition, Patchen Markell (2003) warns that the ideal of mutual recognition is not only impossible,[33] but also deceptive. Forms of mutual recognition can themselves be "the medium of injustice." It is not just the failure to get the powerful to recognize the relatively powerless that contributes to political subordination. Markell argues convincingly that what individuals desire and how they understand their identities and situation can contribute to their subordination. Pursuit of the ideal of mutual recognition can blind citizens to how even "equitable" forms of mutual recognition can contribute to injustice.

Perhaps one of the most insidious problems with the third virtue is the co-option problem. Forms of access can be used to co-opt, and thereby stifle, transformative politics (e.g., Alvarez, 1990; Reed, 1999). They may also be used to stifle citizens' legitimate criticisms. For example, one tactic used by business corporations to control their environmental critics is to gain control of their public forums and organizations. Donations of time and of money are central to this tactic. Such a tactic was used by various businesses to gain control over Earth Day planning committees. In Tucson, the Southwest Environmental Center in Arizona boycotted the 1998 Earth Day Celebration after being told that those participating in the parade were not permitted to criticize the event's sponsors, Raytheon Missile Systems, Waste Management Inc., and HBP Copper. The sponsors wanted Earth Day to be depoliticized, to stress the importance of green consumerism and not to point fingers at the biggest polluters in Tucson – of which these three sponsors were the largest.[34] (Earthfirst! actually crashed the Downtown parade with a banner proclaiming: "Raytheon Presents: Kill the Earth Day.") This example demonstrates how political inclusion can stifle legitimate and important criticism of powerful interests.

The co-option problem teaches us that political incorporation is not always desirable. John Dryzek (1996) makes this point, and argues that marginalized groups should aim at inclusion in the state only when "a) a group's defining concern can be assimilated in an established or emerging state imperative and b) civil society is not unduly depleted by the group's entryway into the state" (475). For Dryzek, marginalized groups must be strategic about when and how they are to be included in the state: "If the interest of an oppositional group cannot be so related to an imperative, then inclusion means that the group will be co-opted or bought off cheaply" (480).

Conclusion

My discussion of the third virtue holds several important lessons that are worth restating. First, good democratic representation requires that democratic citizens not be apathetic and that democratic representatives not be merely responsive. It requires that both representatives and democratic citizens generally understand their political life as a joint enterprise, a way of sharing their fate. This kind of mutual relationship places demands both on citizens and on their representatives. In particular, good democratic representatives will meet the demands of good gatekeeping fully only if they inspire democratic citizens to act in concert with them. To be sure, a democratic representative could, in one limited sense of "represent," adequately represent the concerns of the apathetic – that is, insofar as the representative takes positions that reflect the interests or preferences of apathetic citizens. But that representative's actions would not meet standards of good democratic representation fully, to the extent that the apathetic citizens do not care about that activity.

Second, good democratic representatives will not merely be mouthpieces for their supporters. Good democratic representatives will develop mutual relations with, and make commitments to, their opponents, the dispossessed, and the marginalized. Good democratic representatives will also expand the scope of their mutual relations to all democratic citizens to whatever extent possible. Moreover, good democratic representatives will need to decide with which groups they will develop mutual relations. Sometimes, a good gatekeeper is primarily a door opener, who lets as many people as possible into the political arena. Here, a representative's development of mutual relationships is assessed by her success in promoting inclusion. But at other times, being a good gatekeeper means choosing who to let in and who to keep out of the political arena. The third virtue requires good democratic representatives to exclude as well as include. And in deciding who to let in and who to keep out, a good democratic representative takes into account the complex ways in which power functions in a democratic polity. Who counts as opponents, dispossessed, and marginalized will vary in different circumstances. Being a good democratic representative means being open to the appeals of those who, given the way power is functioning in the polity, need the political resources necessary to be full citizens. And it also means checking illicit exercises of power, by working to minimize the influence of those who seek to exclude unjustly.

Chapter 7

Preferable Democratic Representatives: Real-World Political Virtues

Imagine two elected officials in Country D, Mr. Racist and Ms. Democratic Do-Gooder. Now, both Mr. Racist and Ms. Do-Gooder were legitimately elected in the sense that they were both elected in accordance with Country D's constitutional rules. In Country D, every citizen had one vote. Moreover, both representatives had similar high levels of support. But Mr. Racist achieved his popularity by playing the race card. He gave inflammatory and xenophobic speeches that were known to promote violent outbursts among the citizens. In contrast, Ms. Do-Gooder gained her popularity by reaching out to diverse communities and bridging their differences. She set up public forums in which citizens could listen to and deliberate with each other about their differences. Both Mr. Racist and Ms. Do-Gooder meet some minimal threshold of being legitimate representatives. After all, they each won a fair election. However, who is a better representative from the perspective of democratic theory?

Now imagine two elected officials from a very corrupt Country C, Ms. Buy-Me and Mr. Offensive. Both representatives were able to win elections by "working the system." Each bribed the relevant government officials and ran misleading campaigns against their opponents. Outside observers confirmed that there was serious evidence of voter fraud. Once in office, Ms. Buy-Me helped her wealthy friends at the expense of poor citizens and successfully managed to alienate the public further from politics. Mr. Offensive, renowned for making insulting remarks, directed his particular talent at certain government officials. Indeed, he led an anti-corruption campaign that sought to improve democratic accountability and reinvigorated citizen participation. Both Ms. Buy-Me and Mr. Offensive are in important respects illegitimate representatives. But which representative is preferable?

I hold that Ms. Do-Gooder is, as a democratic representative, preferable to Mr. Racist. Moreover, Mr. Offensive is preferable to Ms. Buy-Me. I take neither claim to be particularly contentious. In fact, I imagine that most political theorists would agree with these assessments, an agreement that reflects the intuitive appeal of my ethics of democratic representation.

The key point is that my ethics of democratic representation articulates the considerations that lie behind those intuitions. It does so by positing certain highly general criteria for comparing and contrasting the performances of Ms. Do-Gooder and Mr. Racist, as well as those of Mr. Offensive and Ms. Buy-Me. If Mr. Offensive builds more critical trust than Ms. Buy-Me does, then he does better at representing in a democratic fashion than does Ms. Buy-Me. If Ms. Do-Gooder links the fate of citizens to democratic institutions and to each other more than Mr. Racist does, then she approximates the virtue of good gatekeeping more than Mr. Racist does. By identifying regulative ideals for judging democratic representatives, my ethics provides reasons for preferring Ms. Do-Gooder to Mr. Racist and for preferring Mr. Offensive to Ms. Buy-Me. These cases illustrate how, at least when confronted with stark choices among representatives, my three virtues are clearly instructive. They also illustrate how the degree to which representatives meet these three ideal standards matters.

However, the test of a system of ethics is not how well it works in an abstract setting at providing justifications for easy choices – but whether that system can illumine the difficult choices we face in the real world. Any adequate ethics of democratic representation must do more than merely encourage democratic citizens to select nonracist representatives over racist ones. It must address how ideals can help democratic citizens negotiate the messy and unpredictable world of contemporary democratic politics. A democratic citizen will sometimes have to choose between looking after her own financial well-being and supporting the democratic institutions she shares with her fellow citizens. She will sometimes need to choose between two representatives, each of whom satisfies different and mutually exclusive virtues. In what follows, I will show how my ethics of democratic representation helps democratic citizens confronted with such difficult choices identify preferable representatives – that is, representatives who are preferable *according to democratic standards*.

What makes a democratic representative preferable to others in difficult circumstances overlaps to some extent with what makes for a good democratic representative. The latter identifies certain highly general criteria that democratic citizens should use in evaluating their representatives as democratic representatives. The former focuses on how democratic citizens should make certain difficult trade-offs, both among those criteria and in weighing the importance of meeting those criteria with other values. The concept of preferability is instructive for negotiating democratic representation in the nonideal world, in which different values cannot always be mutually realized. If democratic citizens are to negotiate the uncertainties, ambiguities, and conflicting obligations of the nonideal world, they must be able to identify preferable democratic representatives.

I begin this chapter by clarifying the meaning of preferability, arguing that the concept of preferability has a substantive, intrinsic dimension, as well as a comparative dimension. A condition of a representative's being preferable is that she be "good enough" – that she approximate the three virtues enough that she does not imperil what legitimate authority democratic institutions enjoy within her polity. In the second section, I consider how evaluations of democratic representatives are system-dependent. I argue that assessments of democratic representatives must attend to the political system as a whole and to the actions of other representatives. In the third section, I return to a question with which I began this project – "How should we evaluate descriptive representatives?" This question falls under the rubric of nonideal theory, because sometimes one needs to make trade-offs between the demands of providing descriptive representation for historically disadvantaged groups and the demands made by democratic representation in general. After suggesting ways in which democratic standards for representation need to be sensitive to the difficulties faced by those who represent marginalized groups, I argue that the standards for evaluating good democratic representatives also apply to descriptive representatives. The fourth section examines the conflicts that can arise among the virtues. The pursuit of one virtue can be incompatible with the achievement of another. Attending to these tensions among the virtues yields important lessons for our understanding of good democratic representation. In the fifth and final section, I defend my account of preferability by arguing that democratic citizens need decent choices of democratic representatives. Choices are decent when the slate of possible candidates includes representatives whose actions make democratic institutions preferable to nondemocratic ones. Democratic citizens need to recognize when all their options are bad, and demand better ones.

Preferability and the Virtues

Preferability, as I understand it, is the status of one representative being *more* desirable than another representative in a specific way: one representative is, on my use of the term, preferable to another if she does a minimally decent job of representing in a democratic fashion and does a better job of representing in a democratic fashion than the other representative does.[1] The relevant standards of assessment are the distinctively *democratic* ones specified, most generally, by the three virtues of democratic representation. Thus, preferable representatives are minimally decent democratic representatives in virtue of complying with the three virtues of democratic representation to a certain level, and they are better democratic representatives than others in virtue of surpassing the others' level of compliance with the three virtues. By providing an account of good democratic representation, my ethics offers this means for determining whether an individual representative is, as a democratic representative, preferable to other available representatives. And it does so by establishing a common political currency for evaluating individual representatives – specifically, by their ability to do a good job of advocating in a democratic fashion.

My understanding of preferability, then, has two dimensions – one intrinsic and substantive, the other comparative. Let me elaborate on each in turn.

The first, intrinsic, dimension of preferability identifies a minimal level to which a democratic representative's behavior must approximate good democratic representation. The first dimension focuses assessments of individual representatives on the extent to which each representative approximates each virtue. In particular, this dimension of preferability requires that a representative approximate the virtues enough so as not to imperil whatever legitimate authority is enjoyed by democratic institutions. Now, one might well ask why preferability does not require merely that a representative be better at representing in a democratic fashion than any other available representative. The answer, in the context of a democratic citizen's deciding whether to support one of a slate of representatives, is to say that the fact that one is preferable to the others implies that he or she is at least minimally choiceworthy, that the citizen should not simply refuse to support any of these representatives. And I am proposing, moreover, that the cutoff for this choiceworthiness is whether a representative imperils what legitimate authority the relevant democratic institutions enjoy. After all, by approximating the virtues, a representative supports the reasons citizens have for preferring democratic institutions as their means for settling political differences, and thereby the legitimate authority of democratic institutions. Thus, preferable democratic representatives must achieve a certain approximation to these ideals as well as surpassing their competitors at representing in a democratic fashion. And this is to say that the intrinsic dimension of preferability is to be determined by holding representatives' performance to the standards set by the three virtues of democratic representation.

The second, comparative, dimension of preferability focuses on the question "Preferable in relation to whom?" Here, judgments about preferable democratic representatives require determining whether a given representative does a better job of representing in a democratic fashion than other representatives. The second dimension requires specifying the relevant comparison class: the other representatives might belong to the same political party or to opposing parties; the other representatives might simply be the remaining names on a ballot, or they might be other members of a grassroots movement who are willing and able to take up a leadership position. This second dimension reflects the fact that available choices are relevant to determining who are preferable democratic representatives. But once the relevant field of available representatives is fixed, judgments of preferability among these representatives are to be guided by the relative degrees to which the candidates approximate the three virtues of democratic representation – at least if the question is which of these representatives is preferable as a democratic representative.

Preferability and System-Dependency

Assessments of the preferability of democratic representatives are system-dependent in two ways.[2] First, judgments regarding the preferability of democratic representatives will depend on the state of the political system as a whole. What is possible and expected of a representative within a democratic polity depends on the norms and values that sustain the legitimacy of that polity's democratic institutions. It matters whether a society prizes democratic institutions because democratic institutions allow one group to maintain power over others, or because they provide fair ways of settling political conflicts. If a society prizes democratic institutions as a means of dominating some of its members, it is apt not to select preferable democratic representatives; for proper assessments of preferable democratic representatives must be based on the norms and values that underlie and justify legitimate democratic institutions.

Second, assessments of preferable democratic representatives are system-dependent because how well a democratic representative can act depends to some degree on what other representatives do or fail to do. More specifically, the degree to which other representatives abide by democratic standards will influence the ability of a representative to excel at representing in a democratic fashion. As was discussed in Chapter 6, good democratic representatives might be unable to develop mutual relations with opponents who exploit religious or class divides. The ability to excel at the virtue of critical trust building will depend on the extent to which opponents mislead and manipulate their constituents. A representative may not be in a position to live up to my ethics of democratic representation, and unavoidably be subject to legitimate criticism as a bad democratic representative, if her fellow political representatives show no regard for the proper functioning of democratic representation.

The second system-dependence of my ethics of democratic representation opens up the possibility that sometimes, this ethics may be too demanding for the real world of democratic politics. Under certain conditions, a representative who follows my ethics of democratic representation can become a dupe of virtue, allowing others to take advantage of her willingness to uphold the legitimacy of democratic institutions. For instance, it is easy to imagine a good democratic representative paying a price for having reached out to the gay and lesbian community because he is running against a candidate who is willing shamelessly to exploit the homophobia of the electorate. In a similar vein, a good democratic representative might lose an election because she was not willing, like her rival, to push-poll. This point underscores my characterization of the virtues of democratic representation as constraints – they rule out options that a representative may naturally be tempted to pursue.

A democratic system that, in effect, punishes good democratic representatives – for example, by rendering them unable to win reelection or to influence public policy outcomes – can perhaps survive, but it is not likely to function properly. Such a system is also more likely to become a tool of domination than is a democratic system that rewards democratic representatives for performing their functions well.

Are Good Descriptive Representatives Good Democratic Representatives?

I want to move to another important question in nonideal theory; namely, should representatives for and from historically disadvantaged groups be held to the same standards of democratic representation as representatives for and from privileged groups? My answer, which I supply is this section, is a qualified, "Yes." Although there are special challenges that descriptive representatives of historically disadvantaged groups face in living up to the three virtues, these difficulties do not excuse these representatives from these standards. At best, these challenges provide mitigating circumstances that should be taken into account when assessing these representatives.

Before turning to these challenges, I want to respond briefly to a general objection some might raise to applying democratic standards to evaluate the performance of descriptive representatives of historically disadvantaged groups. For some (e.g., Williams, 1998) hold that descriptive representation is a distinct form of representation, one that counteracts the injustices committed by democratic representation. To the extent that this position is predicated on restricting democratic representation to formal representatives, the account I have given calls it into question by explaining how our understanding of democratic representation ought to be expanded to include informal representatives. But, more tellingly, on my account, all democratic representation contains an element of descriptive representation. With Jane Mansbridge (2002), I recognize that descriptive representation is an inextricable component of democratic representation. Once we see how democratic representation is to be identified – namely, according to its function in realizing the proper operation of democratic institutions within a democratic polity – we can see that the standards governing good democratic representation are to be applied to all actors who perform that function.

That said, it is important to recognize certain distinctive challenges that descriptive representatives for historically disadvantaged groups face in living up to the standards of democratic representation.

One such challenge arises in a particularly acute form from the fact that some descriptive representatives occupy institutional positions designed with the specific purpose of increasing the representation of historically disadvantaged groups. For example, India's Fourth Amendment, adopted in 1993, reserves one-third of the seats in village councils for women (Rai, 1999). Reserved seats have also been used to guarantee the presence of ethnic groups such as the aboriginal community in Taiwan, the Maori population in New Zealand, and Hungarians and Italians in Slovenia. Some electoral laws specify that party lists of candidates must contain a certain proportion of minority groups or women. In the United States, some electoral districts are specifically drawn in order to increase the number of representatives from certain historically disadvantaged groups. I take the purpose of such institutional reforms to be not merely to increase the numbers of representatives from certain groups but also to improve the substantive representation of those groups – to combat the ways in which public policies ignore and even negatively impact certain groups.[3]

The need for institutional reforms aimed at increasing the number of representatives from historically disadvantaged groups arises because democratic politics has failed certain groups. For example, past betrayals of African-Americans by white representatives necessitate positive steps for increasing the substantive representation of African-Americans. The historical legacy of US democracy gives African-Americans reasons why they should not simply trust the good intentions and avowed promises of white representatives. For this reason, if one occupies a position designed to increase the representation of historically disadvantaged groups by increasing the number of representatives from those groups, doing one's job requires prioritizing the needs of those groups. Descriptive representatives for historically disadvantaged groups who occupy such positions have specific duties or obligations to the groups they represent; for example, facilitating communication in ways that produce trust among marginalized citizens or staying informed about how public policies can adversely impact those citizens. Thus, certain political offices can require descriptive representatives to privilege the interests, opinions, and perspectives of their groups in ways that would be inappropriate for democratic representatives more generally to do.

Such institutional positions can place descriptive representatives for historically disadvantaged groups in a double bind: standards generated from one's institutional position can conflict with the standards that derive from the function of democratic representation. For example, a descriptive representative for radical fundamentalist Muslims or Christians who desire a theocracy and deny that females should have voting rights can only advance the interests, opinions, and perspectives of his group by violating the virtues of democratic representation. Sometimes, descriptive representatives for marginalized groups will have to choose between being a good descriptive representative and being a good democratic representative. If such conflicts exist, then however these descriptive representatives behave in the face of these conflicts, they will violate standards to which they should properly be held. Such conflicts, on my view, do not show that one or the other set of standards should not be applied to these descriptive representatives but, rather, that the assessment of these representatives should take such conflicts into account as a mitigating circumstance.

A further qualification needs to be made regarding the applicability of general democratic standards to descriptive representatives for historically disadvantaged groups. This second qualification is not limited to descriptive representatives for historically disadvantaged groups who occupy certain institutional positions designed to improve the representation of those groups. Indeed, it applies more generally to any descriptive representative of a historically disadvantaged group. It arises from the fact that the democratic standards set by the three virtues place additional burdens on those who represent historically disadvantaged groups. For example, the vulnerability of such a group can make its members less generous to the concerns and interests of other groups. Moreover, the past betrayals of a disadvantaged group by the majority can increase its members' distrust of democratic institutions. Descriptive representatives of historically disadvantaged groups, then, can face additional obstacles to being good democratic representatives. Holding these descriptive representatives to democratic standards in the same way as one does other democratic representatives can be unduly burdensome. Such burdens provide another reason to qualify the application of democratic standards to descriptive representatives of historically disadvantaged groups.

Even though democratic standards can be more restrictive or burdensome on descriptive representatives for historically disadvantaged groups, I nevertheless contend that these descriptive representatives can and should also be evaluated by their ability to realize the three virtues of democratic representation. I do so for three main reasons.

First, to hold descriptive representatives for historically disadvantaged groups to democratic standards is to recognize that representatives of privileged groups are not the only ones who can give democracy a bad name. The existence of what Cathy Cohen (1999) terms "secondary marginalization" – that is, how leaders of historically disadvantaged groups can police and regulate the identity of certain subgroups of historically disadvantaged groups – shows that members of historically disadvantaged groups can be dominated by their own members. Attempts to improve the representation of historically disadvantaged groups can themselves marginalize, stigmatize, and degrade certain members of those groups. We should not assume, then, that all descriptive representatives of historically disadvantaged groups will advance the interests, perspectives, and values of marginalized citizens. Indeed, since elites of historically disadvantaged groups can fail to exercise good democratic representation, their presence can undermine the legitimacy of democratic institutions. Such descriptive representatives are not located exclusively in the formal governmental sphere. It is thus important to recognize that there can be multiple sites of power within a democracy, and to attend to how these sites can weaken the legitimacy of democratic institutions. Democratic standards need to be applied to all representatives who occupy such sites, including descriptive representatives for historically disadvantaged groups, if democratic institutions are to settle disputes fairly and peacefully.

The second reason for insisting that descriptive representatives should not be exempted from democratic standards arises from a danger of gyroscopic representation – namely, the danger that gyroscopic representation can make insularity into a virtue. Descriptive representatives of historically disadvantaged groups are particularly apt to fall into acting as gyroscopic representatives, because the justifications commonly given for having such descriptive representatives emphasize how their membership in certain groups provides them with good internal resources for determining how the interests of these groups should be understood and advocated for. To see the danger of proceeding simply as a gyroscopic representative, it is useful to attend to the case of a representative who is not a descriptive representative of a historically disadvantaged group. When President George W. Bush doesn't, as he claims, read the newspapers or watch television to gauge public opinion before determining what he should do, he is acting as a gyroscopic representative should. But, I would argue, he is not acting as a democratic representative should. For President Bush's dismissal of public opinion reflects a willingness to cut himself off from dissent, thereby precluding the development of mutual relations with much of the electorate. To assume that a descriptive representative can, simply by appealing to her own internal state, adequately understand the interests, opinions, and perspectives of her group is to fail to see the importance of her exhibiting the third virtue. Historically disadvantaged groups are not homogeneous, and their interests are not always crystallized prior to and independently of the development of proper mutual relations with their representatives.[4] In this respect, too, exempting descriptive representatives of historically disadvantaged groups from the democratic standards set by the virtues leaves stigmatized members of historically disadvantaged groups more vulnerable. Descriptive representatives are less likely to do the hard work of developing mutual relations with all members of the groups they represent – for example, fostering a crystallization of interests within these groups that avoids secondary marginalization – if they are not expected to do so.

A further danger associated with the isolation of descriptive representation is that it risks eroding the ties that can develop across different groups of citizens and the ties that bind all citizens within the polity to democratic institutions. To accept that descriptive representatives for historically disadvantaged groups need to listen only to their gyroscope is troubling, because it can enhance undesirable divisiveness; for example, the "us versus them" mentality ("real blacks," "real Americans," or "real women" are ones who speak, feel, and think like me). Such divisiveness can undermine the mutual respect among democratic citizens that makes democracy work. Democratic citizens need to resist understanding the identity of the groups to which they belong in ways that demonize other citizens. And holding descriptive representatives for historically disadvantaged groups to the standards set by the three virtues is vitally important for insuring that democratic representation, rather than contributing to this divisiveness, functions to foster understanding across the various groups that comprise a polity and to link the fates of citizens in ways that makes the polity resistant to this divisiveness.

June Jordan (1995) captures this need to put aside divisive politics and build connections among democratic citizens:

> The ultimate connection [among us] cannot be the enemy. The ultimate connection must be the need that we find between us. It is not only who you are, in other words, but what we can do for each other that will determine the connection. (30)

In a democracy, citizens cannot go it alone no matter how much they want to, and this is something that they need to recognize (Dean, 1996). And this point holds especially true for members of historically disadvantaged groups. It follows that focusing exclusively on the needs of their "constituents" is especially wrong for descriptive representatives of historically disadvantaged groups, if only for instrumental reasons. And when democratic representatives, including such descriptive representatives, lead democratic citizens to reach out to one another, out of a "need we find between us" as democratic citizens of the same polity, the representatives will be linking fate in the manner that the virtue of good gatekeeping requires.

The third and final reason for applying democratic standards to the descriptive representation of historically disadvantaged groups comes from the nature of the virtues themselves. Built into my conception of democratic representation are the values of equality, self-governance, and inclusion. But the same values underlie the case for providing descriptive representation for historically disadvantaged groups. The fact that the same values provide the reason for the very existence both of democratic and descriptive representation necessitates that both forms of representation ultimately be held to the same normative standards. Indeed, this point underscores how, as I claimed earlier, democratic standards need to be applied to descriptive representatives of historically disadvantaged groups, insofar as these representatives, like representatives for dominant groups, can act to undermine and weaken a commitment to equality, self-governance, and inclusion.

Indeed, democratic representation and descriptive representation of historically disadvantaged groups are most likely to be mutually supporting when democratic citizens employ the virtues of democratic representatives for selecting or rejecting, or supporting or denouncing, their representatives – be those representatives descriptive or nondescriptive. After all, descriptive representation is not likely to revitalize democratic institutions or to increase the amount of trust that historically disadvantaged groups have in democratic institutions unless descriptive representatives are good democratic representatives. Indeed, descriptive representation is only likely to satisfy its democratic promise when all citizens, be they from marginalized groups or privileged groups, select their representatives using the three virtues of democratic representation.

Choosing among the Virtues

Democratic representatives can face difficult choices about which virtues they should pursue.[5] For sometimes, under nonideal circumstances, the three virtues of democratic representation come into tension with one another: one virtue can be realized only by forgoing another.[6] In some cases, when the virtues come into tension with each other, it will be obvious which virtue one ought to privilege in that circumstance. But in this section, I will be focusing on more difficult cases, in which the right choice among the virtues is not obvious. Indeed, I will argue that, in some circumstances, there may be no one right choice about which of two conflicting virtues one ought to privilege.[7]

Consider, in particular, how the virtue of fair-mindedness can conflict with the virtue of good gatekeeping. Effectiveness, even tempered by the concern for equality, is not necessarily consistent with inclusiveness. For example, Ewald Engelen (2004) argues persuasively that Dutch Work Councils – that is, workplace legislative bodies set up in the Netherlands to represent workers' interests in private firms[8] – have to balance the need for effective representation with the demand for inclusiveness. Engelen contends that including all workers from the workplace – for example, temps and part-time workers – would compromise the Councils' effectiveness by decreasing the leverage they have in negotiating fair terms with employers for their workers. Determining the extent to which Dutch Work Councils need more descriptive representation for marginalized groups within the relevant work force requires taking into consideration contextual factors; for example, whether such inclusiveness decreases a particular Council's effectiveness. To generalize this moral for all democratic representation is to acknowledge that tensions can arise between the virtue of fair-mindedness and the virtue of good gatekeeping.[9]

Consider a second instance of tension among the virtues – namely, a case in which the virtue of good gatekeeping conflicts with the virtue of critical trust building. Being a good critical trust builder can require providing opportunities for developing the capacity for self-governance to those citizens who have been denied it. In some cases, however, this will require limiting the participation of some citizens. To the extent that such limitations can exclude those citizens, the virtue of critical trust building can come into conflict with the virtue of good gatekeeping.

The leaders of the Student Non-Violent Coordinating Committee (SNCC), a civil rights organization in the 1960s, faced just such a conflict between the virtue of critical trust building and that of good gatekeeping when they had to consider the question whether they should constrain the participation of Northerners, most of whom were white, in SNCC's decision-making. Emily Stoper (1989) describes the conclusion that SNCC leaders reached:

There were so many Northerners that at the meeting it was decided that Northerners could not participate in decision-making. This decision was made sort of by mutual agreement after discussion, because the Northerners recognized that the thrust of the action came from the South. . . . The Southerners wanted it that way, at that meeting, because of the divergent levels of political thinking both within the Northern group and between the North and the politically unsophisticated Deep South. (265–6)

In order to develop the Southerners' capacity for self-governance, SNCC members decided to limit the ways in which Northerners were included and recognized within the organization.[10] Sometimes, it is not possible to develop some citizens' capacity of self-governance without constraining the ways in which some citizens understand themselves as being part of a group. And although, in this instance, the exclusion of Northerners was reached with their willing consent, a similar tension some time later led to the expulsion of all whites from SNCC. In the latter case, building critical trust with blacks came at a genuine cost to realizing the virtue of good gatekeeping; specifically, to the linking of black and white fates.

Finally, consider how the virtue of fair-mindedness can conflict with the virtue of critical trust building. This tension is possible because acting to promote the value of self-governance is not necessarily consistent with acting to promote the value of equality. Consider that when one promotes citizens' capacities to govern themselves, one cannot guarantee what sorts of ends citizens will use those capacities to pursue. Within the US, citizens have sought out inequitable and inegalitarian ends including slavery, Jim Crow laws, and gender inequality. The freedom that comes with self-governance opens up the possibility that democratic citizens will act to undermine the equal standing of all citizens and thereby the legitimacy of democratic institutions.

Recognizing that the virtues can be in tension with one another raises a natural question: How should democratic citizens and their representatives decide which virtues to prioritize when they conflict with each other? Unfortunately, this question defies easy answers. There is, I believe, no lexical ordering of the virtues. I do not have an argument for this position. It simply seems to me that each of the values underlying the virtues – equality, self-governance, and inclusion – is equally fundamental, and equally fundamentally important, to democracy. And given that there is no proper lexical ordering of the virtues, I am inclined to infer from the existence of tension among the virtues that there can be more than one way to excel at representing in a democratic fashion. This point goes beyond the weaker one that standards of evaluation of good democratic representatives will be impossible to generalize across different polities, to the extent that they rely partially on democratic citizens' understanding of democratic norms as well as the ways in which democratic citizens "connect" to their representatives. The present point is that the tensions among the virtues open up the possibility that an adequate ethics of democratic representation should not, even as interpreted by citizens for their given polity, prescribe only one way of advocating in a democratic fashion. Moreover, the fundamental values reflected by the three virtues are incommensurable: there is no common unit of measurement that can be used to rank the virtues. From these claims, it follows that one cannot calculate what makes for good democratic representation as one does an algebra problem, by simply plugging in the relevant values to determine the correct answer. That said, identifying the tensions among the virtues, I would argue, puts democratic citizens in a better position than they otherwise would be to identify preferable democratic representatives.

Four important morals for the assessment of democratic representatives can be drawn from recognizing that there are tensions among the virtues. First, these tensions suggest that if one pursues good democratic representation in too narrow a way – for example, focusing exclusively on only one virtue – one may lose sight of the other functions and their corresponding virtues of democratic representation. *In other words, it is a mistake to evaluate democratic representatives by employing only one of the virtues as one's standard.* The tendency to fall into such a one-eyed approach partially explains how some past democratic reformers have gone far astray.

Consider, for example, how in the early 1900s Progressive reformers endorsed reforms that were intended to promote accessibility – for example, public hearings – as means for providing responsive and accountable government. These reforms, however, ended up providing inroads to government through which special interests have gained power in contemporary democratic practices, limiting accountability, and further marginalizing resource-poor groups. Indeed, these reforms reflected more than a general naïveté about democratic politics. They reflect a preoccupation with political inclusion, and so with the virtue of good gatekeeping, at the expense of attending to what is required by the virtues of fair-mindedness and critical trust building. For these reformers overlooked how increasing the number of points of access to government would end up requiring more political resources, not less, in order to monitor and influence the workings of government, and this amounts to a lack of sensitivity to the real political equality required by the virtue of fair-mindedness. They also failed to see what democratic citizens need in order to have adequate capacities for critical trust: special interests have been masterful in manipulating the trust of citizens. Reformers who fail to recognize the potentially competing demands of the three virtues of democratic representation will be unable to negotiate these demands.

Second, in order that democratic citizens be in a position to evaluate their representatives properly, and not be vulnerable to being easily disillusioned with democracy, we need to be upfront about the tensions among the virtues, and not downplay the challenges that good democratic representatives will face in trying to live up to the three virtues of democratic representation. Unless democratic citizens generally recognize the tensions among the different virtues, tensions that may preclude a representative's realizing an important democratic value in a given circumstance, they are apt to be too harsh in evaluating representatives who face difficult choices among the virtues. Indeed, because there can be no clearly correct choice regarding which of the conflicting virtues to privilege, one cannot hope for a consensus within the democratic polity about just how a democratic representative should handle such tensions. These points suggest that unless democratic citizens appreciate the difficult choices among the different virtues that representatives sometimes have to make, they are likely to become too easily disenchanted with democratic institutions.[11]

In thinking about how democratic citizens need to appreciate the difficult tensions inherent in democratic representation, we should not pretend that all democratic citizens will "love" good democratic representation. After all, good democratic representation is likely to be in tension with many democratic citizens' preferences. The point isn't simply that good democratic representation can be demanding and onerous, taking citizens away from far more pleasant activities than politics, such as sleeping or relaxing with friends. Good democratic representation can also require confronting disagreements and compromising one's political ideals. Neither activity is likely to be fully embraced by citizens, even if they are willing to tolerate some disagreements and some compromises. In short, any adequate ethics of democratic representation will not paint an overly rosy picture of good democratic representation. And, in particular, it will not assume unanimity within the polity about how ideal standards of democratic representation are to be approximated. It will, rather, acknowledge that tensions inevitably arise among the virtues. And such acknowledgement will help equip democratic citizens for determining how such tensions should be reconciled.

A third lesson to be drawn from the tensions among the virtues of good democratic representation is that, in employing these virtues to assess their representatives, democratic citizens will need to determine not only whether a representative has realized each virtue to the maximum extent possible, but also whether a representative confronted with a conflict among the virtues chose one over the other, and so violated democratic standards, for the right sorts of considerations. On the assumption that, at times at least, there is no one right answer about how to resolve tensions among the virtues, democratic citizens should not be asking themselves if a representative made the right choice. They should be asking, rather, whether she went about making this difficult choice in the right way – in light of a keen appreciation of the claims that each of the virtues makes on her. They should, in particular, appreciate how when two virtues conflict, a representative might, with full appreciation of what she is doing, properly choose to violate a democratic standard set by one of the virtues in the service of fulfilling the requirements of another.

The fourth lesson that emerges from identifying tensions among the virtues is that it may serve a democratic polity to have representatives who exhibit a variety of ways of being a good democratic representative. I take it that although every good democratic representative ought to exhibit all three virtues to some degree, a good democratic representative might nonetheless properly exhibit one of the virtues to a higher degree than another, when the two stand in some tension.[12] If so, it would seem that a polity's having democratic representatives who exhibit different ways of privileging the virtues to one another may not only be consistent with, but even contribute to, its realizing good democratic representation. This amounts to a further sort of system-dependence of the preferability of democratic representatives. If it is healthy for a given polity to have some democratic representatives who privilege one virtue and other democratic representatives who privilege another, then whether one good candidate is preferable to another may be a function of what other sorts of good democratic representatives are already serving that polity.[13]

In reflecting on these morals that I have drawn from the tensions among the virtues, it is important to keep in mind that the democratic virtues collectively provide a general framework that democratic citizens can use to generate more determinate standards for assessing particular representatives. On my account, democratic citizens, with their distinctive views and preferences, play an important role in specifying how the highly general standards that the virtues set are to be applied to particular representatives. Democratic citizens will need to address how, within their polity, the values of political equality, self-governance, and inclusion are to be invoked in using democratic institutions to settle political conflicts fairly and peacefully. Thus, my ethics of democratic representation does not purport to settle all disputes about who are better representatives. What the virtues do is focus citizens' attention on the impact that a representative can have on democratic institutions. The virtues also lay out in a general way how the advocacy work of democratic representatives should be informed by democratic norms and values. Although the virtues of fair-mindedness, critical trust building, and good gatekeeping can come into tension with one another, they still provide democratic citizens with indispensable tools for determining how democratic representatives should realize the proper operation of democratic institutions and thereby perform the function of democratic representation.

Bad Democratic Representatives

Democratic citizens do not always have the best choice of representatives.[14] Sometimes, there are no "good" democratic representatives available. Under such conditions, democratic citizens can be forced to choose among representatives who realize only some, or even none, of the three virtues of democratic representation. Such representatives might advocate with excessive partiality, employ methods that weaken the capacities of citizens to rule themselves, and seek nonmutual relations. I take such representatives, who in failing to exhibit the virtues risk undermining the legitimacy of democratic institutions, to be *bad democratic representatives*. Moreover, insofar as the operation of democratic institutions determines the quality of representatives available to a populace, the fact that democratic citizens must choose among bad democratic representatives should be taken as evidence that their democratic institutions are failing them.[15]

Here, I part ways with James Madison, who famously argued that the institutional design of governments can adequately counteract the selfish motivations of individual political actors. According to Madison (see Madison et al., 1987 [1788]), one best controls such motivations by placing self-interested political actors in competition with one another. For Madison, such competition serves best to rein in human vice:

> If men were angels, no government would be necessary. If angels were to govern men, neither external nor internal controls on government would be necessary. In framing a government which is to be administered by men over men, the great difficulty lies in this: you must first enable the government to control the governed; and in the next place oblige it to control itself. (51)

In contrast to Madison, I argue that institutional designs are less likely to protect democratic citizens when those citizens no longer value the norms and values that make democratic institutions legitimate, or when citizens fail to press for representatives who will behave in light of those norms and values. The choice of representatives is therefore vital not for installing angels, but for providing preferable democratic representatives – that is, representatives who are "good enough" to support the legitimacy of democratic institutions.

Implicit in my ethics of democratic representation is the assumption that some degree of commitment to democratic institutions, and not simply to the norms and values that justify them, on the part of representatives is also necessary. If representatives are not loyal to democratic institutions, then those institutions are in a precarious situation, for they are threatened from within. Without this loyalty, representatives are apt to undermine the genuine reasons that democratic citizens have for preferring democratic to nondemocratic political institutions.

Assessments of the operation of democratic institutions therefore should take into account the quality of the representatives who work within and around those institutions, as well the quality of candidate representatives that these institutions provide. Representative democracies can only function properly to the extent that their formal and informal representatives are preferable representatives.

This is not to deny the importance of institutional design.[16] But in attending to questions of institutional design, we need also to attend to how institutional design can impact the quality of the representatives citizens have to choose among. For example, participants in current debates about whether formal representatives should be selected by primaries or membership ballots should, among other things, attend to whether one of these methods for the selection of formal representatives provides more preferable democratic representatives than does the other. Conversely, these methods could be evaluated by the degree to which they weed out bad democratic representatives.

Thus, it is not enough to say that democratic citizens have some choice: they need a decent choice among representatives. And that decent choice requires having some candidate representatives who adequately approximate the three virtues. Such candidates give citizens a good enough choice. Of course, the number of representatives who approximate the virtues or the level of approximation to the virtues necessary to give democratic citizens a "good enough" choice of representatives will vary, depending on circumstances. After all, one can imagine a circumstance in which having one candidate who excels at developing critical trust gives citizens an option that would address the most pressing needs within their polity. Clearly, it is beyond the scope of this project to determine how much representatives need to approximate the virtues or how many preferable representatives are needed in order, in a given circumstance, for a polity to enjoy representation that maintains the legitimacy of its democratic institutions. For now, I want only to claim that if democratic citizens have sufficiently bad choices of representatives, then the desirability of their having choices is significantly weakened.

Furthermore, articulating the virtues will help to stave democratic citizens off from selecting bad democratic representatives only if these citizens have an adequate degree of self-understanding. How citizens understand and negotiate the problems that accompany democratic representation will affect the moral status of democratic institutions. In particular, democratic citizens must continue to appreciate the value of democratic representation even in the face of its problems and remain committed to employing fair procedures in negotiating political conflict. Otherwise, the operation of democratic institutions will devolve and democracy will end up getting a bad name. Indeed, on my account, democratic citizens play an important role in preserving and shaping the genuine normative reasons that they have for preferring democratic institutions to nondemocratic ones. Recall that, in positing some highly general criteria for good democratic representation, my ethics of democratic representation still leaves room for citizens, in collective discussion and debate, to articulate more determinate criteria, and to determine how the general criteria should be applied under certain circumstances. These criteria, or idealized standards, that I pose provide a framework for this discussion and debate, and determine proper boundaries within which further, more determinate, evaluations of good democratic representation should take place.

The degree to which democratic citizens have some say in the meaning of the virtues is the degree to which the virtues of democratic representation, as I've described them, remain indeterminate. Such indeterminacies can allow for anti-democratic influences – that is, norms and values that can undermine the legitimacy of democratic institutions – to "slip in" to our understandings of the virtues. Such indeterminacies open up the possibility that, even when democratic citizens work, through putting pressure on their representatives, to insure the proper operation of their democratic institutions, they may value the wrong things about their representative institutions, choose representatives who corrupt democratic institutions, and be manipulated by democratic rhetoric. Democratic representation can be put to bad, and profoundly undemocratic, ends. Democratic institutions can be used to dominate other citizens, not to rule with them.

To get a sense of how the virtues, by way of the democratic values that inform them, are open to being misappropriated, an example helps. Consider Cathy Cohen's claim (1997) that certain understandings of inclusion and equality have led to the exclusion of gays and lesbians. The understanding of inclusion in question, one Cohen terms the "ethnic model" of inclusion, maintains that as long as citizens pursue political equality and attempt to prove that they deserve their political equality, they will be fully incorporated into a democratic polity. The problem with this model, on Cohen's view, is that attempts to prove one's desert backfire for certain groups – specifically, gay and lesbian citizens. In particular, attempts to prove that one deserves equality can disadvantage marginalized groups such as homosexuals, when the standards of merit to which they must appeal reflect the norms of the dominant society, such as norms of heterosexuals. The rhetoric of equality ends up masking how the attempts of certain marginalized groups to be included in the public policy-making processes are blocked by members of privileged groups as well as by members of other marginalized groups. For example, Cohen describes how the National Association for the Advancement of Colored People (NAACP) refused money from the D.C. Coalition of Black Lesbians, Gay Men, and Bisexuals and how presidential candidate Bob Dole returned a check from the Log Cabin Republicans, a conservative organization of lesbian and gay men. In these cases, an initially attractive conception of inclusion, together with a predominating pernicious norm of equality, not only led to the exclusion of gays and lesbians, but did so in a way that left Dole and the NAACP political cover. Dole and the NAACP could, by appeal to the ethnic model, claim that they are not representatives of gays and lesbians, and that gays and lesbians need to make their donations to different representatives. The problem is that – contrary to the ethnic model of inclusion – hard work, professional success, and money cannot secure representation for these gays and lesbians, as they can for heterosexuals.

Indeed, the potential for misappropriating the virtues is inherent in the virtues themselves. These virtues, and the democratic values that inform them, are complex, and prone to being misappropriated in ways that serve entrenched interests (despite having an initial air of plausibility). In such circumstances, representatives can justify what are in fact profoundly undemocratic actions by invoking the values of equality, self-governance, and inclusion. Democratic citizens need to be aware of how democratic ideals can be misappropriated, and how comforting rhetoric can blind citizens to the misappropriation of these ideals.

Consequently, I issue my ethics of democratic representation with a warning. The warning isn't just that democratic representation should not be treated as a universal panacea for social and political injustices. It isn't even, as I've argued, that good democratic representation is difficult, requiring representatives to convince citizens and other representatives that they should work together to preserve fair and legitimate procedures for settling political conflicts, even if that means sacrificing their own interests for the sake of those procedures. The warning is that if its use in a democratic polity is to be beneficial, and not positively harmful, to that polity, my ethics of democratic representation must itself be treated with care and discernment.

That said, if it is to function properly, a democratic polity cannot do without the virtues of democratic representation. Democratic citizens will only be able to press for good democratic representation, and decide how much good democratic representation they need, when they understand the characteristic activity of democratic representatives and have an appreciation of what it is to excel at this activity. I have argued that good democratic representatives are ones who manifest the virtue of fair-mindedness, the virtue of critical trust building, and the virtue of good gatekeeping. These virtues focus democratic citizens' attention on the adverse impact that representatives can have on democratic institutions, and delineate the boundaries that good democratic representatives do not cross. If they are to be in a position to appreciate good democratic representatives, and to guard against being beguiled by bad ones, democratic citizens need to understand these virtues.

Notes

Chapter 1, pages 1–26

1   For different approaches to the evaluation of democratic institutions, see Andrew Rehfeld (2005), Dennis Thompson (2002), Melissa Williams (1998), Thomas Christiano (1996), and Lani Guinier (1994).

2   See, for example, Edmund Burke's famous discussion of how representatives should act as trustees of the "common good" or "communion of interest" (1968 [1790], 1999 [1774]), James Madison's understanding of the "natural aristocracy" (see Madison et al., 1987 [1788]), and John Stuart Mill's discussion of the deliberative function of representatives (1991 [1861]). All three identify different standards for evaluating representatives. Moreover, there are a number of recent and important works on the ethics of public officials; for example, Arthur Applbaum (1999), Andrew Sabl (2002), and Dennis Thompson (2005). Although these works provide important insights into how democratic citizens should evaluate their representatives, none of them focuses, as I do, on evaluating democratic representatives in light of their characteristic activity as *democratic* representatives.

3   For my purposes, any political actor who advances public policies and claims to act on another individual's or group's behalf will count as a political *representative*. My definition of political representation differs from that of Hanna Pitkin (1967), who structures her discussion of representation around formalistic representation, and its mechanisms of authorization and accountability. It also differs from the definition offered by Andrew Rehfeld's general theory of political representation. Rehfeld (2006) identifies representation simply by reference to a relevant audience accepting a person as its representative. On my account, political representation occurs even when the represented fail to accept the authority of the representative. My ethics of democratic representation specifies the norms that democratic citizens should use for identifying preferable representatives.

4 I want, however, to leave open whether every political representative who represents in a democratic fashion, even excellently, is a democratic representative. A political representative is a democratic representative only if she has the requisite authority and accountability to advocate politically on behalf of democratic citizens. As we shall see in Chapter 3, the requisite authority and accountability need not be derived from the ballot box. There, I discuss the nature of this authority and accountability, arguing that they need to be understood broadly enough to encompass informal democratic representatives.

5 Democratic institutions can have many different sources of legitimacy; compare Jürgen Habermas (1976), Melvin Richter (1982), John Schaar (1981), and Sheldon Wolin (1981). For my purposes, I understand the legitimacy of democratic institutions as their normative authority to adjudicate political disputes.

6 Some may argue that presidents should not be considered political representatives. After all, their office is more often associated with terms such as "leader" or "statesman" than with the term "representative." However, given the role that contemporary US presidents have in advancing public policies, presidents are properly considered representatives and should be assessed by an ethics of democratic representation. Of course, presidents, like other political representatives, can be held to standards distinctive of their office (see Chapter 3). But it is important to evaluate presidents also by their ability to fulfill the function common to all democratic representatives.

7 From here on out, I will use the term "representative" to refer strictly to *political representatives*.

8 When I say that democratic institutions are *fully democratic* to the extent that democratic representatives realize the virtues, I am making claims both about the fairness and the legitimacy of these institutions.

9 Of course, good democratic representatives can advance democratic as well as nondemocratic norms and values. For instance, a good democratic representative who manages her staff well can advance the value of efficiency, a value that is surely important to being effective and thereby to being a good democratic representative; however, efficiency is not a value distinctive of democratic institutions and therefore is not characteristic of good democratic representatives. My focus on the norms and values distinctive of democratic institutions should not be taken to imply that other values – for example, efficiency – are less important.

10 The virtues of democratic representation that are necessary for the proper functioning of democratic institutions are also necessary for their survival. Here, it is instructive to contrast my view with that of Andrew Sabl. Sabl (2005) argues that democratic theorists need to distinguish between virtues necessary for a liberal polity to survive (in his terminology, *core virtues*) and virtues necessary for the polity's progress (*ideal virtues*). To the extent to

which my understanding of proper functioning may be assimilated to Sabl's conception of progress, we are disagreeing about the need to distinguish two classes of political virtues.

11 Political science has recently experienced a renewed fascination with the purpose and function of civic society in representative democracies – see, for example, Simone Chambers and Will Kymlicka (2002) and Mark Warren (2001a). In particular, Robert Putnam (1993) has focused on the importance of connections between citizens, what he calls "social capital," for sustaining democratic commitments. For a discussion of the connection between civic society and political institutions, see Theda Skocpol and Morris Fiorina (1999).

12 According to my view, informal representatives – that is, representatives who are not authorized by formal governmental procedures – play an invaluable function in democratic institutions. To ignore informal representatives is to overlook an important way in which democratic citizens are currently represented. After all, lobbyists, public relations firms, and leaders of interest groups and social movements all play crucial roles in setting policy agendas, in writing and implementing public policies, and in empowering citizens. For a discussion on the need for poor groups to rely on the social capital of other groups, see Mark Warren (2001b).

13 Jane Mansbridge (1983) identifies two types of democratic relations – adversarial and unitary. Adversarial democracy occurs when citizens' interests conflict, while unitary democracy occurs when citizens have shared interests. Although unitary democracy is certainly a political reality, democratic representatives should be evaluated by their ability to negotiate the conflicts among citizens, not by how they advance those policies with which every citizen agrees.

14 There is a rich and insightful philosophical literature on virtue theory; see, for example, Julia Annas (1994), Roger Crisp and Michael Slote (1997), Michael Slote (1993), Julia Driver (2000), and Rosalind Hursthouse (1999). Virtue theory is an approach to ethics that maintains that the basic judgments in ethics are judgments about character. Understanding the question "How should one live?" requires a conception of a virtuous person, a conception that "is grasped, as it were from the inside out" (McDowell, 1979, 331). The focus of this literature is primarily on the individual within a particular social role; for example, on the character that is distinctive of one who is a good friend. It suggests that one needs to understand the characteristic excellence corresponding to a given function by viewing the individual within a certain social role.

   In addition, there is a growing literature on the role of virtues in contemporary political theory; see Alasdair MacIntyre (1984), John Chapman and William Galston (1992), Richard Dagger (1997), Julia Annas (1996), Stephen

Macedo (1990), William Galston (1991), Onora O'Neill (1996), and Gerald Mara (1997, 2000). This literature typically addresses the virtues of liberal citizens, such as "the capacity to discern, and the restraint to respect, the rights of others" (Galston, 1991, 224). Its emphasis is on the virtues of liberal citizens as opposed to those of representatives. When the morality of public officials is discussed, it is typically in Machiavellian terms – that is, how one can balance moral commitments with the duties and obligations of public officials (Thompson, 1987; Walzer, 1974). Such discussions focus on the question of whether, and if so how, public officials need sometimes to be "bad" in order to do "good."

15   For a theoretical discussion of the importance of selecting candidates by character, see Mansbridge (2002).

16   Some may be reluctant to adopt the language of political character because they are skeptical about whether people in fact have stable dispositions of the sort that character requires.

Let me also note here that some common, and at least initially plausible, reasons for being wary of virtue theory in the realm of moral theory do not apply to my ethics of representation. Some virtue theorists ground morality in a distinctively human function, common to all members of the species, and many find positing such a function both untenable in light of modern biology and downright dangerous. But my adaptation of Aristotle's function argument does not assume any such function for a human being. It only posits a function for democratic institutions and democratic representatives. Insofar as these are human creations, or artifacts, it seems entirely unobjectionable to ascribe functions to them.

17   One notable exception is Nadia Urbinati (2000, 2002). Urbinati advances the view that representation is advocacy and is thus similar to my view in an important respect. However, her focus is primarily on the importance of advocacy for deliberative democracy, and she does not draw on an account of representation as advocacy with the aim of improving our understanding of democratic representation.

Chapter 2, pages 27–51

1   In the literature, the representation of historically disadvantaged groups by members of those groups is signified by a variety of other terms, such as "mirror representation," "group representation," "the politics of presence," or "self-representation." There are important differences among these different terms, but they won't concern me here.

2   Jane Mansbridge (1999) argues that descriptive representation of historically disadvantaged groups is only necessary under certain contingent conditions.

She identifies four contingent conditions that could justify preferring descriptive representatives to nondescriptive representatives: "(1) adequate communication in contexts of mistrust, (2) innovative thinking in contexts of uncrystallized, not fully articulated, interests, . . . (3) creating a social meaning of 'ability to rule' for members of a group in historical contexts where the ability has been seriously questioned and (4) increasing the polity's de facto legitimacy in contexts of past discrimination" (628). For Mansbridge, descriptive representatives are needed when marginalized groups distrust relatively more privileged citizens and when marginalized groups possess political preferences that have not been fully formed. For Mansbridge, descriptive representatives are necessary only when descriptive representatives perform certain functions in certain contingent contexts. Mansbridge's discussion provides some important insights into the difficult issue of determining when descriptive representation is necessary. Implicitly, her work offers some general criteria for evaluating descriptive representatives – that is, by their ability to satisfy these different functions. However, her emphasis on identifying the contingent conditions under which descriptive representation is preferable to nondescriptive representation makes the actual choice of descriptive representatives secondary, if not irrelevant. Mansbridge does not address the question of whether some descriptive representatives might be better suited for fulfilling these functions than other descriptive representatives.

3   For arguments against descriptive representation, see J. Roland Pennock (1979), A. Phillips Griffiths and Richard Wollheim (1960), and Hanna Pitkin (1967).

4   Although the reasons they advance differ significantly, these theorists sound a common theme: in order to be fully democratic, a society that has denied full political membership to certain groups must be strongly committed to including those groups in its political life.

5   The number of arguments for descriptive representation has multiplied as empirical findings have refined our understanding of the effect of descriptive representation. For instance, Claudine Gay (2001) found that the election of African-American representatives to Congress decreases white political involvement and only rarely increases African-Americans' political engagement.

6   But it is not universally held that this is the sole, or best, measure of the adequacy of democratic representation of historically disadvantaged groups. See Cathy Cohen, Kathleen B. Jones, and Joan C. Tronto (1997).

7   My initial attempt to articulate standards for descriptive representatives can be found in Suzanne Dovi (2002).

8   For a discussion of the impact of personal influence within the formal governmental institutions, see Mark Hansen (1991).

9   Melissa Williams (1998, 16) provides a helpful definition of the marginalized groups that require descriptive representation. Such groups have four features:

(1) social and political inequalities have been structured along the lines of group membership; (2) membership in these groups is not usually experienced as voluntary; (3) membership in these groups is not usually experienced as mutable; and (4) generally, negative meanings are assigned to group identity by the broader society or the dominant culture. Williams focuses on the experiences of women and African-Americans, arguing that if any groups deserve descriptive representation, it is these two groups. Williams's definition of marginalized groups is less helpful when democratic citizens need to choose among representatives who all belong to historically excluded groups.

10   Here, it is important to distinguish between representatives who occupy positions designed to increase the representation of historically disadvantaged groups – for example, party quotas or reserved seats – and representatives who are members of historically disadvantaged groups and who win an election. The latter are "happenstance descriptive representatives" in that they did not necessarily run as descriptive representatives for a particular group, nor do they necessarily understand their job as requiring certain obligations to historically disadvantaged groups. I would like to thank Jane Mansbridge for this term.

11   Of course, all US citizens – and thereby members of certain historically disadvantaged groups – can choose who runs for a particular office during the primaries for national elections. However, the ability of the members of a historically disadvantaged group to choose their representatives *autonomously* depends on a range of contingent factors, such as their population within any given electoral district. Given the lower rates of political participation by historically disadvantaged groups – for example, in voting and donating money to candidates – the autonomy argument loses some of its appeal. For it ignores the fact that historically disadvantaged groups do not always control who runs for office or occupies institutional positions aimed at increasing the number of descriptive representatives. For instance, party list quotas are often determined by party elites, who may or may not be members of a historically disadvantaged group.

12   For an excellent exchange about the problems with pluralization, see Stephen Macedo (1998a,b) and Richard Flathman (1998).

13   By recommending that democratic states cultivate a multiplicity of norms and values, William Connolly (1995) ignores how some norms and values can displace others. Should democratic institutions try to preserve dying standards? Should they only cultivate those tastes that are themselves consistent with pluralism? Connolly's account leaves such questions unanswered.

14   "Emergency procedures" are increasingly used in Congress to pass rules. Of the 191 total rules the Rules Committee reported for the 108th Congress, 116 were done as emergency measures (Slaughter, 2005, 34). Under regular rules, Members of the House are given 48 hours to examine the text of a piece of

legislation, and thereby to work with staff and legislative counsel to draft amendments. In contrast, emergency procedures prevent Members from reading, let alone deliberating, conference reports. For instance, Members were given as little as "40 seconds a page" to read the 299-page conference report on the dividend tax bill (Slaughter, 2005, 40).

15 For a discussion of the reasons why whites were asked to leave, see Bob Moses's account in Henry Hampton and Steve Fayer (1990, 182).

Chapter 3, pages 52–99

1 For an insightful discussion of just elections, see Dennis Thompson (2002).

2 For a general discussion of the literature on interest groups, see Frank Baumgartner and Beth Leech (1998).

3 According to Julian Lee (2004), as a result of the largely negative view of government, "more and more services have been contracted out to Non-Governmental Organizations . . . , leading the global non-profit sector to be worth over $1 trillion globally" (3).

4 Of course, the line between formal and informal representatives can blur. For example, different branches of government often lobby each other (Cammisa, 1995). As a result, formal representatives can act as informal representatives in influencing other branches of office: for example, when members of the Executive branch lobby legislatures, their attempts to influence public policy go beyond their formal responsibilities. Moreover, some policy advocates are appointed by elected public officials to their advocacy positions; for example, to boards of nonprofits or to bureaucracies. In being so appointed, an informal representative can derive his or her authority to engage in advocacy work from the political authority of a formal representative.

5 There have been some important recent advances in political ethics. For example, Arthur Applbaum (1999) articulates the criteria the public officials should use for determining how they should exercise their official discretion. Dennis Thompson (2005) argues that we should stop evaluating public officials in terms of individual vices (such as sexual misconduct). Instead, our understanding of public responsibility needs to be understood in terms of institutional vices (such as abuse of power and lack of accountability). However, the recent literature does not explicitly link its ethics to the function of democratic representation.

6 Andrew Sabl (2002) is an important exception. Sabl's discussion links the ethics of public officials to their particular office. Sabl examines the contrasting obligations of the senator, the activist, and the organizer. My ethics of democratic representation complements Sabl's work in that it articulates the constraints placed on all political actors who advocate public policies within

a democracy. To the extent that senators, activists, and organizers are responsible for certain functions within a democratic polity, then my ethics spells out certain implicit assumptions in Sabl's work about what makes his standards democratic.

7   Interestingly, some have challenged the legitimacy of social movements by implicitly appealing to democratic norms. For example, Phillip Green (1993) poses a challenge of this sort when he notes that "There is simply no way of determining who gave them [the suffragettes] the right to block traffic in London," in the context of raising questions about the legitimacy of their engaging in this action (16).

8   Most notably, Nancy Fraser (1996) has argued against Jürgen Habermas that the public sphere should not be understood as a homogeneous space. For Fraser, it is important to recognize how "members of subordinated social groups – women, workers, people of colour, and gays and lesbians – have repeatedly found it advantageous to constitute alternative publics"(123). Fraser calls these alternative publics "subaltern counterpublics" and understands their functions as providing an arena in which subordinated social groups can "formulate oppositional interpretations of their identities, interests and needs." My work assumes that democratic representation does not simply take place within the formal governmental institutions, but also within other regions of the public sphere – including the political arenas of subaltern counterpublics.

9   Here I follow Kenneth Goldstein (1999), who argues that these three developments have changed the nature of interest representation in the US.

10   William Greider (1992) estimates that Americans collectively elect over 500,000 formal representatives.

11   Of course, democratic citizens have always been represented by other actors besides their elected officials. Political parties, religious organizations, schools, social movements, and civic associations have always played an important role conveying both citizens' preferences and the intensity of those preferences to elected officials (Dahl, 1989). My contention is that with changes in the nature of formal representation, these informal modes of representation have grown to play an indispensable role in the proper operation of our democratic polity. I should note that, insofar as it attends to these informal actors, my understanding of democratic representation draws on preexisting theories of interest-group representation or pluralism. My view diverges from these theories, however, by focusing on how interest group representation can contribute to the proper functioning of a democratic polity in such a way that it constitutes democratic advocacy.

12   The vulnerability created by the proliferation of political representatives is aggravated by the fact that such representatives can work for nonstate actors, such as international nongovernmental organizations (INGOs). One's representatives are no longer limited to the domestic sphere.

13 By "authority" here, and throughout, I have in mind not just the bare positivist notion of enjoying deference, but a richer notion on which a democratic representative's having authority requires that he have a *legitimate* claim to having what he says on behalf of his constituency's position heard and given weight. Notice that the authority under discussion is, at least in the first instance, not the authority to pass laws that democratic citizens ought to obey, an authority that democratic representatives arguably enjoy only in virtue of being duly elected to a legislature. In this respect, there seems to be a crucial difference between the authority enjoyed by formal representatives and that enjoyed by informal ones. Here, I am indebted to a helpful comment by Thomas Christiano.

14 In fact, one reason to attend to the variety of sources for the authority of democratic representatives is that informal representatives increasingly work for organizations whose members do not elect the heads of these organizations (Berry, 1984).

15 Robert Salisbury (1984) claims that policy advocates most commonly have authority to act in virtue of their institutional affiliation.

16 Of course, this form of authorization can be subject to manipulation. Consider some recent practices of corporations facing lawsuits of sexual discrimination hiring female spokespeople and female lawyers to argue their cases. The appeal of their arguments to the intended audience is enhanced when these arguments come from females. Similarly, one industry's memo urged lobbyists to "DRESS DOWN" like "REAL WORKER types" for an event promoting the Republican tax cut's impact on blue-collar families. See Michael Grunwald (2001).

17 Initially, SNCC was a very nonhierarchical organization, in which any member could act as a spokesperson for SNCC simply by virtue of his or her membership.

18 Being arrested and possibly subjecting themselves to police brutality also raised the consciousness of white SNCC members by showing them the extent of the cruelty in the existing political system. White SNCC members often did not have any previous exposure to injustice – that is, they had never been confronted by racist violence, racial discrimination, or such conditions of poverty.

19 Democratic theorists recognize this point. After all, procedural theories allow for the possibility that substantive criteria can play a role in assessing the outcomes of formal procedures; however, their focus is on fair formal procedures. Such procedures are considered necessary but not sufficient for democratic legitimacy. Nevertheless, contemporary political theory has failed to articulate substantive criteria for determining whether an individual representative is acting in ways that are illegitimate, because they undermine the normative legitimacy of democratic institutions. It has failed to offer a benchmark by which democratic representatives can be judged. See Amy Gutmann and

Dennis Thompson (2004) and Charles Beitz (1990) for a discussion of the importance of substance and procedure.

20 The advantage of focusing on governmental authorization procedures is that such a focus also brings to view the mechanisms for sanctioning political representatives who veer too far from the expressed preferences of their constituents. After all, it is harder to punish – let alone de-authorize – representatives who derive their authority from their social location or representatives who gain their authority from formative experiences.

21 Hanna Pitkin is not alone in pointing out the importance of authorization and accountability for political representation. In her most recent discussion of representation, Iris Marion Young (2000) describes the important relationship between authorization and accountability. In particular, she argues that we should think of democratic representation as "a dynamic process that moves between moments of authorization and moments of accountability" (129). For Young, the movement between these moments makes the process "democratic." A representative process is democratic to the degree that citizens authorize their representatives and then can hold them accountable.

22 Ruth Grant and Robert Keohane (2005) attempt to explain how accountability is possible for organizations, especially international organizations, that are not typically considered democratic.

23 Of course, these different accountability mechanisms provide citizens different degrees of protection from abusive acts of power.

24 For democracies, "those who are affected" often coincide with "those who authorize a power-wielder" according to Grant and Keohane; however, they warn that "the mechanisms of accountability that can work so well to make governments responsive to their own citizens also work against the interests of non-citizens affected by government policies" (2005, 40).

25 Hanna Pitkin (1967) recommends discarding the delegate–trustee dichotomy because of its failure to accommodate the forms of aggregation and compromise necessary in representative institutions. Despite Pitkin's recommendations, most political scientists continue to use the delegate/trustee dichotomy.

26 Richard Fenno's understanding of constituency is complicated further by Jane Mansbridge's recent claim (2002) that representatives act for individuals who live outside the electoral district. For instance, Jane Mansbridge noted how Barney Frank (D-MA), who is gay and who champions gay and lesbian causes, is a representative for gays and lesbians who live outside his electoral district.

27 Amy Gutmann and Dennis Thompson (1985) argue that because of the different constituencies, political representation is best understood as multidimensional. Gutmann and Thompson identify four different constituencies: parties, disadvantaged groups, all members of their electoral district, and the

majority of the electoral district. It would seem that political representatives are not just intermediaries, but *multiple* intermediaries.

28 Some have hoped to reconcile such conflicts by insisting that the proper standard for evaluating a representative's actions is the "best interest" of a constituency. However, such a qualification does not eliminate the difficulties of defining interests and constituency boundaries.

29 Typically, improper influence can be identified by examining whether the representative profited incommensurably or whether there is a pattern of questionable financial dealings surrounding a policy decision. In fact, the most common way of identifying conflicts of interest is in terms of finances. Dennis Thompson (2002) disagrees, arguing that other kinds of motivations should also signal a conflict of interest; for example, ideological commitments or religious affiliations. For an excellent contemporary discussion of conflicts of interest, see Andrew Stark (2000).

30 A significant advantage of adopting this standard is that it can explain why Americans dislike their representatives profiting from their activities as representatives. According to John Hibbing and Elizabeth Theiss-Morse (2002), Americans are not so much worried about special interests as they are about representatives personally profiting from their office.

31 Interestingly, in this respect the autonomy standard flies in the face of arguments about the desirability of descriptive representation of historically disadvantaged groups for democratic institutions. See Chapter 2, as well as Suzanne Dovi (2002).

32 One of the best defenses of the position that professional norms are to be used for the assessment of democratic representatives is Andrew Sabl (2002). Sabl identifies different standards for assessing elected representatives, activists, and organizers. For Sabl, the ethics that govern a political actor depends on her particular office.

33 For a discussion of the parallels between elected representatives and professionals, see Vanessa Merton (1985).

34 Although being a politician has often become a career for political actors, it is important to stress that representatives can have different goals depending on the stage of their career. Famously, Richard Fenno notes two career stages for House members. In the early stages of careers, a member's constituency relationship is expansionist, trying to develop stronger connections to his constituency. In the later stage, a politician is protectionist, and thereby acting in ways to consolidate existing connections and support levels (Fenno, 2002, 25). Fenno's distinction of different career stages suggests that representatives will uphold different standards for evaluating their own performance based on their personal ambitions.

35 My account of Representative Tom DeLay's actions draws heavily on the work of Robert Kuttner (2004).

36   The inability to debate or amend the Medicare bill arguably contributed to
     the debacle that occurred when it was implemented. People were faced with the
     choice of more than three dozen drug plans, with different premiums, deduct-
     ibles, co-payments, and lists of covered drugs. Beneficiaries had difficulties
     comparing programs. Hundreds of thousands of Medicaid beneficiaries, whose
     drug coverage was automatically transferred to the Medicare program, were
     denied or overcharged because of glitches in the systems (Wolf, 2006).

37   Some proponents of the constituent-interest view may be sympathetic to this
     development of their position. Hanna Pitkin (2004) may be expressing this
     sympathy when she acknowledges that her understanding of representation
     did not adequately take into account a democratic context.

38   DeLay's parliamentary tactics could also be criticized for limiting the auto-
     nomy of other representatives; however, such a criticism employs a different
     understanding of the autonomy standards than the one I use here. The altern-
     ative understanding of autonomy focuses on the institutional conditions
     necessary for autonomous deliberations.

39   Joseph Schumpeter (1976) famously held that interest group representation is
     vital for making democratic institutions responsive and accountable. Zealously
     advancing one's group's interests should not be lamented; rather, zealous
     advocacy should be properly countered by zealous advocacy on the part of
     one's opponents. From his perspective, such behavior fosters competition
     and competition among representatives is how democratic institutions remain
     responsive and accountable to those being represented. His view, in short,
     is that democratic institutions function well when representatives advocate
     zealously for their constituents.

40   For a defense of understanding democratic institutions as anti-domination,
     see Ian Shapiro (2003).

41   I borrow this term from Mark Tessler (2006), who uses it to describe recent
     survey findings from the Middle East of people who value democratic institu-
     tions but who do not favor democratic values. See also Mark Tessler and
     Ebru Altinoglu (2004) and Mark Tessler and Eleanor Gao (2005).

42   In fact, how democratic representatives respond to conflicts about the proper
     behavior of representatives is partially indicative of the extent to which they
     excel at representing in a democratic fashion. Acting in ways that categoric-
     ally deny access of relevant parties or stifle public deliberations is unacceptable
     from the perspective of democratic standards. This is true even if citizens
     wish to avoid hearing bad news. This is true even if the citizens who don't
     wish to hear their opponents are in the majority.

43   For a discussion of why neutrality is inadequate for settling political disputes,
     see Amy Gutmann and Dennis Thompson (2004, ch. 3).

44   The importance of political disagreements can vary, and James Buchanan
     and Gordon Tullock (1962) are right to hold that democracy should address

those of moderate importance. Here is how Ian Shapiro (2003) summarizes their view: "Democracy is best suited to issues of moderate importance on their account. Issues of high importance should be insulated from it, while issues of low importance might even be delegated to administrators" (18).

45 While it is possible to imagine advocacy under totalitarian forms of government, the legitimacy of such advocacy would differ significantly from that of the US, whose imperfect representative democracy, by definition, extols the virtues of citizen participation. Although contemporary political scientists and theorists have recognized the extent to which the USA may rely on the apathy and lack of participation of its citizens, its ideals nonetheless espouse a commitment to treating seriously the preferences of citizens as an integral part of the political process.

46 My emphasis of the location of advocacy also reflects certain political realities within the US – namely, the blurring of the distinction between formal and informal representation. Jeffrey Birnbaum (1992, 3) describes how "Washington has become a club in which the line between those inside and those outside the government is not clearly drawn. Corporate lobbyists have so suffused the culture of the city that at times they seem to be part of the government itself." Moreover, informal representatives can act like formal representatives – for example, write the official public legislation – and formal representatives can act like informal ones; for example, branches of government now lobby each other (Cammisa, 1995). Many traditional state functions – for example, monitoring of environmental programs or provision of social services – are contracted out or performed by non-governmental organizations. Perhaps one of the most interesting shifts is the extent to which informal representatives have become objects of envy, the better lifestyles and pay having produced what Birnbaum (1992) calls "lobbyist envy." Some formal representatives enter the political arena with the hope of becoming informal representatives. In other words, one uses one's credentials as a formal representative to become an informal one. The fluid relationship between the career paths of formal and informal representatives indicates that democratic theorists need to rethink the tendency to treat advocacy as a secondary form of representation. It also suggests that our normative understandings of democratic representation should reflect the fluid relationship between formal and informal actors. Since both formal and informal representatives are crucial for doing the central function of representatives, any adequate account of democratic representation cannot ignore advocacy.

47 Such translations can lend themselves to abuse, allowing the possibility of manipulative and disturbing presentation of issues. For a discussion of how power can manipulate preferences, see Steven Lukes (1974). Advocacy has the power to influence the reactions of citizens and other representatives.

48 The connections between political advocacy and democratic deliberations should be readily apparent. By engaging in a war of words and political resources, advocacy is the alternative to political violence.

49 Just as time and interest prevent all citizens from engaging in a direct democracy, representative institutions would not function well if every citizen advocated for himself or herself. Democratic representation works to some extent because certain citizens take a back seat in politics.

50 For a discussion of how political resources can be cumulative, see Sidney Verba, Kay Schlozman, and Henry Brady (1995).

51 By particularistic concerns, I mean the social and economic well-being of constituents. Now as we shall see, the social and economic well-being of constituents can adversely impact their political status, affecting their ability to engage fully in democratic politics. For this reason, democratic representatives perceive the perspectives, interests, and opinions of democratic citizens through a particular light – that is, by the extent to which such perspectives, interests, and opinions can adversely harm the fairness and justice of democratic institutions.

52 We also know that democratic representatives can justify their flaws in a particular way – that is, by claiming to act in their constituents' name and thereby by invoking the authority of democratic institutions. Democratic representatives can justify their nasty, brutal, small-minded behavior by claiming to act democratically. The degree to which they try to justify such behavior by employing democratic norms is the degree that representatives can weaken democratic citizens' desire for democratic institutions.

53 For an important discussion of how the concept of equality justifies democratic authority, see Thomas Christiano (1996, ch. 2).

54 Other notorious examples of representatives who have politically survived multiple run-ins with the law include DC Mayor Marion Barry, Louisiana's Governor Huey Long, and Boston's Mayor James Curley.

55 For a discussion of the reasons why Congress can have a senator or congressman expulsed, see Deschler (1977) and Cannon (1935). The Fourteenth Amendment also provides a "disqualification" provision in Section 3, where a person can be "disqualified" from holding Congressional office for engaging in insurrection or rebellion against the US or giving aid or comfort to our enemies after having taken an oath to support the Constitution.

56 Such a view is mainly associated with Bernard Manin (1997).

57 The dynamic relationship between democratic citizens and their institutions suggests that representatives who act within these institutions cannot help in an important sense educating citizens about democratic institutions. They lead by example. When democratic representatives educate citizens about their reasons for preferring certain policies and for making certain sacrifices for the health of their political institutions, these representatives can influence why democratic citizens value those institutions.

58 Here my position draws partially on the empirical work of John Hibbing and Elizabeth Theiss-Morse (2002). They recommend encouraging citizen participation that is based on an honest appreciation of democratic institutions. More specifically, Hibbing and Theiss-Morse contend that democratic citizens need to appreciate that "disagreements can occur among people of good heart and that some debating and compromising will be necessary to resolve those disagreements" (10). When citizens have reasonable expectations, they will be less likely "to take the first opportunity to tune out politics."

Chapter 4, pages 100–23

1 In arguing that Rabbi Kahane was a bad democratic representative, I do not mean to imply that he should be denied the right to advance whatever policy preference he wants (although he was banned from the Knesset in 1988 under a law against racism). Rather, my contention is simply that Rabbi Kahane was a bad democratic representative because he advanced political preferences that (regardless of whether those preferences were legal or even constitutional) violated the norms and values characteristic of democratic institutions.

2 Not all democratic citizens have equal political standing in democratic governments: for example, children, the mentally disabled, and convicted felons lack equal political standing despite being democratic citizens. Only democratic citizens who possess certain qualifications enjoy that standing. For an insightful discussion of the different qualifications for full democratic citizenship, see Judith Failer (2002).

3 Pitkin's discussion of political representation has been particularly influential on empirical political scientists. However, unlike Pitkin, most political scientists simply equate interests with policy preferences. In this way, current practice of empirical political scientists assumes that good representation should be delegates, not trustees – or, in other words, that good representatives are ones who obey the policy preferences of a majority of their constituents. For an argument against using correlations between representatives and constituents to measure representativeness, see Christopher Achen (1975, 1977).

4 Here, I follow many democratic theorists who specify that democratic theory requires both procedural and substantive standards for the proper use of democratic authority: "one person, one vote" is an example of a procedural standard, while civil liberties, such as freedom of association and a free press, are examples of substantive standards. The latter standards put restrictions on what democratic ends can be set by citizens through the exercise of democratic procedures. So, Dahl (1998), for example, recognizes that democratic citizens should not be given the power to enslave themselves. And this is just to claim that following the preferences of citizens, even the majority of citizens, is not sufficient for determining democratic ends.

5   For instance, Thomas Christiano (1996) offers a revised (and much improved) understanding of equality, one that renders equality compatible with liberty. For Christiano, equal person freedom is the basic principle of democracy. Based on Christiano's understanding of equal person freedom, citizens need to have access to "the same socially important means" to carry out their choices (1996, 18).

6   As discussed in Chapter 3, having properly designed democratic institutions alone is insufficient for two reasons. First, the ability of democratic institutions to settle disputes will depend on the behavior of political actors. After all, democratic procedures allow participants to make and change the rules of those procedures. For this reason, democratic institutions are particularly vulnerable to the whims of the political representatives. Second, even if one trusts democratic institutions to settle disputes fairly regardless of the commitment of particular representatives to democratic values, one must acknowledge the extent to which individuals who are not formally elected act as democratic representatives in contemporary democracies. The influence of social movements, interest groups, and transnational nongovernmental organizations on the making of public policy all call to question the assumption that institutions alone are sufficient to secure good democratic representation.

7   For a detailed discussion of how the rise of liberty and equality in America was accompanied by the rise of slavery, see Edmund Morgan (1975). See also Rogers Smith (1997).

8   My discussion of the different approaches to equality draws heavily on Jennifer Hochschild (1996).

9   For an extensive discussion of the concept of formal equality, see Wendy Williams (1982).

10 Implicit within the conception of civic equality, as held by those who advance a threshold approach, are standards for determining the minimal level of resources necessary for realizing one's humanity; for example, the minimal level of security or caloric intake. I have in mind here Martha Nussbaum's (2000) capabilities approach to humanitarian assistance. On this approach, a society in which all possess the same or a similar deficit of resources would still be judged to be a society that has not achieved civic equality – since all members of the society have fallen below the standards necessary for human flourishing within that society and thus, in an important sense, lack any genuine political standing at all.

11 For a discussion of the changing status of African-Americans during the Reconstruction, see W. E. B. Dubois (1969), especially Chapter 2.

12 For a full discussion of different notions of fairness, see Jennifer Hochschild (1981).

13 Moreover, being able to pass or implement purely symbolic legislation that does not adversely impact the normative legitimacy of democratic institutions would have no bearing on whether a representative excels at the first virtue.

14 I thus challenge a standard view on which strong advocacy for policy preferences is itself an indication of a democratic temperament. According to
this way of thinking, active impassioned citizens sustain democratic institutions
(John Stuart Mill, in Mill and Bentham, 1987). Advancing one's interests,
whatever those interests are, is understood as good democratic representation.

15 Most political representatives claim that their public policies advance the
common good and, thereby, the interests of all citizens. For this reason, both
good and bad democratic representatives are likely to use rhetoric that appeals
to the common good. Good democratic representatives, though, should present sound evidence that backs up their claims that a particular policy helps or
harms citizens.

16 I will discuss the relationship between good democratic representation and
good descriptive representation of historically disadvantaged groups more
fully in Chapter 7.

Chapter 5, pages 124–44

1 In the literature, this strategy goes by a variety of other names, such as
"working the district," "going grassroots," or "using the rank and file." Jeffrey
Birnbaum (2000) noted that half of the top ten groups (of the most powerful
interest groups) in 1997 "were propelled there on the strength of their long-
established grassroots networks" (175). In other words, the mobilization of
members, what is known as astroturfing because of its largely artificial
nature, is a crucial component of interest groups' power.

2 Other reforms have been suggested to improve the opportunities that citizens
have for deliberation. Benjamin Barber (1984) has recommended instituting
referenda in two stages. Each of the stages would be separated by more than
a month as a way to promote deliberation. Bruce Ackerman and John Fishkin
(2002) have argued for providing citizens with a "Deliberation Day." Given
these different proposals, it would follow that a measure of a good representative is the degree to which he or she provides incentives and opportunities
for democratic citizens to rule themselves.

3 Robert Goodin (1980) identifies an instance of manipulation by asking
two questions. First, is the interference deceptive? Second, is the interference
contrary to the putative will of those subject to it? Together, these questions
identify the defining features of a manipulative politics.

4 Here, I agree with Arthur Applbaum (1999), who contends that "manipulation, lies, and many sorts of secrets corrode the principle of publicity on which
deliberative democracy depends." Moreover, he adds the following interesting
observation that "these strategies can be justified only when there is precious
little, democratically speaking, to lose (when formal political mandates lack
legitimate jurisdiction and legitimate reasoning and democratic value) or,

perhaps, when there is much democratically to gain (when very important matters of democratic justice hang in the balance)" (235).

5   For a related discussion concerning the episodic nature of the exercise of liberal democratic virtues, see Andrew Sabl (2005).

6   For a more detailed discussion of the limitations of active citizenship, see David Plotke (1997). John Dryzek (1996) has actually argued that inclusion in formal governmental institutions can be counterproductive to certain social movements. For an insightful discussion of listening, see Susan Bickford (1996).

7   For a discussion of how interest groups have tripled since the 1960s, see Jack Walker (1991).

8   My understanding of democratic representation suggests two reasons why the agency of democratic citizens cannot be reserved exclusively for election day. First, not all those who represent democratic citizens are elected, so such a focus ignores the power of informal representatives in representative democracies. Second, the danger of reserving the agency of democratic citizens to the choice of representatives is that it ignores other forms of accountability; for example, fiscal accountability and peer accountability.

9   Here, I explicitly disagree with those theorists who treat political participation as irrelevant to democratic citizenship. Some appeal to the ignorance of democratic citizens to argue that democratic representation should not demand too much from citizens (Schumpeter, 1976). While I agree that democratic citizens can have more important things on their minds than the health of their democratic institutions, and democratic citizens should certainly be free to withdraw from political life if they choose, we should recognize that democratic institutions will be accountable and responsive only if citizens retain the capacities needed for active citizenship. Democratic citizens must be able to participate effectively when they choose to intervene, monitor, deliberate, and mobilize. Such a perspective can acknowledge the fact that many citizens opt out of political engagement much of the time.

10   Here, I follow Martha Nussbaum (1990), who emphasizes the role of choice in determining the proper ways of assessing human development. For Nussbaum, the state should not impose its conception on the good. Rather, the state should provide the conditions that would allow individuals to make their own choices regarding the good. They need to be given "the necessary conditions for the exercise of choice and practical reason (among which will be education, political participation, and the absence of degrading forms of labor)" (216). While Nussbaum stresses the capacities necessary for human flourishing, my focus is on the capacities necessary for the well-functioning of democratic institutions.

11   Given the range of capacities that democratic citizens need, I fully expect arguments about good democratic representatives to dovetail with arguments about the capacities needed for full democratic citizenship.

12 For a discussion of how qualifications for rights are bundled, see Judith Failer (2002).

13 Judith Shklar (1985) notes that "one can imagine only too readily that people might look forward to a state of material comfort without political responsibilities or the conflicts imposed by freedom." She then wisely adds that "the power to govern is the power to influence fear and cruelty" and that "no amount of benevolence can ever suffice to protect an unarmed population against them." For this reason, she contends, representative institutions need to institutionalize suspicion since "only a distrustful population can be relied on to watch out for its rights, to ward off fear, and to be able to make their own projects, whether these be modest or great" (238).

14 Given the tensions between criticism and trust, it would appear that any measure of critical trust must exist along a continuum.

15 For George Kateb (1981), what is morally distinctive of representative institutions is the fact that citizens are able to develop critical distance to their political institutions. For Kateb, democratic citizens are also more likely to be skeptical of political authority and therefore be more vigilant about their own political beliefs and interests. Thus, his view is, like mine, one on which the presence of distrust can be consistent with the flourishing of democratic institutions.

16 Anne Phillips (1995), in contrast, dismisses the role model argument for descriptive representation as irrelevant to democratic theory. However, with David Campbell and Christina Wolbrecht (2006), I contend that democratic representatives influence whether and how citizens talk about politics. Moreover, it is important to think about how democratic representatives – both formal and informal – often by example "mentor" other representatives, teaching them the "rules of the game," such as those governing fundraising. See Amanda Driscoll and Kris Kanthak (2006).

17 For a fuller discussion of moral exemplars, see Suzanne Dovi (2005).

18 The second virtue of democratic representation also seems to leave out of its account the importance of democratic representatives' engaging with certain vulnerable groups, especially those groups that live within democratic borders but who are not citizens; for example, illegal immigrants.

19 These citizens most obviously must rely on the benevolence of those who advance public policies on their behalf.

20 For a different understanding of the rationality of public opinion, see Benjamin Page and Ian Shapiro (1992). For criticisms of existing ways of measuring democratic citizens' capacities, see John Dryzek (2005) and Shawn Rosenberg (2005).

21 Notice that the distribution of capacities throughout the citizenry matters. For this reason, the problem of making democratic representation responsive to constituents' interests needs to be considered in conjunction with the

capacities of elites within disadvantaged groups to serve as good informal representatives. In particular, one needs to take account of these citizens' capacities to represent in a democratic fashion to mitigate the incompetence of other citizens.

Chapter 6, pages 145–78

1　The K Street Project later fell into political disrepute because of its links to Jack Abramoff, a top Washington lobbyist who pleaded guilty to corruption, embezzlement, and bribery charges in January 2006. Abramoff became a "symbol of a system out of control" (Birnbaum and Balz, 2006), leading some to rethink the lawmaker–lobbyist relationship.

2　Note that the term "constituents" is multiply ambiguous (cf. Chapter 3).

3　Contemporary political theorists such as Nancy Fraser (1997, 2000) and Charles Taylor (1992) have argued for the importance of recognition for justice. For a critical discussion of mutual recognition as equals, see Patchen Markell (2003). For Markell, not only is mutual recognition as equals imposs-ible, but its incoherence can blind us to how mutual recognition can be the "medium for injustice" (4). Calls for mutual recognition can, in fact, disguise subordination – that is, the ways of "patterning and arranging the world that allow some people and groups to enjoy a semblance of sovereign agency at others' expense" (2003, 5). Markell points out how the desire for sovereign agency, a concept that underlies conceptions of democracy as self-rule, can thereby sustain forms of injustice. Markell raises the possibility that a little alienation from one's political institutions, and from one's fellow citizens, can be desirable.

4　For example, Richard Fenno (2003, 3) describes the notion of representation that underlies his research as "a home relationship, one that begins in the constituency and ends there."

5　Democratic theorists do place some restrictions on the actions of democratic representatives. For instance, Alvin Goldman (1980) argues that democratic representatives should be responsive so long as the representative does not violate "the negative rights" of democratic citizens. Negative rights are claims not to be treated a certain way; specifically, the claims of citizens that the government should not infringe on their civil and political liberties. Civil and political liberties set boundaries on the actions of democratic representatives. Most of the business of politics is therefore outside the scope of democratic norms. Such a vision of democratic representation ignores how oppression can occur in ways other than depriving citizens of their formal rights.

6　John Dryzek (2005) and Shawn Rosenberg (2005) raise some important objec-tions to the empirical ways of testing democratic citizens' capacities.

7   In contrast to much of the literature on descriptive representation, Iris Marion Young (2000) denies that we should choose representatives for their similarities. For, she argues, to make such choices is to ignore the problem of one person representing the many: the problem that, given the diversity that exists within any constituency, it is impossible for one person to resemble all aspects of his or her constituency. As the only adequate way of dealing with this problem, Young recommends that we adopt an understanding of representation as "a differentiated relationship." She understands representation as a process in which traces of authorization and accountability can be discerned in the actions of representatives. Good democratic representation should be evaluated by the extent to which the relationship between representative and constituents "avoids separation" and "renews connection" (128–30). Young never adequately addresses what kind of connection is needed. My discussion of mutual relations is an attempt to explicate the kinds of separation and connection that are vital to good democratic representation.

8   For a helpful overview of the research on citizen trust and government trustworthiness, see Margaret Levi and Laura Stoker (2000).

9   As discussed in Chapter 5, I also hold trust as an important feature of democratic representation. However, my emphasis on critical trust recognizes that citizens must maintain both a certain skepticism and faith in democratic institutions. My argument is that the existing literature on trust has not adequately incorporated the insight that trust is necessary under conditions of distrust.

10 As noted in Chapter 5, however, the function of democratic citizens includes a passive, or receptive, aspect (cf., n. 2). I should note that Plotke, in stressing the need for active participation by citizens, does not himself discuss the trust paradigm for democratic representation.

11 This mutual recognition puts certain demands on the transparency of a democratic representative's actions. In particular, this recognition demands that democratic representatives do not hide their efforts for democratic reform. Some democratic representatives might, in some circumstances, have good reason to hide such efforts. I have in mind situations in which public disclosure of efforts for democratic reform undermine the prospects of those efforts' success. But such closet democrats can be good democratic representatives only if they avoid vicious hypocrisy. For a discussion of vicious hypocrisy, see Suzanne Dovi (2001).

12 Contemporary political theorists have recognized the importance of mutual recognition among democratic citizens. In particular, Charles Taylor (1992, 25–6) contends that misrecognition or nonrecognition can be a harm and an injustice. A person's identity partially depends on how others recognize that person. What I am suggesting is that there is a particular relation of mutual recognition, specifically between representatives and the represented, that

can partially constitute the identity of constituents, and that this relation must be realized in any healthy indirect democracy.

13   I borrow the term "linked fate" from Michael Dawson (1994). Dawson uses the term to describe how African-Americans believe that their self-interests are linked to the interests of their racial group. In other words, individuals believe that "what happens to the group as a whole affects their own lives" (77). In particular, African-Americans consider having an African-American representative to be an advance for their racial group. Dawson's account of linked fate is limited to the way in which a particular disadvantaged group experiences its identity. In contrast, my view expands his understanding of linked fate so that it captures how representatives can promote that connection and how democratic citizens should understand their identity as democratic citizens.

14   For an interesting biographical account of Mayor Curley, see Beatty (2000).

15   My discussion of Mandela's response to Hani's assassination relies heavily on Kenneth Zagacki (2003).

16   Quoted from Kenneth Zagacki (2003, 716).

17   Richard Fenno (2003b) does not specifically claim that "homestyles" are somehow distinctive of democratic representatives, nor does he explicitly draw the conclusion that such forms of identification serve an important function in democratic polities.

18   In her discussion of the personalized nature of contemporary politics, Judith Shklar (1985) notes that representatives need to satisfy the emotional needs of democratic citizens in addition to their policy preferences. For Shklar, "the rulers, presidents, and lesser elected leaders who cannot satisfy the affective demands of the electorate will not be sufficiently trusted to 'handle' the strains imposed on a government by such disasters as war and economic depressions" (220). Implicit in Shklar's discussion is the claim that gyroscopic representation is particularly necessary in times of crises.

19   David Price (1985) notes that taking a broad view of one's representative role does not have to be "self-sacrificial." He writes that "Legislators often find it politically profitable to cultivate new constituencies, and to appeal over the heads of contending groups to a broader public concerned with one issue or another. Such strategies do not work automatically: legislators must *work* at increasing the salience and attractiveness of their policy stances" (138).

20   For the purposes of my argument here, I limit my discussion to democratic citizens. In this way, I have consciously set aside whether democratic representatives have obligations to noncitizens, such as legal residents, illegal residents, refugees, and citizens of other states. As mentioned before, democratic institutions can possess competing norms of accountability: democratic institutions are supposed to be accountable to those affected by public policies as well as to those who have entrusted them with power. For now, it will

suffice to acknowledge that democratic norms are not entirely clear about how much democratic representatives owe noncitizens.

21 For a discussion of why democracies need to exclude foreigners, see Avery Kolers (2002).

22 Andrew Sabl (2002) goes further, stating that "Responsive senators in theory and in actual practice – neither demonize opponents' positions as false, unjust or stupid, nor expect their opponents ever to be fully persuaded by argument, given that they have distinctive local interests and ideals to uphold" (163).

23 Andrew Sabl (2005) describes "democratic sportsmanship" as a core virtue of liberal democratic citizenship. For Sabl, "democratic citizens must be good losers, willing to accept with good grace and no loss of commitment to the polity, that the democratic game will not always go their way" (216). I would add that democratic representatives also need to win well. When they find a political victory thrilling, they must temper that thrill with the realization that, for the sake of maintaining the legitimacy of democratic institutions, they must avoid indulging in behavior that is apt to humiliate their opponents. A representative's capacity to win or lose gracefully, and not just his willingness to step down when he loses an election or to accept a public policy outcome, is crucial for the well-functioning of democratic institutions.

24 For a discussion of the negative effects of political advertisements on democratic institutions, see Stephen Ansolabehere and Shanto Iyengar (1996).

25 In requiring good democratic representatives to reach out to their opponents, my ethics of democratic representation rejects a growing practice of encouraging only certain targeted citizens to participate in American politics.

26 The dispossessed are by no means limited to the poor. For other groups – for example, the sick, the incarcerated, and certain religious groups – can lack the resources needed to maintain their status as equal citizens.

27 As John Gardner (1973, 55) noted, "All citizens should have equal access to decision-making processes of government, but money makes some citizens more equal than others." Exactly how money favors the well off is an extremely controversial matter. Political scientists have been unable to link the role of money – for example, lobbying or campaign financing – to obtaining certain votes. Money "buys" access, not votes.

28 Mark Warren (2001b) emphasizes how groups that suffer from social and economic inequalities can rely on the mobilization of other groups.

29 Here one should keep in mind that, in developing mutual relations with the poor, a good democratic representative will help the poor develop some kind of shared understanding of their interests. As Virginia Sapiro (1981) reminds us, "political systems are not likely to represent previously unrepresented groups until those groups develop a sense of their own interests and place demands upon the system. This requires the development of political consciousness and political activism based on this new group consciousness" (704).

30   For this reason, I concur with Andrew Sabl (2002) that senators should be evaluated by their "constant opposition to the influence of big money in legislative campaigns and legislators' decisions" (152). This claim, however, should not be limited to senators but extended to all democratic representatives.

31   For those who equate a good representative with a zealous advocate, winning is everything.

32   For a discussion of those theorists who equate democraticization with inclusion, see John Dryzek (1996).

33   At least under certain circumstances, the ideal of mutual recognition can be impossible to achieve. Moreover, as Markell points out, in attempting to approximate this ideal, humans face "practical limits imposed on [them] . . . by the openness and unpredictability of the future" (5). However, a somewhat different lesson can be drawn from these limits – namely, that humans cannot know ahead of time when forms of mutual recognition can be improved. So while Markell calls for a "politics of acknowledgement" – that is, a politics that is aware of how circumstances set limits on how humans can recognize each other – I contend that good democratic representatives should respond to these practical limits by trying to develop mutual relations, and thereby the virtue of good gatekeeping, as much as possible. Note that my understanding of good gatekeeping does not disguise the ways in which good democratic representation can require isolation, alienation, and exclusion; rather, it seeks to minimize those forms of isolation, alienation, and exclusion that can also contribute to subordination.

34   By emphasizing the very individualist message of "What you can do" instead of identifying ways in which the community needs to respond to polluters, the Earth Day parade made political solutions – for example, additional environmental legislation – less likely (see Britell, 1996).

Chapter 7, pages 179–200

1   The term "preferability" is ambiguous. On the one hand, preferability can refer exclusively to the preferences of democratic citizens. According to this first meaning, preferable representatives are those who democratic citizens find more desirable. On the other hand, preferability can refer to the degree to which a representative conforms to a particular set of standards. In the second sense of "preferable," a representative may be preferable to other representatives, regardless of the actual popularity of the representatives among the represented. My understanding of preferability is a version of the second, but does not sever preferability entirely from the actual preferences of democratic citizens. For while the three virtues provide standards for evaluating

representatives, these standards themselves are not, on my account, entirely independent of the perceptions that democratic citizens have of their representatives.

2   For a discussion of system-dependency, see Amy Gutmann and Dennis Thompson (1985). While my understanding of system-dependency draws significantly on their work, it differs in one important respect: whereas Gutmann and Thompson focus exclusively on legislators, my discussion of preferable democratic representatives includes informal as well as formal representatives.

3   For a discussion of the reasons why descriptive representation is necessary, see Chapter 2.

4   Besides, the identities of historically disadvantaged groups are sufficiently complex that they overlap with members of dominant groups as well as with members of other historically disadvantaged groups. The ability of descriptive representatives from those groups to reach out to members of their group requires that they are sensitive to the internal diversity within their group as well as to points of alliance and common ground with other citizens. In order for descriptive representatives to be effective, to develop the political capacities of their constituents, and to foster the right mutual relations, they must be able to reach beyond their groups, as they are narrowly understood. Such insularity is a luxury that descriptive representatives for historically disadvantaged groups cannot afford.

5   Choices among the different virtues are a special class of the difficult choices that good democratic representatives face. Representatives who seek to carry out their democratic commitments must negotiate "the paradox of representation" differently than those who seek merely to do a good job of representing their own constituents. It is important to recognize the distinctive difficulties faced by good democratic representatives, because this helps citizens to recognize the costs associated with democratic representation. Instead of understanding the three virtues of democratic representation as "pure" ideals, it is important to understand how these ideals create certain problems.

6   Michael Walzer (1973) argues that such dilemmas are pervasive in the political arena and that, as a consequence, public officials who enter the political arena cannot govern innocently. I am not prepared to make such a strong claim about the extent to which these different virtues conflict. My point is a more modest one that good democratic representation is difficult and rare.

7   Of course some theorists, such as A. John Simmons (1979), claim that wherever obligations conflict, there is always a right choice about which obligation to privilege. I do not pretend to have given an adequate argument against Simmons here. For a discussion of genuine conflicting obligations, see E. J. Lemmon (1962) and Bernard Williams (1973).

8   These Councils provide voluntary advice to the board of executives on issues such as mergers and reorganizations, and possess a conditional veto on issues such as pensions and grievance procedures.

9   This tension is likely to be aggravated when a group defines itself in opposition to another group. For example, the fact that white supremacists tie their identity to their perception of the inferiority of blacks puts the virtue of fair-mindedness in a direct clash with the virtue of good gatekeeping. For it will, to say the least, be difficult to maintain mutual relations with white supremacists while at the same time seeking to educate them about the equality of races and distancing oneself from their abhorrent views about blacks. Here is a situation in which the good democratic representative will feel the pressure to stand with blacks, even if that means foreclosing any opportunity to maintain mutual relations with white supremacists.

10   Even when citizens consent to having restraints placed on their participation (as in the case of Northern whites in SNCC), such actions would seemingly go against the actions required of the second virtue.

11   Here it is useful to recall a finding by John Hibbing and Elizabeth Theiss-Morse (2002), discussed in Chapter 3: democratic citizens have unreasonable expectations about the amount of agreement that obtains among democratic citizens, and this false expectation leads to their being easily discouraged by democratic politics.

12   The tensions among the virtues thus yields a conclusion similar to one that Andrew Sabl reaches from other considerations: "Different politicians should be seen *as embodying different virtues* – partly because no single role can accomplish all that we want politicians to perform; partly because politicians, like all people, are different from one another and legitimately seek positions that fit comfortably with those differences; and partly because politicians differ in their constituencies, institutions, and social forces to whom they are responsible" (2005, 212). Sabl's understanding of the virtues emphasizes the virtues of those "active in politics," while my account emphasizes the need for both representatives and citizens to be engaged in good democratic representation.

13   For a more detailed discussion of the need for a variety of actors in the political arena, see Suzanne Dovi (2005).

14   Democratic citizens do not necessarily wholeheartedly embrace the representatives whom they have chosen. Often, democratic citizens endorse a particular representative because she is simply the least bad option. Democratic citizens rarely face choices of representatives who embody all aspects of what they are looking for in a representative, let alone a democratic representative. For a discussion of the differences that exist among all representatives and their constituents, see Iris Marion Young (2004).

15   A lot of attention has been paid to the incumbency effect on the chances that representatives will be reelected. In particular, the effect of incumbency is

thought to decrease the accountability of elected officials. From my perspective, the issue is not how long incumbents stay in office but the performance of those representatives in terms of the three virtues. Rather, my ethics suggests that the real issue is whether an incumbent is a bad democratic representative who should be voted out of office.

16   Indeed, the institutional design can play a significant role in shaping the activities of representatives; for example, the types of strategies that representatives use to be effective, or their willingness to approximate the three virtues. For example, the ability of a descriptive representative for African-Americans to realize the virtue of fair-mindedness will depend on the extent to which the redrawing of his electoral district has diluted the black vote.

References

Achen, Christopher 1975: Mass political attitudes and the survey response. *American Political Science Review*, 69, 1218–31.

—— 1977: Measuring representation: perils of the correlation coefficient. *American Journal of Political Science*, 21(4), 805–15.

Acker, Joan 2000: Revisiting class: thinking from gender, race, and organizations. *Social Politics*, Summer, 192–213.

Ackerman, Bruce and John Fishkin 2002: Deliberation day. *Journal of Political Philosophy*, 10(2), 129–33.

Adams, John 1852–65: A defense of the constitutions of government of the United States of America, against the attack of M. Turgot, in his letter to Dr. Price, dated the twenty-second day of March, 1778. In Charles Francis Adams (ed.), *The Works of John Adams*, vol. VI. Boston: Little, Brown, 220.

Alcoff, Linda 1995: The problem of speaking for others. In Judith Roof and Robyn Wiegman (eds.), *Who Can Speak*. Chicago: University of Illinois Press, 97–119.

Alvarez, Sonia 1997: Latin American feminisms "go global": trends of the 1990s and challenges for the new millennium. In Sonia Alvarez (ed.), *Culture of Politics/Politics of Cultures Revisioning Latin American Social Movements*. New York: Westview Press, 731–54.

Annas, Julia 1994: *Morality of Happiness*. Oxford: Oxford University Press.

—— 1996: Aristotle on human nature and political virtue. *The Review of Metaphysics*, 49(4), 731–54.

Ansolabehere, Stephen and Shanto Iyengar 1996: *Going Negative: How Political Advertisements Shrink and Polarize the Electorate*. New York: The Free Press.

Applbaum, Arthur 1999: *Ethics for Adversaries: The Morality of Roles in Public and Professional Life*. Princeton, NJ: Princeton University Press.

Aristotle 1970 [1831]: *Nicomachean Ethics*, trans. J. A. K. Thomson. New York: Penguin.

Arnold, Douglas 1990: *Logic of Congressional Action*. New Haven, CT: Yale University Press.

Baker, Richard 1985: The history of congressional ethics. In Bruce Jennings and Daniel Callahan (eds.), *Representation and Responsibility: Exploring Legislative Ethics*. New York: Plenum Press, pp. 3–27.

Barber, Benjamin 1984: *Strong Democracy*. Berkeley, CA: University of California Press.

Barry, Brian 1990 [1965]: *Political Argument*, 2nd edn. London: Harvester Wheatsheaf.

Baumgartner, Frank and Beth Leech 1998: *Basic Interests: the Importance of Groups in Politics and in Political Science*. Princeton, NJ: Princeton University Press.

Beatty, Jack 2000: *The Rascal King*. New York: DaCapo Press.

Beitz, Charles 1990: *Political Equality*. Princeton, NJ: Princeton University Press.

Berelson, Bernard, Paul Lazarsfeld, and William McPhee 1954: *Voting: A Study of Opinion Formation in a Presidential Campaign*. Chicago: The University of Chicago Press.

Bermeo, Nancy 2003: *Ordinary People in Extraordinary Times: The Citizenry and the Breakdown of Democracy*. Princeton, NJ: Princeton University Press.

Berry, Jeffrey 1984: *The Interest Group Society*. Boston: Little, Brown.

Bickford, Susan 1996: *Dissonance of Democracy: Listening, Conflict, and Citizenship*. Ithaca, NY: Cornell University Press.

—— 1999: Reconfiguring pluralism: identity and institutions in the inegalitarian polity. *American Journal of Political Science*, 43 (January), 86–108.

Birnbaum, Jeffrey H. 1992. *The Lobbyists: How Influence Peddlers Get Their Way in Washington*. New York: Random House.

—— 2000: *The Money Men: The Real Story of Fund-Raising's Influence on Political Power in America*. New York: Crown.

—— and Dan Balz 2006: Case bringing new scrutiny to a system and a profession. *The Washington Post*, January 4, A01.

Britell, Jim 1996: A plan to reform Earth Day. Available at www.britell.com/use/use17.html (accessed February 9, 2006).

Brown, Clyde and Herbert Waltzer 2004: Virtual sources: organized interest and democraticization by the Web. *Social Science Journal*, 41(4), 543–58.

Buchanan, James and Gordon Tullock 1962: *The Calculus of Consent: Logical Foundations of Constitutional Democracy*. Ann Arbor, MI: University of Michigan Press.

Bunce, Valerie 2000: Comparative democraticization: big and bounded generalizations. *Comparative Political Studies*, 33(6), 703–35.

Burke, Edmund 1968 [1790]: *Reflections on the Revolution in France*. London: Penguin.

—— 1999 [1774]: *Select Works of Edmund Burke*. Indianapolis: Liberty Fund.

Cain, Bruce, John Ferejohn, and Morris Fiorina 1987: *The Personal Vote*. Cambridge, MA: Harvard University Press.

Cammisa, Anne Marie 1995: *Governments as Interest Groups: Intergovernmental Lobbying and the Federal System*. London: Praeger.

Campbell, Angus, Philip E. Converse, Warren E. Miller, and Donald E. Stokes 1960: *The American Voter*. New York: Wiley.

Campbell, David and Christina Wolbrecht 2006: See Jane run: women politicians as role models for adolescents. *Journal of Politics*, 68(2), 233–47.

Cannon, C. 1935: *Cannon's Precedents of the House of Representatives*. Washington, DC: US Government Printing Office.

Carens, Joseph 2000: *Culture, Citizenship & Community A Contextual Exploration of Justice as Evenhandedness*. New York: Oxford University Press.

Carson, Clayborne 1982: *In Struggle: SNCC and the Black Awakening of the 1960s*. Cambridge, MA: Harvard University Press.

Chambers, Simone and Jeffrey Kopstein 2001: Bad civil society. *Political Theory*, 29(6), 837–66.

—— and Will Kymlicka (eds.) 2002: *Alternative Conceptions of Civil Society*. Princeton, NJ: Princeton University Press.

Chapman, John and William Galston 1992: *Virtue*. New York: New York University Press.

Christiano, Thomas 1996: *The Rule of the Many*. Boulder, CO: Westview Press.

Cohen, Cathy 1997: Straight gay politics: the limits of an ethnic model of inclusion. In Ian Shapiro and Will Kymlicka (eds.), *Nomos XXXIX: Ethnicity and Group Rights*. New York: New York University, 572–617.

—— 1999: *The Boundaries of Blackness: AIDS and the Breakdown of Black Politics*. Chicago: The University of Chicago Press.

——, Kathleen B. Jones, and Joan C. Tronto 1997: *Women Transforming Politics*. New York: New York University Press.

Cohen, Joshua and Joel Rogers 1995: *Associations and Democracy*. The Real Utopias Project, Erik Olin Wright (ed.), vol. 1. London: Verso.

Collins, Patricia 1990: *Black Feminist Thought: Knowledge, Consciousness, and the Politics of Empowerment*. Boston: Unwin Hyman.

Connolly, William 1995: *The Ethos of Pluralization*. Minneapolis: University of Minnesota Press.

Converse, Philip 1964: The nature of belief systems in mass publics. In David Apter (ed.), *Ideology and Discontent*. New York: The Free Press, 206–61.

Crisp, Roger and Michael Slote 1997: *Virtue Ethics*. Oxford: Oxford University Press.

Dagger, Richard 1997: *Civic Virtues*. New York: Oxford University Press.

Dahl, Robert A. 1989: *Democracy and Its Critics*. New Haven, CT: Yale University Press.

—— 1998: Equality versus inequality. *PS: Political Science and Politics*, 29(4), 639–48.

Dawson, Michael C. 1994. *Behind the Mule: Race and Class in African-American Politics*. Princeton, NJ: Princeton University Press.

Dean, Jodi 1996: *Solidarity of Strangers*. Los Angeles: University of California Press.

d'Entreves, Maurizio Passerin 1992: Hannah Arendt and the idea of citizenship. In Chantal Mouffe (ed.), *Dimensions of Radical Democracy*. London: Verso, 145–68.

Deschler, Lewis 1977: *Deschler's Precedents of the United States House of Representatives*. H. Doc. 94–661. Serial Set No. 13151-2. Washington, DC: US Government Printing Office.

De Tocqueville, Alexis 2003 [1835]: *Democracy in America*, trans. Gerald Bevan. New York: Penguin.

Diamond, Irene and Nancy Hartstock 1981: Beyond interests in politics: a comment on Virginia Sapiro's "When are interests interests? The problem of political representation of women." *The American Political Science Review*, 75(3), 717–21.

Dillard, Angela 2001: *Guess Who's Coming to Dinner Now? Multicultural Conservatism in America*. New York: New York University Press.

di Stefano, Christine 1997: Integrating gender into the political science curriculum: challenges, pitfalls, and opportunities. *PS: Political Science and Politics*, 30(2), 204–6.

Dobel, J. Patrick 1990: *Compromise and Political Action: Political Morality in Liberal and Democratic Life*. New York: Rowman & Littlefield.

Dovi, Suzanne 2001: Making the world safe for hypocrisy? *Polity*, 34(1), 3–33.

—— 2002: Preferable descriptive representatives: or will just any woman, black, or Latino do? *American Political Science Review*, 96, 745–54.

—— 2005: Guilt and the problem of dirty hands. *Constellations: An International Journal of Critical & Democratic Theory*, 12(1), 128–46.

Dowie, Mark 1995: *Losing Ground: American Environmentalism at the Close of the Twentieth Century*. Cambridge, MA: The MIT Press.

Downs, Anthony 1957: *An Economic Theory of Democracy*. New York: Harper.

Driscoll, Amanda and Kristin Kanthak 2006: Patterns of colleague support in the U.S. House: why Democrats have an "old girls network," but Republican women want to be "just one of the boys." Unpublished manuscript, University of Arizona.

Driver, Julia 2000: *Uneasy Virtue*. Cambridge, UK: Cambridge University Press.

Dryzek, John 1996: Political inclusion and the dynamics of democratization. *American Political Science Review*, 90 (September), 475–87.

—— 2005: Handle with care: the deadly hermeneutics of deliberative instrumentation. *Acta Politica*, 40, 197–211.

DuBois, W. E. B. 1969: *The Souls of Black Folk*. New York: Penguin.

Easton, David and Jack Dennis 1967: The child's acquisition of regime norms: political efficacy. *The American Political Science Review*, 61(1), 25–38.

Engelen, Ewald 2004: Problems of descriptive representation in Dutch Work Councils. *Political Studies*, 52, 491–507.

Failer, Judith 2002: *Who Qualifies for Rights?: Homelessness, Mental Illness, and Civil Commitment*. Ithaca, NY: Cornell University Press.

Fenno, Richard F. 2002: *Home Style: House Members in Their Districts*. New York: Longman Classics.

—— 2003: *Going Home: Black Representatives and Their Constituents*. Chicago: The University of Chicago Press.

Flathman, Richard 1998: "It all depends . . . on how one understands liberalism": a brief response to Stephen Macedo. *Political Theory*, 26(1), 81–4.

Fraser, Nancy 1996: Rethinking the public sphere: a contribution to the critique of actually existing democracies. In Cheshire Calhoun (ed.), *Habermas and the Public Sphere*. Cambridge MA: The MIT Press.

—— 1997: *Justice Interruptus: Critical Reflections on the "PostSocialist" Condition*. New York: Routledge.

—— 2000: Rethinking recognition. *New Left Review*, May/June, 107–20.

Galston, William 1991: *Liberal Purposes: Goods, Virtues, and Diversity in the Liberal State*. Cambridge, UK: Cambridge University Press.

Gardner, John 1973: *In Common Cause*. New York: Norton.

Gaventa, John 1982: *Power and Powerlessness: Quiescence and Rebellion in an Applachian Valley*. Urbana, IL: University of Illinois Press.

Gay, Claudine 2001: The effect of black congressional representation on political participation. *American Political Science Review*, 95, 589–602.

—— 2002: Spirals of trust? *American Journal of Political Science*, 4, 717–32.

Goldman, Alvin 1980: *The Moral Foundations of Professional Ethics*. Totowa, NJ: Rowman & Littlefield.

Goldstein, Kenneth M. 1999: *Interest Groups, Lobbying, and Participation in America*. Cambridge, UK: Cambridge University Press.

Goodin, Robert 1980: *Manipulatory Politics*. New Haven, CT: Yale University Press.

Goodwin, Doris 2005: *Team of Rivals: The Political Genius of Abraham Lincoln*. New York: Simon & Schuster.

Gould, Carol 1996: Diversity and democracy: representing differences. In Seyla Benhabib (ed.), *Democracy and Difference: Contesting the Boundaries of the Political*. Princeton, NJ: Princeton University Press, 171–86.

Grant, Ruth and Robert O. Keohane 2005: Accountability and abuses of power in world politics. *American Political Science Review*, 99, 29–44.

Green, Phillip 1993: "Democracy" as a contested idea. In Phillip Green (ed.), *Democracy: Key Concepts in Critical Theory*. Amherst, NY: Humanities Press, 2–18.

Greider, William 1992: *Who Will Tell the People?: The Betrayal of American Democracy*. New York: Simon & Schuster.

Griffiths, A. Phillips and Richard Wollheim 1960: How can one person represent another? *Aristotelian Society*, Suppl. 34, 182–208.

Grunwald, Michael 2001: Business lobbyists asked to discuss onerous rules. *The Washington Post,* December 4, A03.

Guinier, Lani 1994: *The Tyranny of the Majority: Fundamental Fairness in Representative Democracy.* New York: The Free Press.

Gutmann, Amy and Dennis Thompson 1985: The theory of legislative ethics. In Bruce Jennings and Daniel Callahan (eds.), *Representation and Responsibility.* New York: Plenum Press, 167–95.

—— and —— 2004: *Why Deliberative Democracy?* Princeton, NJ: Princeton University Press.

Habermas, Jürgen 1976: *The Legitimation Crisis.* London: Heinemann.

Hampshire, Stuart 2000: *Justice is Conflict.* Princeton, NJ: Princeton University Press.

Hampton, Henry and Steve Fayer (eds.) 1990: *Voices of Freedom: An Oral History of the Civil Rights Movement from the 1950s through the 1980s.* New York: Bantam.

Hansen, Mark 1991: *Gaining Access: Congress and the Farm Lobby, 1919–1981.* Chicago: The University of Chicago Press.

Hardin, Russell 2004: Representing ignorance. *Social Philosophy and Policy,* 21, 76–99.

Hayward, Clarissa 2000: *De-Facing Power.* New York: Cambridge University Press.

Held, David 1995: *Democracy and The Global Order.* Cambridge, UK: Polity Press.

Hibbing, John and Elizabeth Theiss-Morse 2002: *Stealth Democracy.* Cambridge, UK: Cambridge University Press.

Higginbotham, Evelyn 1992: African American women's history and the metalanguage of race. *Signs,* 17, 251–74.

Hochschild, Jennifer 1981: *What's Fair? American Beliefs about Distributive Justice.* Cambridge, MA: Harvard University Press.

—— 1995: *Facing Up to the American Dream: Race, Class, and the Soul of the Nation.* Princeton, NJ: Princeton University Press.

hooks, bell 2000: *Feminist Theory: From Margin to Center.* Cambridge, MA: South End Press.

Houston, Thomas 1985: Ethics in political campaigns. In Bruce Jennings and Daniel Callahan (eds.), *Representation and Responsibility: Exploring Legislative Ethics.* New York: Plenum Press, 67–88.

Hursthouse, Rosalind 1999: *On Virtue Ethics.* Oxford: Oxford University Press.

Jacobs, Lawrence R. and Robert Y. Shapiro 2000: *Politicians Don't Pander: Political Manipulation and the Loss of Democratic Responsiveness.* Chicago: The University of Chicago Press.

Johnson, Dennis 2001: *No Place for Amateurs: How Political Consultants are Reshaping American Democracy.* New York: Routledge.

Jones, Kathleen 1993: *Compassionate Authority: Democracy and the Representation of Women.* New York: Routledge.

Jordon, June 1995: Report from the Bahamas. In Margaret Andersen and Patricia Hill Collins (eds.), *Race, Class, and Gender: An Anthology*, 2nd edn. New York: Wadsworth.

Kateb, George 1981: The moral distinctiveness of representative democracy. *Ethics*, 91(3), 357–74.

Kernel, Samuel 1986: *Going Public: New Strategies of Presidential Leadership*. Washington, DC: Congressional Quarterly Press.

Kingdon, John W. 1984: *Agendas, Alternatives and Public Policies*. New York: HarperCollins.

Kolers, Avery 2002: The territorial state in cosmopolitan justice. *Social Theory & Practice*, 28(1), 29–50.

Kollman, Kenneth 1998: *Outside Lobbying*. Princeton, NJ: Princeton University Press.

Kovach, Hetty, Caroline Neligan, and Simon Burall 2003: *The Global Accountability Report: Power Without Accountability?* London: One World Trust.

Kuttner, Robert 2004: America as a one-party state. *American Prospect*, February 1, 18–24.

Lee, Julian 2004: NGO accountability: rights and responsibilities. Presented at The Programme on NGOs and Civil Society, The Center of Applied Studies in International Negotiations (CASIN), Geneva, Switzerland.

Lemmon, E. J. 1962: Moral dilemmas. *The Philosophical Review*, 71(2), 139–58.

Levi, Margaret and Laura Stoker 2000: Political Trust and trustworthiness. *Annual Review of Political Science*, 3(1), 475–508.

Lippmann, Walter 1922: *Public Opinion*. New York: Macmillan.

Lorde, Audre 1984: *Sister Outsider*. Trumansburg, NY: Crossing Press.

Lukes, Steven 1974: *Power: A Radical View*. New York: Macmillan.

Macdonald, Laura 1997: *Supporting Civil Society: The Political Role of Non-Governmental Organizations in Central America*. New York: St. Martin's Press.

Macedo, Stephen 1990: *Liberal Virtues: Citizenship, Virtue and Community in Liberal Constitutionalism*. Oxford: The Clarendon Press.

—— 1998a: Flathman's liberal shtick. *Political Theory*, 26(1), 85–9.

—— 1998b: Transformative constitutionalism and the case of religion: defending the moderate hegemony of liberalism. *Political Theory*, 26(1), 56–80.

McAdam, Doug 1983: Tactical innovation and the pace of insurgency. *American Sociological Review*, 48, 735–54.

McDowell, John 1979: Virtue and reason. *Monist*, 63, 331–50.

MacIntyre, Alasdair 1984: *After Virtue: A Study In Moral Theory*. South Bend, IN: University of Notre Dame Press.

MacRae, Duncan 1958: *Dimensions of Congressional Voting*. Berkeley, CA: University of California Press.

Madison, James, Alexander Hamilton and John Jay 1987 [1788]: *The Federalist Papers*, ed. Isaac Kramnick. Harmondsworth: Penguin.

Manin, Bernard 1997: *The Principles of Representative Government*. Cambridge, UK: Cambridge University Press.

Mansbridge, Jane 1983: *Beyond Adversarial Democracy*. Chicago: The University of Chicago Press.

—— 1986: *Why We Lost the ERA*. Chicago: The University of Chicago Press.

—— 1999: Should blacks represent blacks and women represent women? A contingent "Yes." *The Journal of Politics*, 61 (August), 628–57.

—— 2002: Rethinking representation. *American Political Science Review*, 97 (November), 515–28.

—— 2004a: Representation revisited: introduction to the case against electoral accountability. *Democracy and Society*, 2(1), 1, 12–13.

—— 2004b: The fallacy of tightening the reins. Keynote address, Austrian Political Science Association, Vienna, Austria, December 10.

Mara, Gerald M. 1997: *Socrates' Discursive Democracy*. Albany, NY: State University of New York Press.

—— 2000: The logos of the wise in the politeia of the many: recent books on Aristotle's political philosophy. *Political Theory*, 28, 835–60.

Markell, Patchen 2003: *Bound By Recognition*. Princeton, NJ: Princeton University Press.

Matland, Richard E. and Donley T. Studlar 1998: Gender and the electoral opportunity structure in the Canadian provinces. *Political Research Quarterly*, 51, 117–49.

Merton, Vanessa 1985: Legislative ethics and professional responsibility. In Bruce Jennings and Daniel Callahan (eds.), *Representation and Responsibility: Exploring Legislative Ethics*. New York: Plenum Press, 303–24.

Mill, John Stuart 1991 [1861]: *Considerations on Representative Government*. New York: Prometheus Books.

—— and Jeremy Bentham 1987: *Utilitarianism and Other Essays*, ed. Alan Ryan. New York: Penguin.

Miller, Warren and J. Merrill Shanks 1996: *The New American Voter*. Cambridge, MA: Harvard University Press.

—— and Donald Stokes 1963: Constituency influence in Congress. *American Political Science Review*, 57, 45–56.

Miller, William Ian 1997: *The Anatomy of Disgust*. Cambridge, MA: Harvard University Press.

Minow, Martha 1991: *Making All the Difference: Inclusion, Exclusion and American Law*. Ithaca, NY: Cornell University Press.

Morgan, Edmund 1975: *American Slavery American Freedom: The Ordeal of Colonial Virginia*. New York: W. W. Norton.

Morrow, Daniel R. 2003: Karl Rove: prince of push polling. Available at www.webdelsol.com/The_Potomac/politics-rove.htm (The Potomac, December 17) (retrieved from www.sourcewatch.org/index.php?title=Push_poll).

Nagel, Jack 1987: *Participation.* Englewood Cliffs, NJ: Prentice Hall.

Neckerman, Kathryn 2004: *Social Inequality.* New York: Russell Sage Foundation.

Nussbaum, Martha 1990: Aristotelian social democracy. In Bruce Douglass and Gerald Mara (eds.), *Liberalism and the Good.* New York: Routledge, 203–52.

—— 2000: *Women and Human Development: The Capabilities Approach.* Cambridge, UK: Cambridge University Press.

O'Donnell, Guillermo 1998: Horizontal accountability in new democracies. *Journal of Democracy,* 9(3), 112–26.

O'Neill, Onora 1996: *Towards Justice and Virtue: A Constructive Account of Practical Reasoning.* Cambridge, UK: Cambridge University Press.

Page, Benjamin and Ian Shapiro 1992: *The Rational Public: Fifty Years of Trends in Americans' Policy Preferences.* Chicago: The University of Chicago Press.

Paolino, Phillip 1995: Group-salient issues and group representation: support for women candidates in the 1992 Senate elections. *American Journal of Political Science,* 39 (May), 294–313.

Parker, Glenn R. and Roger H. Davidson 1979: Why do Americans love their congressmen so much more than their Congress? *Legislative Studies Quarterly,* 4, 53–61.

Pateman, Carole 1970: *Participation and Democratic Theory.* Cambridge, UK: Cambridge University Press.

Pennock, J. Roland 1979: *Democratic Political Theory.* Princeton, NJ: Princeton University Press.

Phillips, Anne 1991: *Engendering Democracy.* College Station: Penn State University.

—— 1995: *Politics of Presence.* New York: The Clarendon Press.

—— 1998: Democracy and representation: or, why should it matter who our representatives are? In Anne Phillips (ed.), *Feminism and Politics.* Oxford: Oxford University Press, 224–40.

Pilger, John 1998: *Hidden Agendas.* New York: New Press.

Pitkin, Hanna Fenichel 1967: *The Concept of Representation.* Berkeley, CA: University of California Press.

—— 2004: Representation and democracy: uneasy alliance. *Scandinavian Political Studies,* 27(3), 335.

Piven, Francis Fox and Richard Cloward 1979: *Poor People's Movements: Why They Succeed, How They Fail.* New York: Vintage.

Plotke, David 1997: Representation is democracy. *Constellations,* 4 (November 1), 19–34.

Popkin, Samuel 1991: *The Reasoning Voter.* Chicago: The University of Chicago Press.

Price, David 1985: Legislative ethics in the new Congress. In Bruce Jennings and Daniel Callahan (eds.), *Representation and Responsibility: Exploring Legislative Ethics.* New York: Plenum Press, 129–45.

Putnam, Robert D. 1993: *Making Democracy Work: Civic Traditions in Modern Italy.* Princeton, NJ: Princeton University Press.

Rai, Shirin M. 1999: Democratic institutions, political representation and women's empowerment: the quota debate in India. *Democratization*, 6(3), 84–99.

Rawls, John 1971: *A Theory of Justice.* Cambridge, MA: Harvard University Press.

Reed, Adolph Jr. 1999: *Stirrings in the Jug.* Minneapolis: University of Minnesota Press.

Rehfeld, Andrew 2005: *The Concept of Constituency: Political Representation, Democratic Legitimacy and Institutional Design.* Cambridge, UK: Cambridge University Press.

—— 2006: Towards a general theory of political representation. *Journal of Politics*, 68(1), 1–21.

Richter, Melvin 1982: Toward a concept of political illegitimacy. *Political Theory*, 10(2), 185–214.

Rosenberg, Shawn 2005: The empirical study of deliberative democracy: setting a research agenda. *Acta Politica*, 40(2), 212–25.

Rosenstone, Steven and John Hansen 1993: *Mobilization, Participation, and Democracy in America.* New York: Macmillan.

Sabl, Andrew 2002: *Ruling Passions: Political Offices and Democratic Ethics.* Princeton, NJ: Princeton University Press.

—— 2005: Virtue for pluralists. *Journal of Moral Philosophy*, 2(2), 207–35.

Salisbury, Robert 1984: Interest representation: the dominance of institutions. *American Political Science Review*, 78(1), 64–76.

Sapiro, Virginia 1981: When are interests interesting? *American Political Science Review*, 75 (September), 701–21.

Saxon, John 1985: The scope of legislative ethics. In Bruce Jennings and Daniel Callahan (eds.), *Representation and Responsibility: Exploring Legislative Ethics.* New York: Plenum Press, 197–219.

Schaar, John 1981: *Legitimacy in the Modern State.* New Brunswick, NJ: Transaction.

Schattschneider, E. E. 1960: *The Semisovereign People.* New York: Holt, Rinehart, and Winston.

Schier, Steven 2000: *By Invitation Only: The Rise of Exclusive Politics in the United States.* Pittsburgh, PA: University of Pittsburgh.

Schumpeter, Joseph 1976: *Capitalism, Socialism, and Democracy.* London: George Allen and Unwin.

Shapiro, Ian 1994: Three ways to be a democrat. *Political Theory*, 22(1), 124–51.

—— 2003: *The State of Democratic Theory.* Princeton, NJ: Princeton University Press.

Shklar, Judith N. 1985: *Ordinary Vices.* Cambridge, MA: The Belknap Press of Harvard University Press.

Simmons, A. John 1979: *Moral Duties and Political Obligations.* Princeton, NJ: Princeton University Press.

Skocpol, Theda and Morris Fiorina 1999: *Civic Engagement in American Democracy.* Washington, DC: Russell Sage Foundation.

Slaughter, Louise 2005: Broken promises: the death of deliberative democracy. A congressional report on the unprecedented erosion of the democratic process in the 108th Congress. Washington, DC: US House of Representatives.

Slim, Hugo 2002: By what authority? The legitimacy and accountability of NGOs. *Journal of Humanitarian Assistance.* Available at www.jha.ac/articles/a082.htm

Slote, Michael 1993: *From Morality to Virtue.* Oxford: Oxford University Press.

Smith, Rogers 1997: *Civic Ideals.* New Haven, CT: Yale University Press.

Stark, Andrew 2000: *Conflict of Interest in American Public Life.* Cambridge, MA: Harvard University Press.

Stasiulis, Daiva 1993: Authentic voice: anti-racist politics in Canadian feminist publishing and literary production. In Sneja Gunew and Anne Yeatman (eds.), *Feminism and the Politics of Difference.* Halifax, NS: Fernwood, 35–60.

Stokes, Donald and Warren Miller 1962: Party government and the saliency of Congress. *Public Opinion Quarterly*, 26, 531–46.

Stoper, Emily 1989: *The Student Nonviolent Coordinating Committee: The Growth of Radicalism in a Civil Rights Organization.* Brooklyn, NY: Carlson Publishing.

Tarrow, Sidney 1994: *Power in Movement.* Cambridge, UK: Cambridge University Press.

Taylor, Charles 1992: *Multiculturalism and "The Politics of Recognition."* Princeton, NJ: Princeton University Press.

Tessler, Mark 2006: Assessing the influence of religious predispositions on citizen values related to governance and democracy: findings from survey research in three dissimilar Arab societies. *Taiwan Journal of Political Science*, 1, 1–12.

—— and Ebru Altinoglu 2004: Political culture in Turkey: connections among attitudes toward democracy, the military, and Islam. *Democratization*, 11 (March), 22–51.

—— and Eleanor Gao 2005: Comparing the influence of religious predispositions and political and economic assessments on citizen values related to democracy and governance. Paper presented at the annual meeting of the International Studies Association, Honolulu.

Thomas, Sue 1991: The impact of women on state legislative policies. *Journal of Politics*, 53 (November), 958–76.

Thompson, Dennis 1970: *The Democratic Citizen.* Cambridge, UK: Cambridge University Press.

—— 1987: *Political Ethics and Public Office.* Cambridge, MA: Harvard University Press.

—— 1999: Democratic secrecy. *Political Science Quarterly*, 114(2), 181–93.

—— 2002: *Just Elections.* Chicago: The University of Chicago Press.

—— 2005: *Restoring Responsibility.* Cambridge, UK: Cambridge University Press.

Truman, David 1951: *The Governmental Process.* New York: Knopf.

Urbinati, Nadia 2000: Representation as advocacy: a study of democratic deliberation. *Political Theory*, 28, 758–86.

—— 2002: *Mill on Democracy: From The Athenian Polis to Representative Government*. Chicago: The University of Chicago Press.

Uslaner, Eric M. 2002: *The Moral Foundations of Trust*. New York: Cambridge University Press.

VanderHei, Jim 2002a: GOP monitoring lobbyists' politics. *The Washington Post*, June 10, A1.

—— 2002b: Reid urges Bush to condemn GOP monitoring of lobbyists. *The Washington Post*, June 11, A5.

Verba, Sidney and Norman Nie 1987: *Participation in America: Political Democracy and Social Equality*. Chicago: The University of Chicago Press.

——, Kay Schlozman, and Henry Brady 1995: *Voice and Equality: Civic Voluntarism in American Politics*. Cambridge, MA: Harvard University Press.

Walker, Jack 1991: *Mobilizing Interest Groups in America: Patrons, Professions and Social Movements*. Ann Arbor, MI: University of Michigan Press.

Walzer, Michael 1974: Political action: the problem of dirty hands. In Marshall Cohen, Thomas Nagel, and Thomas Scanlon (eds.), *War and Moral Responsibility*. Princeton, NJ: Princeton University Press, 62–82.

—— 1996: Opportunism knocks? *New Republic*, 215(12–13), 27.

—— 1999: Deliberation, and what else? In Stephen Macedo (ed.), *Deliberative Politics*. Oxford: Oxford University Press, 58–69.

—— 2000: *Just and Unjust Wars*, 2nd edn. New York: Basic Books.

Warren, Mark 1999: *Democracy and Trust*. New York: Cambridge University Press.

—— 2001a: *Democracy and Association*. Princeton, NJ: Princeton University Press.

—— 2001b: Power and conflict in social capital: community organizing and urban policy. In Bob Edwards, Michael W. Foley, and Mario Diani (eds.), *Beyond Tocqueville: Civil Society and the Social Capital Debate in Comparative Perspective*. Hanover, NH: University of New England Press, 169–82.

Weissberg, Robert 1978: Collective vs. dyadic representation in Congress. *American Political Science Review*, 72(2), 535–47.

Weldon, S. Laurel 2002: Beyond bodies: institutional sources of representation for women in democratic policymaking. *The Journal of Politics*, 64(4), 1153–74.

Williams, Bernard 1973: Ethical consistency. In *Problems of the Self*. Cambridge, UK: Cambridge University Press, 166–86.

Williams, Melissa 1998: *Voice, Trust, and Memory: Marginalized Groups and the Failings of Liberal Representation*. Princeton, NJ: Princeton University Press.

Williams, Wendy 1982: The equality crisis: some reflections on culture, courts, and feminism. *Women's Rights Law Reporter*, 7(3), 175–200.

Wolf, Richard 2006: Government trying to simplify drug plan. *USA TODAY*, February 9, 10A.

Wolin, Sheldon 1981: Max Weber: legitimation, method and the politics of theory. *Political Theory*, 9(3), 401–24.

Young, Iris Marion 1990: *Justice and The Politics of Difference.* Princeton, NJ: Princeton University Press.

—— 1997: Deferring group representation. In Ian Shapiro and Will Kymlicka (eds.), *Nomos XXXIX: Ethnicity and Group Rights.* New York: New York University Press, 349–76.

—— 2000: *Inclusion and Democracy.* Oxford: Oxford University Press.

Zadek, Simon 2003: In defense of non-profit accountability. *Ethical Corporation Magazine,* September, 34–6.

Zagacki, Kenneth 2003: Rhetoric, dialogue, and performance in Nelson Mandela's "Televised Address on the Assassination of Chris Hani." *Rhetoric & Public Affairs,* 6(4), 709–35.

Zaller, John 1992: *The Nature and Origins of Mass Opinion.* New York: Cambridge University Press.

Index

Printed and bound by CPI Group (UK) Ltd, Croydon, CR0 4YY

13/04/2025

14656563-0002